UNIVERSITY OF KNOWLEDGE INCORPORATED

GLENN FRANK, B.A., M.A., Litt.D., L.H.D., LL.D., *Editor-in-Chief*

PRINTED AND BOUND IN THE UNITED STATES
OF AMERICA BY THE CUNEO PRESS, INC.

Every Branch of Knowledge Man Possesses May Be Applied To Some Good Purpose

MAJESTIC WATERFALL IN WESTERN NORWAY

THE UNIVERSITY OF KNOWLEDGE
WONDER BOOKS

GLENN FRANK, EDITOR-IN-CHIEF

TREASURES

OF

TRAVEL IN EUROPE

Written and compiled by
NUMEROUS WORLD TRAVELERS
under the direction
of
MASON WARNER

World Traveler—Foreign News Correspondent
Member
Adventurers' Club of Chicago

•

UNIVERSITY OF KNOWLEDGE, INCORPORATED
CHICAGO - 1940

ACKNOWLEDGMENT

From the misty banks of Iceland to the sunny isles of Greece, and from the land of the midnight sun to the olive groves of southern Yugoslavia we have received pictures of the most interesting places of Europe.

We wish to thank the following organizations most sincerely for their co-operation:

The Art Institute of Chicago

Associated British & Irish Railways, Inc., New York

French Government Tourist Bureau, New York

Railways of France, New York

Press Bureau of the Ministry of Foreign Affairs, Oslo, Norway

Swedish Traffic Association, Stockholm, Sweden

Royal Danish Consulate, Chicago

Finnish Central Chamber of Commerce, Helsingfors, Finland

German Railroads Information Office, New York

Czechoslovak State Railways, New York

United Resorts of Carlsbad, Marienbad, Franzensbad and Teplitz-Schonau

Press Section of the Lithuanian Foreign Office, Kaunas, Lithuania

Chamber of Commerce of Riga, Latvia.

J. BRADFORD PENGELLY
Picture Editor

TABLE OF CONTENTS

Drawing by Raeburn Rohrbach

THE WHITE AREAS REPRESENT COUNTRIES DESCRIBED IN THIS VOLUME

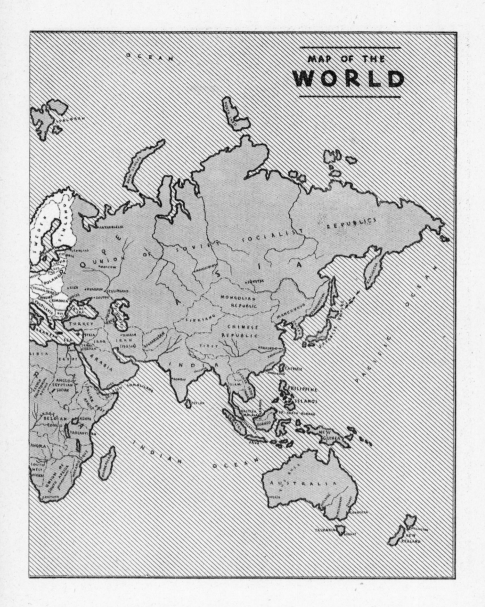

THE SHADED LAND AREAS ARE DESCRIBED IN COMPANION VOLUMES

Paul's Photos, Chicago

OPENING OF BRITISH PARLIAMENT
Showing a royal procession leaving Buckingham Palace for the House of Lords.

THE OAK TREE THAT GREW FROM AN ACORN

AMERICAN CIVILIZATION has grown from an English seed. So much of the political, cultural, and economic life is explicable only in terms of its English origin that it is almost impossible to enumerate the separate parts of our British heritage. America has been a wayward child, now grown to a distinct, self-orphaned manhood, but the marks of English contributions and background are still present.

Time has brought vast differences. The influx of other peoples with other civilizations, the advent of wars, a tendency toward increasing national consciousness, and economic independence— these have made it apparent that the seed of the English oak planted in the New World has grown into a sturdy new species.

[13]

The greatest tie of all has been the common language. In spite of superficial local differences on both sides of the Atlantic, the mother tongue has made English stories, learning, and literature known to Americans to an extent which can scarcely be overestimated. And so it is with startling familiarity that Robin Hood and Friar Tuck have made their Sherwood Forest part of the American literary world. King Alfred and the cakes, Lancelot and Guinevere and King Arthur, Dick Whittington, David Copperfield, Richard the Lion-Hearted, Sir John Falstaff—to any of these it is impossible for an English-speaking person in any land to be a stranger. Who is there who does not know of the ancient gray buildings of Oxford, Wordsworth's Lake District, the colorful pageantry of a regatta on the Thames, or the white chalk cliffs of Dover?

LIVING ON ZERO

Through London's suburb, Greenwich, runs the zero meridian of longitude, the north-south equator, and in many ways this is a fit symbol of Britain's place in the center of the world. England, with Wales, comprises the southern three-fourths of the largest of the British Isles. In size, England and Wales together are only slightly larger than the state of Illinois. The islands lie in the Atlantic Ocean to the west of continental Europe, separated from France by the English Channel which, at the Strait of Dover, its narrowest point, is only eighteen miles wide. The North Sea lies to the east, and across the border to the north is Scotland. The smaller island of Ireland is to the west, separated from England by the Irish Sea and St. George's Channel.

England is low-lying, but not flat in contour. The level of the land rises gradually to the north from the chalk cliffs of the Channel coast and the rolling South Downs and Cornish hills, to the rugged Welsh highlands, and along the western coast to the low mountains of the Lake District and the Cheviot Hills along the Scottish border. The great central plain is lined with many rivers, and the shore line is characterized by lofty cliffs and long beaches. The foundations for British industrial and commercial greatness lie in the coal and iron deposits which underly the central portion of the island. Great Britain includes the Isle of Man, in the Irish Sea; the Isle of Wight, lying off the south coast of Hampshire; and the Channel Islands, the most famous three of which, Jersey, Alderney, and Guernsey, have given their names to fine dairy cattle.

VAST CITY OF FOG

In southeastern England in the valley of the River Thames, lies the great city of London. There is really no phrase, no concise set of words which describes this vast English metropolis. Like all great metropolitan centers its great extent, its varied life, and enormous population, defy all generalizations. Naturally, a number of familiar names spring to the mind as soon as the city is mentioned, such as Piccadilly, Regent Street, the Tower, London Bridge, and a hundred others.

THE TOWER OF LONDON

Across the sweeping curve of the Thames stretches the great Tower Bridge, two immense towers with battlements and spires and between them two crossings of the river. One is a drawbridge for vehicular traffic at the foot of the towers; the other, an elevated footbridge suspended from tower to tower. At one end of the Bridge is the historic Tower of London. The Tower has been a vigilant watchdog of Britain's domestic safety for centuries, and the scene of countless beheadings and imprisonments. Now it stands with its massive stonework and tall fur-capped sentries, a grim reminder of its past.

Courtesy The Art Institute of Chicago

TOWER OF LONDON AND TOWER BRIDGE

Among the treasures from the past which the Tower guards are the Crown Jewels, huge diamonds and sapphires and rubies of matchless beauty and untold worth. Here in the part known as Wakefield Tower, is the ruby of the Black Prince, and here too is the Star of Africa, a huge priceless gem, weighing 516½ carats. The Yeomen of the Guard, emerging from their sentry boxes, which resemble tall phone booths, are still picturesque, even though they are not required to wear the square beards of the past. Their queer, flat caps, bright scarlet uniforms, rosetted shoes and garters present an imposing sight as they pace along the battlements in pairs, holding their tasseled maces.

LONDON BRIDGE

The original London Bridge was built in Roman times, as far back as 43 A.D., when the city was a small fortified village covering only a few square miles on the river bank. The early Bridge was used not only as a thoroughfare across the Thames, but also as a site for houses and shops. It was destroyed in the Great Fire in the seventeenth century, along with most of the city. The fire cleared the way for a new London, and gave Sir Christopher Wren, the great architectural genius, an opportunity to propose his city-planning program. He is responsible for the magnificent dome and exquisite beauty of St. Paul's Cathedral, innumerable London churches, Greenwich and Chelsea hospitals, Marlborough House, and a great number of other London buildings and residences. The Whispering Gallery of St. Paul's one of the famous engineering feats with which Wren made this church outstanding among the great cathedrals of the world.

THE LITTLE OLD LADY OF THREADNEEDLE STREET

Near St. Paul's is the Bank of England, guardian of the economic fate not only of England but of a major part of the world. The Bank is housed in an unostentatious building which covers more than four acres, in the financial district off Cheapside. Across from it is the classic front of the Royal Exchange, facing the square with its simple columns and Grecian frieze.

Beyond the Bank is the Guildhall, hoary with tradition. The grotesque wooden images of Gog and Magog, London's antique guardian gods, leer down on the elaborate doings of the lord mayor

Courtesy The Art Institute of Chicago

ST. PAUL'S CATHEDRAL IN LONDON
Outstanding work of Sir Christopher Wren.

and the sheriff. Here the great banquets and public celebrations take place, and in the halls the Cabinet ministers are fêted on Lord Mayor's Day. This is the neighborhood of the ravages of the Great Plague which was followed by the Great Fire. The latter disaster is commemorated by the Monument, another of Wren's works, a two-hundred-foot stone column with symbolic flames leaping at its top.

PROFANITY MADE BILLINGSGATE FAMOUS

Back toward London Bridge is the market of Billingsgate, named for one of the gates of the ancient city, where the pungent language of the fishwives and traders became such a byword that the place-name is a synonym for violent words. Following along Cheapside into Oxford Street, which, with its hum of commerce, rivals the famous Regent Street and Bond Street, one reaches the British Museum. The Museum is one of the outstanding institu-

Courtesy The Art Institute of Chicago

SOUTH FAÇADE OF THE BRITISH MUSEUM IN LONDON

tions of its kind in the world. The Elgin Marbles, brought from the Parthenon, are only the most widely known of the myriad treasures of world history which the Museum contains. Here too is the Rosetta stone without which scholars would have had insuperable difficulties in learning something of the ancient civilizations of the East.

Site of the famous theater by that name is Drury Lane, from whose narrow way have emerged many of the great actors and plays of the English-speaking world. It is rivaled in tradition only by the old district on the other side of the Thames in Southwark, where stand the theaters in which Shakespeare himself acted. Back toward the Thames is Fleet Street, renowned as a newspaper center although in recent times many of the newspapers have sought other homes. Here, again in sight of St. Paul's, are the Law Courts, which are described as "new" in old London, though they have been standing there since 1882. Across from the domain of the bewigged and gowned guardians of the British Law is the Temple, originally the headquarters of the Knights Templar. Now a legal center, it is one of the few institutions privileged to admit young lawyers to the bar.

"ORANGES AND LEMONS"

West of Fleet Street is the Strand, one of the world's great thoroughfares. In the Strand are two noted churches, one being the church of St. Clement Danes, whose bells are immortalized by the bit of nursery doggerel stating that, "Oranges and lemons say the bells of St. Clement's." The other is a gracefully beautiful structure, also in the middle of the avenue, the church of St. Mary-in-the-Strand, where in old times May Day revelers danced about the maypole. Near at hand is Covent Garden with its great market, and farther up the river bank, along which in earlier days the Strand extended, is the British National Gallery. The portrait gallery is one of the best known in Europe, and together with the Wallace collection and the Tate gallery represents England's claim to fame in the world of painting.

At the foot of the Strand is Trafalgar Square. Near the Square is the original Charing Cross, one of the series of markers along the road from Lincoln to Westminster, where halts were called in the funeral procession of Queen Margaret, wife of Edward I. The Square is named to commemorate Nelson's great victory on the seas which gave England control of the Mediterranean. The Nelson Monument towers in the open square, a tall column 170 feet high, with the figure of Lord Nelson looking down on the fountains of the area beneath.

All about Pall Mall are the places of ceremony and pomp with which English life is made colorful. Here is Marlborough House, another of Wren's works, built for the famed Duke of Marlborough. Opposite is St. James's Palace, the seat of the Court of St. James, and one of the brightest stars in the entire diplomatic constellation. Close by, too, is Buckingham Palace, the royal residence. The changing of the guard which takes place every morning when any of the royal family is in residence is among the most familiar yet colorfully impressive sights anywhere

BOWLING GREEN

Buckingham Palace looks out on the broad expanse of the Mall. Both the Mall and Pall Mall must own a sort of kinship with an American city in Kentucky and a district of lower Manhattan, for the words are derived from the French *pêle mêle*, a sort of bowling imported by Charles I. Adjoining the Mall is one

Paul's Photos, Chicago

FLOWER SELLER ON
LONDON STREET

of the many London parks and one of the most attractive, St. James's Park, part of the eighteen thousand acres of parks, squares and open courts which relieve a feeling of crowdedness in the great city.

East of the famous buildings about the Mall is Piccadilly Circus, throbbing with the roar of London traffic and at night bright with a thousand lights. Piccadilly, perhaps the most famous of all the two thousand miles of streets in London County, lies in the heart of London. To the west is Hyde Park and around it the fashionable residence district of the West Side.

HYDE PARK IDIOSYNCRASIES

Greatest of London's many parks is Hyde Park, 364 acres of natural beauty on the West Side. The British call the broad, shaded avenue which leads to the Serpentine Lagoon "Rotten Row," in the same spirit, perhaps, in which the graceful tower of the cathedral in old Boston is named the Boston Stump. But no names can destroy the pleasant loveliness of the great park. The Marble Arch at Tyburn in the northern end of the park was erected to honor the Duke of Wellington's victory over Napoleon, but Tyburn itself is the location of the grim pit where Cromwell's exhumed and beheaded body was for the second time buried. An effigy of Peter Pan, a memorial to his creator, Sir James Barrie, stands by the Serpentine Lake.

Other parks brighten the city to the north and west. Kensington Gardens and Kew Gardens are world-famous for their beds of innumerable gay flowers. The Zoölogical Gardens satisfy the universal urge of civilized man to see his fellow earth-dwellers. All the squirrels in nearby Regent's Park are said to be descended from one pair which escaped from the Zoo. Hampstead Heath is another of London's great parks, the natural beauty of green trees and fields all the more welcome in the drabness of the city.

INTERIOR OF THE FAMOUS WESTMINSTER ABBEY
Where the coronation of British kings takes place.

"THE KING IS DEAD; LONG LIVE THE KING"

Back again toward the Thames, past the glorious cluster in the vicinity of St. James's Park, the visitor comes to another illustrious group of buildings. Beautiful Westminster Abbey, with its tall Gothic towers, is regarded with reverence by Englishmen and all who would pay honor to great men of the past. Here is the burial place of English kings and queens as well as of great statesmen and poets. To those illustrious dead who are not buried in the shrine, tribute has been paid by including their effigies or tablets dedicated to them. The Poet's Corner is a famous spot, and the old Coronation Chair, in the chapel of Edward the Confessor, is familiar to everyone. Beneath the chair is the hoary Stone of Destiny, symbol of Scottish royal power.

Here within the cloisters is the ancient Chapter House, where almost from its beginning until the time of Edward VI, the House of Commons held its sessions. Westminster Bridge and the graceful sweep of the Embankment adorn the river at this point, and beyond Westminster Abbey rise the towers of the Houses of Parliament. Between these and the Abbey is the parish church, St. Margaret's, one of London's many churches, handsome with its spacious windows and great square tower.

STANDING ROOM ONLY

The sign might well hang in the House of Commons, for here there are only 476 green leather seats for the more than six hundred members of Britain's governing body. The House, at times sober and businesslike, and at other times riotous almost to the point of violence, works at its task of guiding the fate of the Commonwealth of Nations, always itself guided by the spirit of the great leaders who have gone before it. Here, too, is the House of Lords, better lighted and furnished, with red leather-upholstered benches instead of green. In the Upper House are the figures of the eighteen rebellious Barons who forced King John to sign the Magna Charta. The Lord Chancellor sits at his ease on a couch called the Woolsack when he presides over the sessions of the Lords of the Realm.

King John was power-hungry and his rule was as tyrannical as Richard's had been slipshod. The combination was fatal. Encouraged by the freedom they had gained under the absent Richard,

Courtesy The Art Institute of Chicago

SEAT OF THE BRITISH GOVERNMENT
Houses of Parliament in London.

the nobles were doubly incensed by the hardships they suffered under John. They rebelled in 1215, and John was forced to sign the Magna Charta. The first tentative expression of actual democratic form was the first House of Commons, which met in 1265. The qualifications of the members and their electors were so definitely based on property-holding that there was little chance of the representation of the poor masses, but it was a beginning. In a world only beginning to emerge from feudalism, it was a radical step.

THERE IS NO LEASE

The tenant of the celebrated residence at Number 10 Downing Street has no lease on the official residence, situated close to the Houses of Parliament. Here have lived generations of British Prime Ministers and from behind locked-door sessions in Number 10 have come decisions which have rocked the world. Looking back at the Houses of Parliament from Westminster Bridge one sees a magnificent façade of Gothic buildings rising above the waters of the Thames. In the tower is perhaps the most famous clock in the world, Big Ben, sounding his chimes over London. On the other side of the Thames is Southwark Cathedral, a vast Norman structure near which William Shakespeare lived while he was writing such plays as *Midsummer Night's Dream, Merchant of Venice,* and *Troilus and Cressida.* In Southwark, too, John Harvard, who later went to America and donated the money to found the university which bears his name, was baptized in 1607.

"THE CONSTABLE COUNTRY"

The great lobe of England that projects into the sea between the mouth of the Thames and into that arm of water known as The Wash is East Anglia, one of the early Saxon kingdoms. The counties of Essex, Suffolk, Norfolk, and Cambridge make up what

NORWICH
CATHEDRAL

Courtesy The Art Institute of Chicago

is often called the "Constable country," though it might as well be known as the Gainsborough country, except that the sound of the latter lacks the alliterative value of the former. Both of the painters sprang from, knew, and loved this quiet, sunny countryside. Not the least of the charm of this part of England is the multitude of captivating names, a charm which is not exclusively East Anglia's. But Chipping Barnet, Shoeburyness, Barking Braintree, Swaffham, Wells-next-the-Sea, and Diss are hard to equal.

Norwich is the ancient capital of East Anglia, and here in the prominent city of Norfolk is the boiling down of the life of the kingdom; so that a narrow, winding medieval lane, paved with cobblestones and lined with overhanging houses and quaint little shops can lead into a modern busy street such as Prince of Wales Road. Chief among the many churches which dot the city is Norwich Cathedral. This beautiful structure is a heritage from Norman days along with the other great feature of the Norwich skyline, the castle.

FLOWERS IN THE MOAT

Passing from the busy atmosphere of Tombland into the contrasting stillness of the Close, through the picturesque gate of St. Ethelbert, one comes to where the huge square castle, rising on the hill from the level of city rooftops, dominates the picture. Below it are the famed Norwich cattle market, and the gracious castle meadow and park. The bridge leading to the castle crosses the former moat, now a rich garden filled with bright flowers. The once gloomy interior serves as a museum of Angliana and a small gallery is also housed here. The museum itself is in the keep, the old castle dungeon, and beneath arching stone pillars where unhappy prisoners had their necks stretched in torture, the visitor now cranes his neck to see the traces of ancient life.

Beyond the Castle Meadow is the city's ancient Market Place, an oval open square between the Guildhall and the Church of St. Peter Mancroft. Trading here goes on under a gay patchwork of canvas-roofed stalls in much the same way as it has for centuries. Many other market places are scattered about in the southern end of the town: in Orford Hill is the old hog market, close by is the cattle market, and to the west in Rampant Horse Street is the place where roped horses once pranced and the time-honored art of horse trading was carried on. The Guildhall on the north side of the Market Place is an interesting bit of medieval building, with its checkered walls and huge clock. Within it are the administrative offices of the city; and the council assembly room with its beautiful stained glass window, as well as the Mace Room where are kept the city relics and plate; and the jail, where among the modern cells are preserved some of the terrors of the gaols of the Middle Ages.

SHAKESPEARE ON AN OPEN PROSCENIUM

In a picturesquely paved alley running from Charing Cross to St. John Maddermarket Church is the home of Nugent Monck's Norwich Players, the Maddermarket Theater. Here in a theater constructed like the Elizabethan houses in which Shakespeare first produced his plays and he himself acted, the work of the Bard is being successfully carried on. The Shakespearean dramas are interspersed for variety with other plays, but it is in *Julius Caesar* or *As You Like It*, played on an open stage with the original tang of the genius, that the Maddermarket is at its best.

Three miles south of the city is the excavation of Caistor-next-Norwich, where the Roman remains which everywhere mark this section of England are being exposed. The antique forum, the Roman paving, the baths, and many coins and pieces of pottery prove this excavation to be among the finest and best preserved anywhere in the country. To the east are the Broads, for much of East Anglia is low and flat, where mills turn in the wind to keep the water from completely overflowing the land. The Broads themselves are winding watercourses, sometimes as narrow as rivers, occasionally spreading out like broad lakes. For a hundred and fifty miles, they add a pleasant touch of blue water to the green of the inland East Anglia landscape. But they are not allowed to remain mere idle landscape features; the Broads are a popular resort district where yachtsmen from all of England gather and boating is carried on to an extent that is made possible by the long sheltered waterways.

Norwich is the hub of a wheel whose spokes reach out toward the coast. To the westward almost on the tip of The Wash is historic King's Lynn with its old buildings and quaint musty atmosphere, and on the way is another delightful town bearing the quaint name of Dumpling Green. A few miles from King's Lynn is Sandringham, where Edward VII maintained a famous country residence, an imposing building nestling in a pleasant country of woodlands and rolling hills. From here all the way round the curve of the shore to the mouth of the Thames is a holiday land of beaches and resorts. It is a land mellow with memories of invasions, for the coast was always a prey to pillagers from the sea. The Roman remains, the influence of the Danish control, are part of the life of East Anglia. Hunstanton, Wells-next-the-Sea, Lowestoft, Felixstowe, and hundreds of other towns are watering-places which capitalize on the happy combination of sunny skies and sea breezes possessed by the coast.

ONE FOR THE LAND, ANOTHER FOR THE SEA

The picturesque church at Blakeney in the northern part of East Anglia is a simple church with an ordinary bell tower at the shoreward end, but at the other end rises another tower used as a lighthouse. On a grassy heath overlooking the reaches of the North Sea, the lighthouse throws its beams far out over the water. At Cromer, along the coast to the eastward, the white sand of the beach is backed by high imposing cliffs, reminiscent of the great white chalks of Dover.

The Yare River, which flows through Norwich, empties into the sea at Great Yarmouth, a city where the waterfront location serves the double purpose of providing a watering-place for pleasure-seekers and of harboring a thriving and ancient fishing fleet. Like Kent and London and a score of other places, Great Yarmouth and its vicinity have been called "Dickens Land," partly because of allusions in the writings of the great novelist—many scenes in *David Copperfield* are laid here—and partly because of the Dickensian atmosphere which pervades it. Great Yarmouth is one of the ancient ports of the eastern coast of England. It is still one of the great fishing centers, sending its fleets out over the water from Dogger Banks to as far as Iceland for the cargoes of fish which pour into the city of London. In other towns of Norfolk and Suffolk the Dickens touch immortalized the picturesque sights; Ipswich and Bury St. Edmunds bear the stamp of Pickwick's wanderings. At Bury St. Edmunds is the shrine of Edmund, the last king of East Anglia. He was killed and subsequently canonized for his refusal to deny Christianity; here, too, is the grave of Queen Mary.

THATCHED ROOFS AND OIL PAINT

In the point of land which lies between the arms of the Stour and the Orwell rivers is the district which Constable loved and painted. Here are the quiet scenes of homely beauty—thatched roofs on little vine-covered cottages, old mills by clear streams, a precious part of the tradition of rural England. To the west is Sudbury, rich in associations with another great painter—Gainsborough. Throughout the whole of East Anglia are these little towns, not famous perhaps, but all abounding in historical memories, and all filled with a strange historic atmosphere of their own. Among the green fields and woodlands they lie, each different from the other, and again different from any place else in the world. They go on with the slow flow of life, treasuring their own particular ruins or churches or other buildings, and also their own particular peculiarities of name: Haveringatte-Bower, Saffron Walden, Saxmundham, Castle Rising, or Brightlingsea.

One of the prominent racing centers in a country which loves its racing is Newmarket in Suffolk. Here is a great sporting country, for besides the race meetings there is to be found some of the most excellent partridge shooting in England.

Another interesting spot is Colchester, a port in northern Essex, where the oyster is so prominent a part of everyday life and local industry that an annual oyster festival is held, and English gourmets from everywhere are attracted by the Colchester delicacy. Colchester is also the scene of some of the better-known Roman diggings, and is in the heart of the famous rose-growing district of the east.

SLIP OF THE TONGUE

When King Henry II uttered the ill-fated, petulant wish that someone would remove a man who was constantly a thorn in his side, he brought upon himself the terrible stigma of having caused some of his courtiers brutally to murder Thomas à Becket, Archbishop of Canterbury, in his cathedral. Before or after the Reformation, Canterbury has been the religious capital of England, and its archbishop the leading prelate. Henry himself, when the deed became known, walked all the way to Canterbury, in barefooted humility to atone for the monstrous crime for which he felt himself directly or indirectly responsible.

ROMAN RUINS, CANTERBURY

Several centuries before the erection of the cathedral, Augustine was sent to England by Pope Gregory the Great and became Archbishop of Canterbury. It is to St. Augustine that the English Church was indebted for the foundation of its loyalty to Rome and its dependence on the Holy See, a connection which saved England from the isolation of the Celtic Church. The name of St. Augustine is among the greatest in the roster of early Church missionaries. The archbishopric has seen many great men come and go. Anselm, when he was an old man, filled the position till his death; and there were Justus, and Morton, and many another name, great in the history of the Church. The cathedral itself is majestic in its proportions. The delicate tracery of its towers, the great windows and massive buttresses, the intricate stonework and lofty interior; all are overpowering in their beauty. An atmosphere of silence filled the aisles and transepts.

"WHITE CLIFFS OF ALBION"

East of Canterbury is the land of Kent, the Albion which the Romans saw when they crossed the Channel from Gaul. The towering and impressive chalk cliffs of Dover which gave the name to the island, mark the dropping off of the rolling, green Kentish hills to the sunny beaches which form a playground for all who are attracted by the rolling of the surf in the sun. The entire coastline is dotted with seaside resorts: Margate, Whitstable, Folkestone, Ramsgate, and Deal, to name only a few. Deal and the quaint and almost Elizabethan town of Sandwich are the site of the landing of Caesar's legions in 54 B.C. The pleasant county of inland Kent is a region of moated castles surrounded by fields of hops and fragrant orchards—in the spring, pink with blossoms and fragrant with their scent. Another favorite health resort is Tunbridge Wells, an inland spot halfway between London and the Channel. Farther along the coast is Hastings, where King Harold died, pierced by an arrow, and William of Normandy began his conquest of Britain.

The Normans crossed the English Channel to Britain in 1066, and the Battle of Hastings saw the possession of England again change hands. William set about organizing his newly-acquired kingdom in a systematic manner. He commanded the compilation of the *Domesday Book,* a rough census of the population

and wealth of his realm. He dispatched Norman dukes and other
nobles to govern the district and set up an intricate feudal hier-
archy after Continental models. This set in motion the endless
battles for power between the kings and the nobility which
everywhere marked the feudal system. In the tenth century under the early kings, the nobles in England had succeeded in establishing an organization with dubious powers known as the Witen-
agemot, with which they and their successors sometimes attempted to check the power of the Crown. In this body of jealous
nobles it would have been difficult to see any element of democracy, but it was this germ which developed through slow centuries into the British Parliament. Opposition must come
from those who have power to oppose, and under feudalism this
group could scarcely have been the mass of the people. Under
Norman feudalism the balance shifted from side to side. King
Henry II, an able ruler, held his vassals in check with much success. But Richard I, called Coeur de Lion, who spent all but one
year of his reign in foreign lands, fighting in the Crusades, lost
ground heavily, and when his treacherous brother ascended to
the throne the power of kings sank to new depths.

A FOREIGN PORT LEFT HIGH AND DRY

Like several of the old cities of the southern coast, Rye has
been deserted by the sea and now stands inland, secure in its
memories of the nautical glory it once possessed. A medieval
port, Rye became the home of many Belgians and the twelfth-
century tower looks like one imported from Ypres. The days of
smuggling, piracy, and driving off of invaders are gone, however,
in more ways than one for picturesque little Rye. Nearby, on
the borders of Romney Marsh, is the quiet town of Hythe, which
boasts of being the earliest borough in England. The line of
cliffs commences again, as the traveler proceeds westward along
the coast, and the rolling South Downs appear inland. Here at
Seaford are the beautiful Seven Sisters Cliffs, rivaling those at
Dover. Here, too, is perhaps the most famous of all the English
seaside resorts, Brighton. Nearby are other resorts: Littlehampton,
Bognor Regis, and Worthing. Bognor Regis is the seat of the Duke
of Norfolk, England's premier duke.

Rudyard Kipling, the English author, called Sussex his home
county, although born in Bombay, India. He was educated in

Courtesy The Art Institute of Chicago

THE NEEDLES, ISLE OF WIGHT

England and though his writings dealt more often with India than with his home land, he loved through all his life the green country of the South Downs. In the western end of the county is another of England's vast cathedrals. Chichester Cathedral, founded in the seventh century, is a monument to the conversions of that early Wilfred who landed on the British shore to carry Christianity to the pagans of England. The long roof and tall spire, rising above the massive towers, blend with the countryside, and there is real beauty in the retrochoir and in the paintings with which the interior is adorned.

The Isle of Wight lies in a bend in the English Channel close to the Hampshire coast. The island serves as a breakwater to two major English ports; across on the mainland is the great naval base of Portsmouth, and farther inshore is Southampton on a deep arm of the sea. The harbor of Portsmouth is more than four miles in length and overlooks the protected roadstead of Spithead. Here is a three-hundred-acre dockyard, and down the Portsmouth ways have slipped the greatest of British warships. At the end of the Southampton Water, a deep narrow bay slicing into the shore, lies Southampton, a port which has been famous since the days of Saxon England and in which today can be seen the largest ocean liners from all over the world lying at anchor.

The home of Lord Tennyson through most of his life was the Isle of Wight, and here the poet wrote much of his best work.

The island also boasts Osborne House, which was designed by Queen Victoria and Prince Albert. The quasi-Italian villa was the beloved home of the Queen and her Consort during the early years of their life together. Because of the matchless climate of the little island, the ailing Keats lived here for a time, listening to "perhaps the self-same song that found a path through the sad heart of Ruth, when, sick for home, she stood in tears amid the alien corn."

VICTORIA, REGINA, IMPERATRIX . . .

The long reign of Queen Victoria, which lasted sixty-six years, witnessed the fulfilment of that destiny toward which England had been climbing. Gladstone, Peel, Cobden, Disraeli, Bright, these towering ministers fostered the liberalism typified by free trade and broad suffrage at home and widened the range of British power in the Crimean War, in the Boer War, in the struggles in India. Britain grew to be the great creditor of the world, leader in trade and manufacturing as she was in empire building. Her son, Edward VII, ruled for only nine years until 1910, when he was succeeded by George V, and early in his reign Britain entered the World War. Pouring her resources into the mad mêlée, England at the finish of the war shared the exhaustion of all Europe, though she gained colonial territory, and the unrest which followed the war marked her reconstruction. In 1924 the socialist Labor Party came into control of the government, but in the turmoil of the 1929 depression the Laborites were swept out of power. During the post-war years England has taken a place among the leaders of movements striving for international peace. King George VI, successor to the brief reign of Edward VIII, who abdicated before his coronation, has taken his place in the long line of rulers of the empire upon which "the sun never sets."

Charles I came to Carrisbrooke on the Isle of Wight as a visitor, but he soon found himself a prisoner, and sensing that this was the beginning of the end the dauntless cavalier-king wilted tragically. His hair turned gray, and after two desperate and unsuccessful attempts at escape from imprisonment in London he was executed in the street in front of Whitehall Palace.

Now, however, the island is a peaceful and popular vacation land. The quaint island towns, the pleasant sea air and sunshine, and the sixty-five miles of scenic coast, including the white, tusk-like Needles on the western tip, are exceptionally attractive.

RETURN OF DIVINE RIGHT

The Stuarts of Scotland followed Elizabeth, the last of the Tudor line, and James Stuart, King of the Scots, reigned as James I of England. The liberality which the Tudors had to some extent shown in acceptance of a parliamentary form of government was in no way shared by the Stuarts. James's reign was a constant struggle with Parliament over his belief in the "divine right of kings," and a series of difficulties over his strong Catholicism in a now Protestant England. Charles I, who followed James, continued the bitter wrangle, and he simply refused to call the representatives together. For eleven years Parliament did not meet, but when it at last came together in the famous Long Parliament, Charles was dethroned and beheaded. Cromwell, the strongest of the revolting leaders, established the severe British Commonwealth, with himself as Lord Protector. For fifteen years he ruled the islands with an iron hand, but the bitter hatred which he inspired left short reign to his son, who had not the strength of his father, and Cromwell's body was exhumed and beheaded. After a short return to Stuart rule under Charles II, the English revolted. Charles fled, and the new rulers, William of Orange and Queen Mary, entered the scene as joint sovereigns following the "Bloodless Revolution" of 1688.

Though William, a foreigner, was not well liked, he was an intelligent man and a capable king. He brought an end to the religious struggles which had for so long torn his country. He gave free rein to Parliament and made his ministers responsible to it. Anne, who succeeded to the throne, left behind her the legislative union with Scotland and, under the leadership of such men as Marlborough, an increasing empire.

CALLED NEW AT THE AGE OF NINE HUNDRED YEARS

In western Hampshire is the New Forest, which William the Conqueror laid out by the simple process of demolishing all human habitation within its borders. Here generations of kings hunted the red deer which formerly roamed about through the forest's hundred and forty square miles. Now the Crown has opened most

Courtesy The Art Institute of Chicago

WINCHESTER CATHEDRAL FROM THE NORTHWEST

of it to the public, and in this bewitchingly beautiful woodland of ancient beech and oak, where shaggy wild ponies run at large, is some of the most picturesque scenery in England.

Twenty miles apart are two of the South Country's great cathedrals: Winchester, the second longest in Europe, and Salisbury, whose spire is the tallest in all England. The little city of Winchester, which is more than a thousand years old, was until the time of William of Normandy the capital of England. Here Egbert, the first king of all England, held his court, and here his grandson, Alfred the Great, was tutored by the venerable St. Swithin, bishop of the cathedral. St. Swithin was buried outside the cathedral, according to his own desires, and when the hundred years had passed, at the end of which time he was to be moved into the church, a rain of forty days postponed the transference. From this event sprang the legend:

> "Saint Swithin's day, if thou dost rain,
> For forty days it will remain;
> Saint Swithin's day, if thou be fair,
> For forty days 'twill rain na mair."

The cathedral itself stretches its vast length in the ancient town, and in its spacious interior is much of England's absorbing antiquity as well as much of modern carved and sculptured beauty.

Only a few miles to the west of old Winchester is Salisbury, whose cathedral is one of the most admired in England. It is the only English cathedral to be built without interruption of the construction; in less than forty years the airy spire and the edifice, in graceful symmetry, took form and were completed. This achievement in the thirteenth century made something of a record. The banded spire tapers to a delicate point more than four hundred feet above the surrounding land, and it is an exquisite landmark that can be seen for many miles.

THE WISE MAN AND THE OYSTER

With the withdrawal of the Romans came a new source of trouble for the Britons, in the form of invading tribes of Picts and Scots from the North. These untamed marauders harassed the more civilized Celts until they were forced to call for assistance. But, like the two quarrelers who called in a mediator to decide which should have an oyster, they found themselves with the two halves of the shell and the mediator with the oyster. The Angles and Saxons and Jutes not only drove out the Picts and Scots; they subjected the Britons and settled down to possess the rich land. These new rulers were Germanic tribes and pagans, but they were gradually absorbed as they were on the one hand assimilated into the remainder of the population and on the other hand converted to Christianity, chiefly by the heroic efforts of St. Augustine, sent by Pope Gregory in 597. The tribes gradually organized the seven kingdoms of England, until in the ninth century one of these minor kings mustered enough power to rise as overlord of all of them. This was King Egbert of Wessex, the first king of England, whose ancestry was claimed by all but a half dozen of the long line of English rulers.

ALFRED AND THE DANES

Best known of these early kings is Alfred the Great. He came to the throne in the midst of a new series of invasions which were ravaging a great share of western Europe. The new scourge was that of the Danes. In his wars Alfred succeeded in driving the Danes out of a part of England, and he maintained a tenuous overlordship of the sections of the island in which they remained. After his death the perilous equilibrium he had achieved was upset and by 1013 the Danes were able to call their kings the rulers of England. Their power was short-lived. Less than thirty years after the accession of the first Danish king of England, the fourth and last, Hardecanute, was succeeded by Edward the Confessor, and the crown returned to the English line.

Close to Salisbury is the impressive mystery of the ancient ruin of Stonehenge. The amazing circle of ponderous stones, imported by unknown means and certainly with inconceivably great effort, stands surrounded by an earth wall and dry moat. The stones are roughly hewn into squared surfaces and surmounted by flat rocks to form what, at a time perhaps two thousand years ago, resembled a massive picket fence. The date of each year was determined in those primitive days by drawing a line through the center of the circle to the Heel stone, which

Courtesy The Art Institute of Chicago

WEATHERED SANDSTONE MEGALITH AT STONEHENGE
DATING FROM PREHISTORIC TIMES

stands at a distance. When the rising sun came to this point the Druids knew that the summer solstice had been reached. The ancient sacrifice stone also remains in the mighty ruin, which is certain to inspire awe in all who see it.

TESS AND JUDE

Dorset is the county which gave birth to Thomas Hardy, and here were laid the scenes of *Tess of the D'Urbervilles* and *Jude the Obscure*. The green hills and the crumbling red sandstone of the shore display little of the dark imagination of the novelist and poet, however. It was to these hills that the dying Lawrence came: Lawrence of Arabia, one of the most picturesque Englishmen of the twentieth century. The land is a shrine for those who know and love his diverse writings. Farther west, in Devonshire, is another of England's renowned cathedrals. Exeter is a town of timbered medieval buildings. The cathedral is remarkable in a land of remarkable cathedrals. The two massive towers

Courtesy The Art Institute of Chicago

EXETER CATHEDRAL FROM THE SOUTHEAST

possess walls nine feet thick, and the complex loveliness of the
small spires and flying buttresses gives an appearance of strength
which is not belied by its solid construction. The three-hundred-
foot nave, from which rise the columns which spread into exquisite fan vaulting, is graced by a beautiful rose window. Here
too is the unusual minstrels' gallery where angels are depicted,
each playing a different instrument.

Devonshire is the land of *Lorna Doone,* and in its fair
country wandered Coleridge and Wordsworth and Southey. The
historic port of Plymouth was a point of departure for many of
the country's great seamen. The *Mayflower* set sail from this port,
carrying the Pilgrim Fathers to America, and it was from here
that Drake and Raleigh, Frobisher and Grenville set forth on
their voyages of exploration in the New World and on their
valiant conquest of the Spanish Armada.

THE VIRGIN QUEEN

Third of the offspring of Henry VIII to rule England, Elizabeth, the daughter of Anne Boleyn, succeeded to the throne in
1558, and under her rule England rose to heights hitherto unknown in the history of the island. Shakespeare, Bacon, Spenser,
Drake, Raleigh: these Elizabethans brought to their country a
Golden Age, inspired, cajoled, loved, spurned, hated, by Queen
Elizabeth, one of the outstanding figures of English history. Under
Elizabeth England experienced a scientific and literary renaissance, a spread of international prestige marked by the defeat of
the Spanish Armada, and a growth of strong national feeling.

Cornwall is the tip of the great arm of England that stretches
out into the sea at its southwestern corner. From the Devon border, the waters lap the Cornish shores, Bristol Channel on the
north and on the south the English Channel, meeting at the
famous promontory of Land's End. Cornwall has always been
isolated and different from the rest of England. While the other
subdivisions of England are counties, Cornwall retains the status
of a duchy, the eldest son of the king being Duke of Cornwall
as well as Prince of Wales. Cornwall remained Celtic, like parts
of Wales and Scotland, because of its remoteness, and Angles,
Saxons, and Danes never conquered the Cornishmen. Their language persisted until only a little over a century ago, a Gaelic
stock much like that of the Bretons across the Channel. The

A CHARMING
CORNWALL
VILLAGE

Life moves in a leisurely way in old English villages like this one, Bodinick, in sunny Cornwall

Paul's Photos, Chicago

land is rich in legends: here is Tintagel, an ancient fortress overlooking the sea, where King Arthur was born, and the echoes of the castle ring in many of the Arthurian legends. Here too the ill-starred Tristram brought the Irish Princess Isolde as a bride for his uncle, the traditionally villainous King Mark. Almost at Land's End is Penzance, whose rollicking pirates have charmed many a delighted Gilbert and Sullivan audience.

"AS I WAS GOING TO ST. IVES"

The traveler to St. Ives today is not likely to find the nursery-rhyme man with seven wives and the other multiplying problems, but in this little fishing village a few miles north of Penzance he is sure to find much else of interest. There is an artists' colony here, a sure sign that the land and its inhabitants are both charming and picturesque. The English Channel shore of Cornwall is almost tropical in climate. Starting out in the sea with the Scilly Isles, whose chief industry is the raising of flowers, the southern coast has been called the Cornish Riviera. Its villages are situated on little forested inlets that are reminiscent of the Louisiana bayous. The most active harbor is old Falmouth, but another storied place is Truro, on the rugged Cornish coast, with its beautiful cathedral which is different from most famous English churches in being new. Cornwall, back of the romantic seashore, is a region of mines, known to the ancient Phoenicians, and today still doing a flourishing trade in the smelting of tin and tungsten.

The rugged scenery of the West Country is perhaps best in the wild plateaus of Dartmoor and its smaller cousin Exmoor. These untamed moors with their rocky peaks and great boulders, or tors, of which the best known is Yes Tor, fascinate the imagination because of their lofty aloofness. Shaggy ponies and surefooted sheep inhabit the Dartmoor ranges, and in the red sandstone reaches of Exmoor are to be found the last of the famous red deer which English huntsmen have chased from time immemorial.

THE BRINGING OF THE HOLY GRAIL

Eastward again, into Somerset and Glastonbury, in whose famous abbey King Arthur was buried, according to legend. Here it was that Joseph of Arimathea came from Palestine after Christ's resurrection, bringing with him the Holy Grail, which plays so prominent a part in the Arthurian tales. In Glastonbury Joseph is said to have thrust his staff, cut from the holy thorn tree, into the ground, and it sent out roots and grew, and blooms today. Glastonbury is said to have been the scene of the pathetic hesitation of Sir Bedivere, when Arthur bade him cast Excalibur into the waters which surrounded the Abbey. When at last the sword was thrown, an arm "clothed in white samite" rose mysteriously from the water and grasped it.

Only a few miles from Glastonbury is Wells, with one of the smallest, and one of the most exquisite, cathedrals in all England. The skilfully carved front, reminiscent of the great cathedral at Chartres, is only an outward expression of the intricate grace of the interior. North and east of Wells is Bath, where mineral springs have made a popular health resort since before the times of the Roman occupation. Perhaps the best-known character of the place is Chaucer's charming Wife of Bath, with her two

Paul's Photos, Chicago

FAMOUS GORGE OF THE RIVER AVON
Beyond the suspension bridge is the city of Bristol.

small dogs in the pilgrimage to Canterbury, but Dickens enjoyed the place, and Jane Austen also has written of it. Its tremendous increase of popularity in the eighteenth century was due to the visits of Beau Nash, who led all the glittering lights of British society to the pleasant spot. All about Bath are places of interest. From here the Cotswolds, with their quaint villages and shepherds, Cheddar Gorge, and the Wookey Hole caves with their underground traceries and stalactites, are easily accessible. Bristol is an ancient trading town, from which Cabot sailed on his epoch-making voyage to America. Outside of the church of St. Mary Redcliffe is the grave of Thomas Chatterton, who by various forged hoaxes succeeded in making fools of half the wise men of England.

Forefather of the famous Massachusetts fishing port, Gloucester, connected by canal with the Severn and thus with the sea, is an active trading center in the west of England. The city contains an ancient cathedral and here too is the New Inn, which certainly is not new, with an inner court, above which is a balcony from which spectators used to watch plays being acted in the space beneath.

SUNDIAL ON ALL SOULS COLLEGE, OXFORD

OXFORD

In the entire English-speaking world there is probably no other institution of education which possesses greater prestige than Oxford University. Since the thirteenth century Oxford has held a distinguished place among the great universities of the world, and among her sons are numbered many of England's greatest statesmen, poets, authors, and intellectual leaders. Situated along the banks of the upper Thames, the school, with its many hallowed buildings, stands secure in quiet dignity against the inroads of time. The university comprises twenty-one colleges, each with a history and tradition of its own, and each with its own roll of distinquished graduates. Some of the more famous of these colleges: Balliol, Christ Church, Magdalen, Brasenose, Jesus, and Corpus Christi, are known all over the world. Here among the ancient Gothic buildings gowned students walk, attending lectures, combing libraries, or conferring with their tutors, or "dons." Attached to the university is the Bodleian Library, founded by Sir Thomas Bodley in 1597 and containing over half a million volumes. The library ranks next to that of the British Museum in point of value to scholarship.

North of Oxford is Warwickshire and in it Stratford-on-Avon, the birthplace of one of the true literary titans. Shakespeare's mighty name has made quiet little Stratford a mecca for his devotees, and thirty thousand of them visit the town every year. Shaded by the elms which are so numerous in the county that they have been called the "Warwickshire weeds," the town lies along the banks of the lovely Avon river. The town has innumerable relics of the great poet, most of them authentic. In the church are the registry with the record of his baptism and burial, and the memorial stone with the famous inscription composed, it is believed, by himself, which reads:

"Good friend, for Jesus' sake forbear
    To dig the dust encloséd here;
Blest be the man that spares these stones
    And curst be he that moves my bones."

His birthplace, the cottage where he courted Anne Hathaway, and the manor grounds where he is said to have poached game, and other reminders of the playwright are in and around Stratford. Here also is the beautiful modern Shakespeare Memorial Theater, which was destroyed by fire in 1926 but rebuilt by public subscription in 1932.

Only a few miles from Stratford-on-Avon is a cluster of famous place names—Warwick, with its storied castle, and Rugby, the scene of *Tom Brown's School Days*, which has given its

Courtesy The Art Institute of Chicago

STRATFORD-ON-AVON, HOME OF SHAKESPEARE

name to the game which ranks with cricket in the attention of English sportsmen. Nearby is Kenilworth, and in the village is the inn in which Sir Walter Scott began the writing of his novel, *Kenilworth*. The castle, a ruin since the time of Cromwell's depredations, is here, an unforgettable place to the readers of Scott's novels.

Coventry was the home of the famous Coventry plays, and the miracle and mystery pageants of the Middle Ages. It is also the scene of the valiant ride of Lady Godiva, who according to the story rode naked, except for the cloak of her long hair, through the streets of the town on a white horse, in order to effect the repeal of a burdensome tax imposed by her husband, the Earl of Mercia.

Near Banbury, in the county of Northampton, is Sulgrave Manor, the home of George Washington's ancestors. Sold by Henry VIII to Lawrence Washington, the perfectly restored home was the residence of the family until the departure of John, grandfather of George Washington, for the New World. In the

Courtesy Associated British and Irish Railways, Inc.

SULGRAVE MANOR, ORIGINAL HOME OF THE WASHINGTON
FAMILY FROM WHICH GEORGE WASHINGTON CAME

spandrel over the doorway of Sulgrave Manor is the Washington coat-of-arms, whose stars and stripes inspired the design of the arms and flag of the newly formed United States. In the church can still be seen the old Washington family pew.

THE KING'S ENGLISH IS GERMAN

Washington's famous antagonist, George III, came to the throne because of a religious freak. There were no more Protestant Stuarts in 1714 and the Crown went to the House of Hanover. The foreign king, George I, spoke no English and cared nothing for his new kingdom; so it was left in the hands of the Whigs and the great Prime Minister Walpole, who with his balance-of-power doctrine laid the basis for much of British foreign policy since that day. George II cared scarcely more for his island kingdom except insofar as its military activities could enhance his reputation as a soldier. The Empire grew in America and India in his reign under the leadership of such men as Wolfe and Clive.

George III, however, was bent on the direct and absolute control of England and all its colonies. He looked back with a great deal of longing to the days when the "divine right of kings" was not questioned, and fought with his ministers, his Parliament, and eventually lost his American colonies from Maine to Georgia. England was now, despite this loss, on the way toward her dominating position in world affairs. Nelson, by the victory at Trafalgar, assured the status of England as "mistress of the seas," and the growth of the Empire was imminent.

ELEVEN POETS WENT TO SCHOOL

Rivaling Oxford University is historic Cambridge, almost as old and in some ways as great as its fellow. Among those who attended the institution were such poets as Wordsworth, Milton, Spenser, Dryden, Byron, Gray, Herrick, Tennyson, Sidney, Housman, and Brooke. The buildings along the broad King's Parade are impressive, and the river-shore loveliness of the "Backs" is unforgettable. Among her seventeen great colleges, Cambridge numbers Trinity, St. John's, Jesus, and King's. King's College boasts a superb Tudor chapel, and among other famous spots in the university are Erasmus Court in Queen's College, Trinity's

Courtesy The Art Institute of Chicago

ON THE CAM RIVER, CAMBRIDGE

Great Court, and the imposing gateway of St. John's. The exquisite fan vaulting and stained glass windows of King's College chapel make it one of the most beautiful of all college churches; Wordsworth made it immortal in one of his sonnets. Among the new buildings in the grounds of sweeping lawns and shady groves is the New Library, erected by donations of the Rockefeller organization. This great library is matched by the old College Library, with its quarter million volumes, another masterpiece of Sir Christopher Wren. East and northeast of Cambridge is the region of the fens, where the whirling sails of windmills over the green flat meadows make the district a miniature replica of Holland, complete with dikes and waterways.

On the northwest coast of The Wash is the ancestor of the American city of Boston. Here Brewster and other of the Pilgrims were tried in the ancient Law Court, in 1607, charged with conspiring to flee England. The great landmark of the town is the lofty church tower called the Boston Stump. Notwithstanding its unlovely name, the tower itself is truly lovely in proportion and line.

VENISON AND GREEN SWARD

West of Lincolnshire is Nottingham, an old town in a district which will always be familiar because of the stories of Robin Hood and his merry men. In the famous tales of Robin Hood, Friar Tuck, Little John, and Alan-a-Dale, the green reaches of Sherwood Forest, and Nottingham with its villainous sheriff, have become known and loved. Getting back into Lincolnshire, the visitor finds one of the lovely cathedrals of central England. Lincoln Cathedral displays the paradox of a sense of unity imparted by a diversity of styles skilfully combined. Rising over an intricate façade are twin towers of simple lines and dark peaks; rising almost next to these two there is another tower, more massive and almost as tall. This great shaft is a beautiful mass of exquisitely fine stonework. The three towers rise high above the surrounding town and the rest of the church, the latter displaying humorously grotesque gargoyles with their gaping grins and weird faces.

One of the curious things about York is its white walls, high and long and perfectly preserved. Coming into the county from Lincoln, perhaps by way of historic Doncaster which is not now dependent on its history for its fame, since the St. Leger horse

HUNTING EGGS AT FLAMBOROUGH HEAD

Daring Yorkshire hunters risk their lives to secure prized eggs of sea birds.

Paul's Photos, Chicago

race meetings are held there, one notices the walls among the first of York's many sights. They are not the first to catch the eye, however; it is York Cathedral, one of the great cathedrals of the North. The great structure can be seen from the same white walls which almost surround the city and along whose parapet the visitor can walk just as the York sentrymen walked six hundred years ago. The vast cathedral ranks among the most glorious in all Europe, with its fine stone tracery and unbelievably beautiful Five Sisters window. Among the winding, picturesque medieval streets is the charm of the city, streets bearing such odd names as the Shambles and Whipmawhopmagate, and fully as absorbing as their names. Roman remains are plentiful in Yorkshire, too, including a great angular tower built by the legionaries. And, to exemplify the ancient atmosphere of York, the curfew is still rung every night in this old town.

The exhausting century of war with France was begun by Edward III, in whose mind rankled the French inroads on lands in

France which he controlled as well as the French aid which the Scots had received in their battles with his predecessors. The interminable struggle abroad, in which the balance wavered first to one side and then the other, ended with the English faring badly against a France which was inspired by Jeanne d'Arc. Meanwhile the break-up of feudalism and the growing desire for democracy made home conditions unsettled. Richard II was compelled to abdicate, and the Parliament succeeded in naming his successor, Henry IV.

THE TUDORS OFFER A PINK ROSE

The internal difficulties of England in the fifteenth century were further complicated by the thirty years of struggle between the two royal houses of Lancaster and York. These feuds were known as the Wars of the Roses, the emblem of the house of Lancaster being a red rose, and that of York a white rose. The kingship changed hands again and again as the tide of battle turned this way and that. The final victory went to the House of York, but this temporary peace was upset by the seizure of the throne by Richard III.

He was in turn overthrown after a short reign and the old difficulties were solved by the accession of Henry VII of the House of Tudor, in whose veins flowed the blood of both the Lancastrians and the Yorkists. Perhaps the most significant result of the wars was the removal of the great chess pieces, the noblemen, leaving the king with far greater authority than before because there were fewer rebellious noblemen to contest it.

The great York Minster is only the center of many churches and abbeys of the county, however. Ripon Cathedral is an ancient wonder, from whose tower the curfew has been rung for more than a thousand years. The city has an official horn blower, another medieval survival, who blows his trumpet in the Town Hall square. Nearby are the ruins of Fountains Abbey, where, according to legend, Robin Hood was killed. In the southern part of the county is Selby Abbey, founded by William the Conqueror, which, in deference to its exalted builder, is permitted to dress its choir in red; the only other abbey so honored is Westminster. Farther to the north, the traveler enters the Durham country, where, as the island begins to narrow, the old Roman roads begin to converge as they approach the old Roman Wall

Courtesy Associated British Railways, Inc.

DURHAM CASTLE AND CATHEDRAL

which was built in defense against Scottish invasions. Durham, with the River Wear flowing deep in its valley, rises to the crest of the hills where stand the cathedral, with its massive square towers, and the castle.

COALS TO NEWCASTLE

Still farther into the north country is the great industrial and shipbuilding city of Newcastle-on-Tyne. From here to the Scottish border stretches the rugged county of Northumberland, which is studded with innumerable mighty fortresses and watch towers. This hardy region bore the brunt of the attacks of the sea invaders from the north, being their first port of call as they voyaged southward. It has also been the buffer county in the border raids by the Scottish chiefs and in the many wars with the Scots. The border itself rises into the rugged beauty of the Cheviot Hills, from which the famous tweed derives its name; here, now that border warfare has ceased, is one of the noted sheep growing regions.

Nearly as impressive as the Great Wall of China, the Roman Wall, built in defense against Scottish invasion, stretches in solitary strength from Wallsend-on-Tyne, near Newcastle, westward

Paul's Photos, Chicago

NEAR BUSY NEWCASTLE
Desmond Dale, one of the most beautiful spots in Northern England, is a
popular retreat near the industrial city of Newcastle.

across the moors of Northumberland to Carlisle and beyond in Cumberland county. Along its seventy-three miles, undulating over hill and valley from the North Sea to the Irish Sea, are regularly spaced fortresses, and there are also to be seen the remains of two Roman towns, Chester and Borcovicus. Chester is derived from the Latin word "castra" meaning camp; this is the explanation for the Winchesters and Chichesters and Gloucesters and Worcesters. They were Roman outposts almost two thousand years ago. The outlines of baths, villas, temples and barracks are still evident in the remains. The Wall itself is, in the segments that are still intact, some ten feet in height and in many places eight feet thick, constructed of regular stone cubic blocks.

Caesar and his Roman legions came across the English Channel in 55 B.C. and wrested a foothold on British soil from the fierce but unorganized Celts, but his invasion was more one of exploration and adventure than of conquest. It was not until a hundred years later that Agricola brought about the Roman control of

Britain, and he was unable to penetrate Scotland and much of the hinterland. The Romans as usual built roads and erected fortifications and in many ways tried to impress their civilization on that of the Britons. But when in the hectic later days of the Empire the Roman troops were removed, little of significance remained to tell of their occupation. On the other hand Christianity had become a part of British life, despite the active discouragement of the proconsuls.

"WHAT VALE SHALL BE MY HARBOR?"

Turning again south in Cumberland, the visitor enters the famous Lake Country of northern England. The wild scenery of this wilderness brought Wordsworth home again after his schooling and revolutionary fling. Here too came Coleridge and Southey, and the three held momentous discussions in the inspiring country. Keats and Shelley felt the lure of the dark lakes and towering peaks. The Derwent Water and Rydal Water, where De Quincey wrote his finest prose, are two of the most beautiful of the lakes, and Windermere, the longest, is also prob-

Courtesy The Art Institute of Chicago

RYDAL WATER, ONE OF THE BEAUTIFUL LAKES IN
ENGLAND'S FAMOUS LAKE DISTRICT

ably the most famous. From the deep blue waters rise the lofty crags of Skiddaw, Scawfell, and Helvellyn, blanketed with dense forests and green rocky clearings, to a height of more than three thousand feet, the highest point in England. Other steep cliffs abound, testing the skill of the expert climber, for distance above sea-level has nothing to do with ruggedness, and Pillar Rock and the Great Gable are two whose summits are achievements. Any summit in the district, however, is worth the effort of scaling it. The hazy vistas of verdure-clad hills in contrast with the placid blue of waters beneath, are unrivaled in England and in some respects anywhere in the world.

So swam Young Lochinvar who came out of the West. The river empties into the Irish Sea just north of the Lancashire border, and as one proceeds south into Lancashire he sees the wild hills of the Lake Country in miniature. The coast is a series of holiday centers, chief of which are Blackpool, which is the closest British approximation of Coney Island, and Southport. In Southport is the other extreme, a showy sophisticated resort reminiscent of continental boulevards, and boasting a multitude of golf courses.

In the Irish Sea, midway between the shores of Ireland, Scotland, and England, lies the Isle of Man, one of the rarest oddities in all Europe. From the height of Snaefell, the island's highest peak, all three of the countries can be seen. The most famous residents of the island are the tailless cats, which have emigrated more freely than the Manx people. The Manx speak a Gaelic language, and have their own government. Their constitution is the oldest in the world, and provides for a governor and the Tynwald Court, a legislature of two houses, the assembly called the House of Keys. Upon passage, a law must be read aloud from Tynwald Hill on July Fifth in both English and Manx, in order to be valid. The bay in which Douglas, the capital, is situated is typical of the natural beauty of the Isle. At each end of the bay is a mountain, like a sentinel guarding the harbor from intrusion. A tiny dot of land off the southern tip of the Isle of Man is called humorously the Calf of Man.

A NEW KIND OF MARTYR

Lancashire is the great beginning, from the north, of England's industrial district. This is the county of cotton, where streets and houses and statues—all are blackened with the ever present soot of the mills. In this busy sector of England the industrial revolution reared its head in the eighteenth century, and with it came a new sort of martyr. Kay, forced to flee the country by angry competitors because of his "flying shuttle," was the first; he died in France, penniless. Hargreaves, inventor of the spinning jenny, saw his epoch-making machine destroyed, and Arkwright suffered a like fate after his "rollers" vastly increased production. Crompton, inventor of the cross between Hargreaves' and Arkwright's machines, was forced to keep secret all his work; but his "mule" is still used in the great cotton district. Cartwright made possible the widespread use of these discoveries by the application of steam power, and with this event, the revolution was on. Blackburn, Bolton, and Manchester are three of the best known of the Lancashire factory cities.

Manchester is the smoky metropolis of Lancashire, converted into a port accessible to 15,000-ton ships by virtue of its Ship Canal. But the city is not entirely to be understood in the light of its mills and warehouses and slums; the first free library established in Europe, together with one of the world's finest private libraries, show a spirit in the metropolis which is in no way part of the industrial phase. The John Rylands Library, accumulated by an industrialist and his wife, contains a vast and rich selection of priceless books, among which is the earliest printed work produced in Europe and still preserved. This is *St. Christopher*, laboriously transferred by wooden blocks, containing odd pictures and designs.

THE CITY THAT STEAM BUILT

It is strange that Liverpool, England's greatest seaport, should have sprung up, like a mushroom, almost overnight. Until 1709 the city did not even boast a dock. But like a mushroom, the sudden growth of the external greatness was possible only because of the long underground period of preparation. The broad estuary of the Mersey River, the proximity of the great steel and coal centers, and the growing importance of the trade with the Americas contributed the firm foundation on which a port as noteworthy as Liverpool could grow. The complexity of the loading and unloading facilities is almost unbelievable; the six miles of wharves include eighty-seven docks, and the warehouses are enormous. All this display of commercial strength became possible only with the introduction of steam navigation and the hegemony of New York City in the world of international trade.

The immense floating landing stage, which provides a solution for the varying levels of the tides on the Mersey, is nearly two miles long. Under the river is the amazing new Mersey Tunnel.

Unlike most English churches the great Liverpool cathedral is new, a symbol of the busy modernity of England's second largest city. Among Liverpool's other buildings are its four colleges, St. George's Hall, and the Walker Art Gallery. In Birkenhead, not far from the great metropolis, is the model village of the great Lever soap works, as well as its impressive library.

One of England's prominent railroad cities, Birmingham's industries include railway coach building, brass working, electroplating, automobile making, munition making, and the production of a tremendous variety of other metal goods.

The whole city reflects its industrial pre-eminence. The university maintains departments for study of town planning and oil engineering and also works with the industrialists on problems of mining research and others. The streets of Birmingham are busy arteries, and they are being swiftly adapted to the strenuous conditions imposed on them by the city's commerce.

METAL WORKS AND THE ENGLISH ALPS

East of Liverpool and Manchester is another famous pair of industrial cities; Sheffield and Leeds are to metals what Manchester and Bolton are to cloth. Here and in the neighboring cities of Yorkshire's West Riding the night skyline is aglow with the red glare from blast furnaces. The fame of Sheffield's cutlery is world-wide. Not far from these smelting cities is the English Peak District, sometimes called the English Switzerland because of the fantastic limestone cliffs, and the vast caverns rearing gleaming stalagmites, and dripping pearly stalactites, rather than on account of any marked resemblance to the Alpine grandeur. But with or without any similarity to Switzerland, the Peak District is a fascinating surface of many-faceted England.

Swinging southeast, from historic Stoke-upon-Trent the traveler passes through Derby into the three hunting counties: Nottingham, Leicester, and Rutland. Here the honored sport of riding to hounds reaches its greatest popularity; and the huntsmen, equipped with horn, topper, and steed, ride in pursuit of the coveted brush of the unfortunate fox. Leicester was, according to legend, the residence of King Lear and his perfidious daughters. West and south from Leicester is Birmingham, which, like its godchild in the United States, is a famous coal- and ore-producing city.

THE HOME OF CHARLES DARWIN

Westward toward the Welsh border, one passes through the busy industrial city of Wolverhampton, which has made keys and locks since the Elizabethan era. The traveler is now in Shropshire, the pleasant region of rolling upland pastures which Housman described in the poems of the "Shropshire Lad." In this county is Shrewsbury, the birthplace of Charles Darwin and the place where Samuel Butler and Sir Philip Sidney received their education. Nearby is the ruin of Ludlow Castle, in which Milton's *Comus* was first presented.

North of peaceful Shropshire lie Cheshire and the ancient city of Chester. Although the county may not have any wonders to compare with the Duchess' amazing Cheshire Cat, which Lewis Carroll describes, the medieval city of Chester, with its surrounding walls, is a truly remarkable place. Nowhere else in England do old walls completely encircle their town, and they have perhaps been instrumental in guarding the atmosphere of antiquity which still fills Chester. The narrow streets passing between houses and shops in the timber-and-plaster style of a distant day, and the "Rows," which are footways running along the streets through the first stories of the buildings, arouse the curiosity of the visitor. Chester Cathedral is a massive, fortress-like edifice towering over the rooftops of the town.

THE LAND OF Y'S AND LL'S

From Chester the traveler's road leads westward through Rhyl and Llandudno, the "Queen of Welsh watering places," taking him to Wales. The resort town of Bangor stands beneath the towering summit of Snowdon, loftiest peak among the craggy mountains of North Wales. From Snowdon's summit can be seen the distant shore of Ireland, the peaks of the Lake Country, and the crest of Snaefell, on the Isle of Man. Remote in their mountainous land, the Welsh still retain considerable use of their Gaelic language. The result of survival by isolation can be seen exemplified in the ancient circle of the Druids preserved in the center of the town. West of Bangor is the island of Anglesey, where the Druids made their last stand against the Romans.

Courtesy The Art Institute of Chicago

RUINS OF TINTERN ABBEY, FROM CHAPEL HILL
This famous old church, immortalized by Wordsworth, is one of
the many spots of interest to the visitor in England.

Courtesy The Art Institute of Chicago

CARNARVON CASTLE IN WALES
Built late in the thirteenth century as the castle of Edward I, Carnarvon Castle
was the birthplace of Edward II, the first Prince of Wales.

Parys Mountain is deep red in color, and the crude copper mines of the Romans can be seen along its slopes.

Returning from Anglesey to the mainland across the Menai Strait, the visitor encounters Carnarvon Castle, whose mighty walls stand practically intact today, just as they stood six and a half centuries ago. The walls are tremendously thick, bulking from ten to twenty feet, and the massive structure of the old pile is a wonder seldom equaled. The Welsh coast is a popular resort country from Pwllheli and Aberystwyth to Fishguard on the southern shore of Cardigan Bay, and there is a noted sulphur spa in the interior country at Llandrindod Wells.

South Wales is famed as a rich coal mining region, and Cardiff is the focus. The Black Mountains of the south are less fiercely rugged than the mountains of the north and west, but they are not the less beautiful for that, and beneath them are the coal deposits which give them a far greater value than that of mere scenery. In South Wales are located many medieval castles, among which those at Pembroke, Llanstephan, Carew, and Laugharne are outstanding. Near the famous River Severn in southeastern Wales is the beautiful valley of the Wye.

Courtesy The Art Institute of Chicago

SCOTT MONUMENT IN EDINBURGH

HELL'S GLEN, NEAR LOCH GOIL-HEAD, SCOTLAND

"YOU TAKE THE HIGH ROAD"

SCOTLAND stirs one's imagination. It is the land of the heather, of the fighting highlander, of heroic Bruce, of tragic Mary, Queen of Scots, of Glencoe. A small sea-carved country, Scotland has an area of some thirty thousand square miles, and more than two thousand miles of winding coastline. Practically no spot in Scotland is more than forty miles from the sea. The country lies between the North Sea and the Atlantic, and includes the northern end of the largest of the British Isles.

Highlands and Lowlands form the two main divisions of the country. The Highlands are jagged hills separated by deep valleys and indented with sea lochs resembling the fjords of Norway. These narrow, cliff-walled bays are really submerged valleys, results of a sinking of the land in recent geologic times. Numerous glen lochs or lakes also dot the scantily populated Highlands. A range of hills less lofty than those of the Highlands extends northward into Scotland from the Cheviots which lie along the English border.

The Lowlands, with one-tenth the area of Scotland, contain two-thirds of the five million population. Here are located the harbors, the mines, and the factories of the country.

As a result of a cold, damp climate and a rocky soil, Scotland is poor in vegetation. Few trees grow at an elevation of more than two thousand feet and even at lower elevations forests are not abundant. Peat moors and marshy grasslands predominate in the Highland landscape, and at many points on the coast are vast tracts of sand dunes.

The only large animals found in Scotland are deer, if the fabulous sea monsters, such as the famous creature of Loch Ness, are excepted. The rest of the larger animals are extinct; the last wolf, it is believed, was killed in 1600. On the other hand, the country abounds with grouse. Many wealthy Englishmen have shooting boxes or houses in Scotland for use during the grouse season. The Scotch lochs are also noted for their salmon, which are another lodestone for sportsmen. How strong this lure is can be seen from the Gilbert and Sullivan rhyme in which the members of parliament are told:

"You shall sit, if he sees reason
Through the grouse and salmon season."

In northern Scotland there are still many people who speak Gaelic, the ancient language of the Scotch. Some ten thousand speak only Gaelic and another one hundred fifty thousand speak both Gaelic and English.

The main agricultural crop of Scotland is oats. Fishing is an important vocation, the main catch being herring. Scotland also possesses extensive coal and iron mines. Iron and steel, shipbuilding, textiles and electrical machinery account for most of Scotland's industry. The manufacture of whisky is one of Scotland's best-known activities; the chief distilleries are located in the north. All but seven of the distilleries in the United Kingdom are in Scotland.

Near the mouth of the Clyde River is located the great shipbuilding city of Glasgow. With a population of over a million it is the largest commercial city of Scotland and ranks high among the great cities of the commonwealth. One of the earliest subway systems in the world was built in Glasgow, and the structure is symbolic of the increasing progressiveness of the city.

Paul's Photos, Chicago

LAUNCHING OF THE GREAT LINER "QUEEN MARY"
At Clydebank, Glasgow, Scotland.

Among the modern streets and buildings rises the great cathedral
with its many-pillared crypt, one of the few buildings which are
as old as the twelfth century. Glasgow has some fascinating historical associations. It is supposed to have been founded in 539
by St. Mungo who came here from the Orkney Islands to preach.

"BY THE BONNY BANKS OF CLYDE"

On the bank of the Clyde River is Glasgow Green, a very
old public park, where gay festivities of the annual Fair are
held each July. South of the city is Langside, where Mary, Queen
of Scots, was defeated in 1568.

Ascending the valley of the Clyde, one is continually reminded of Scotland's romantic past. Near Hamilton is the Both-

Courtesy The Art Institute of Chicago
GLASGOW CATHEDRAL AND NECROPOLIS

Paul's Photos, Chicago
ROTHESAY ON THE FIRTH OF CLYDE, SCOTLAND
In the center of this Scottish seaport and watering place are the
ruins of Rothesay castle, built 800 years ago.

Homer Smith photo. Chicago

GEORGE V BRIDGE, GLASGOW, SCOTLAND

well Bridge, scene of a battle between the Scotch Covenanters and the royal forces in 1689.

Some twenty-five miles upstream from Glasgow, the Clyde has a number of falls. Although they are not very high, they present a beautiful scene. Just below the falls is found the cave in which William Wallace hid after he had slain an English sheriff. Wallace was one of the courageous leaders under whom the Scots attempted to unite for independence. Inspired by this patriot, the Scotch held the superior English forces for a time in check, but eventually the Scots met defeat and Wallace was hanged, drawn, and quartered.

ROBBIE BURNS

South of Glasgow, the poet Burns is a living memory. A small cottage in Alloway was his birthplace. On the river bank is a monument (in his honor) containing many relics of the poet. In Ayr, not far from Galloway, are many scenes of his poems —the inn of Tam 'o Shanter, and the Auld Brig.

One of the oldest churches in Scotland, the Abbey Church, is situated on a bank of the Clyde. Part of the church, which was built in 1163, is a picturesque ruin but a part is intact and is still used for services.

Courtesy The Art Institute of Chicago

BIRTHPLACE OF ROBERT BURNS, FAMED SCOTTISH POET, AT AYR

On the shore of the Firth of Clyde are many bathing beaches and yachting stations which, during the summer, are very popular. On the island of Arran, in the Firth itself, is some of the finest scenery in Scotland. The island has but few buildings because the Hamilton family, owners of a large part of it, have discouraged artificial disfigurement of Arran's natural beauty.

West of Arran Island is the long peninsula of Kintyre, where are found many remains of the prehistoric peoples of Scotland— primitive burial mounds and sepulchral pillars.

RUGGED MAJESTY

Only a few hours from Glasgow's grimy streets can be found some of the finest scenery in all Europe. Even nearer is Loch Lomond, the best-known of all Scotland's lakes. Boats steam the scenic length of this twenty-three mile lake, at whose lower end is a cluster of beautiful islands. A narrow strip of land separates the upper end from the sea loch, Loch Lang. Loch Lomond abounds in historical and legendary associations. Near the water's edge, partly concealed by fallen rocks, is Rob Roy's Cave. It is supposed to have provided a place of refuge for Rob Roy, for whom the cave is named, and for Robert Bruce, who raised the

"THE BONNY, BONNY BANKS OF LOCH LOMOND"

banner of revolt and administered a sound thrashing to the English at Bannockburn in 1314, thus preserving the independence of Scotland for many centuries.

THE LADY OF THE LAKE

Loch Katrine has figured prominently in poetry. It and Sir Walter Scott's *Lady of the Lake* are inseparable. It inspired the admiration of Coleridge, Wordsworth, and other poets.

By coach one goes through the famous pass, the Trossachs, into the neighboring lake country, a scene of even greater loveliness. Here are Loch Achray and Loch Vennachar. The rugged peaks of Mount Ben Venue can be seen from various parts of this exquisitely beautiful country. Loch Earn has been for a long time a most popular stopping place. In this neighborhood the Highlands and the Lowlands may be said to meet.

Throughout this region the tourist must travel by steamer and coach until he reaches Aberfoyle and Callander, for no railroads defile this beautiful countryside.

Going in the direction of Stirling, one passes Glenfinglas, where the Stuarts chased deer. The entire district is a constant reminder of the *Lady of the Lake*. Among the Scotch ballads

Courtesy The Art Institute of Chicago
STIRLING CASTLE, FROM THE BACK WALK

is one commemorating the battle between Fitzjames and Roderick Dhu at Coilantogle Ford. After passing through many beautiful glen villages, one reaches Stirling.

Every nook and cranny in Stirling has historical associations. Its history reaches back to the days when Rome had its legions in Britain. This was the site of a Roman station. The remains of the road built by the Romans can still be traced.

Stirling Castle, from which seven battlefields can be seen, was built in the early days of feudalism. In 1304 it was besieged by Edward I, who attempted to gain control of the Scotch crown and precipitated the War for Independence.

Not far from Stirling is the famous battlefield, Falkirk, where Wallace was defeated by the English. On the same field Bonnie Prince Charlie, a familiar figure in literature, also made a daring and dramatic but unsuccessful stand in 1745.

Another reminder of Scotland's past is the castle of Lochleven, several miles from Stirling. Now in ruins, it was once the prison of Mary, Queen of Scots.

EDINBURGH

Though scarcely half the size of Glasgow, Edinburgh, the capital, is both the political and cultural center of the country. Because it is built on several hills, it has been called "The Modern Athens." Its resemblance to Athens is more than physical. It has long been a center of art and culture. More than any other city of Scotland it is filled with historical associations.

The city is divided into two parts, the Old and New Towns. The New, comparatively speaking, was completed in 1815. Lately a new New Town has been growing up alongside the older New Town.

One of the most prominent topographical features of Edinburgh is Calton Hill. From its top one may obtain a striking view of the whole city. On its summit is Nelson's Monument; also, the old Royal Observatory. Every day at one o'clock, an electric signal causes a time ball to drop at the same instant that a gun is fired at the castle.

From Calton Hill one may see Princes Street, *the* thoroughfare of Edinburgh, bordered on one side by the chief hotels of the city and on the other by beautiful gardens. It ranks high among the finest thoroughfares in Europe.

Courtesy Associated British and Irish Railways, Inc.

EDINBURGH FROM CALTON HILL

Courtesy The Art Institute of Chicago

EDINBURGH CASTLE AND NATIONAL GALLERY

Located off Princes Street is the National Gallery of Painting. It contains many of the paintings of the masters, including Van Dyck, Titian, Rembrandt, Raeburn, and Gainsborough.

THE FIFTH AVENUE OF EDINBURGH

Rivaling Princes Street in elegance is George Street, on which are located many fine offices, buildings, and shops. The Music Hall, the place where most of Edinburgh's balls and concerts are given, is located midway on the street. At the far end of George Street is located St. Andrew Square, the chief place of business in the city. On the square is the birthplace of the famous historian and philosopher, David Hume.

One of the finest collections of antiquities in Scotland is housed in the Antiquarian Museum, located north of St. Andrew Square on Queen Street. Here are found relics of prehistoric England and Scotland. It also contains items of a historic nature, such as Rob Roy's purse, the pulpit of John Knox, and the blue ribbon which Bonnie Prince Charlie wore as a Knight of the Garter. In one of the northern suburbs of Edinburgh, one may see Edinburgh Academy, the most important day school of the city. Many illustrious names can be found among the former students of the school—Professor James Clerk Maxwell, the physicist, Robert Louis Stevenson, and Andrew Lang.

Separating the Old Town from the New is the ravine containing beautiful Princes Gardens. The Old Town is picturesque and decidedly unsymmetrical. On a precipitous rock, which has been compared to the Acropolis in Athens, is Edinburgh Castle, the focal point about which the city has been built. The long and colorful history of this castle goes back to the eleventh century. Previous to this period Scotland was divided, but during this century the four Scot kingdoms, which had been warring among themselves, were united. Their first ruler was the King Duncan mentioned in Shakespeare's *Macbeth*. A Macbeth actually existed, and it was he who slew Duncan in 1040 in order to gain the throne.

In Edinburgh Castle Mary, Queen of Scots, gave birth to the boy who was later to be James I of England.

High Street runs from the castle esplanade down to Holyrood. Near the castle is the Assembly Hall, the meeting-place of the General Assembly of the Church of Scotland. Farther down is James' Court, built over two hundred years ago, for a time the residence of David Hume and of Boswell. Parliament Square contains a paving stone marked J. K., 1572. This, it is believed, covers the body of John Knox.

St. Giles' Church, the old parish church of Edinburgh, is another reminder of the city's past. Here almost three centuries ago, the Solemn League and Covenant, which brought on war with England, was entered into. Beyond the church is the Parliament House, which was formerly the meeting-place of the Scotch parliament and has housed the Supreme Courts since the Act of Union with England. The Parliament House was built during the period 1632-1640. Adjoining this building is the Advocates' Library, one of the five libraries in Great Britain receiving every book published in that country. It contains one of the finest collections in Scotland.

HOLYROOD

Perhaps the most famous building in Edinburgh is Holyrood Palace, the ancient seat of Scottish royalty. It was constructed early in the twelfth century by David I, was destroyed by fire in 1650, and was rebuilt by Charles II. At various times it has been occupied by the reigning monarch—as recently as 1927,

Courtesy The Art Institute of Chicago

HOLYROOD, EDINBURGH, FROM CALTON HILL

by King George V and Queen Mary. The most interesting part of the palace is the apartment of Mary, Queen of Scots. In the Queen's bedroom, in 1566, occurred the murder of her Italian secretary and favorite, Rizzio.

In one of the winding streets of the Old Town, Sir Walter Scott was born. Here are the remnants of some of the most picturesque buildings in Edinburgh, called "lands." Because of lack of space the "lands" were built high and closely together, much like our modern apartment houses. The main street of the quarter is known as the "Royal Mile." Through this thoroughfare passed both criminals and martyrs to their death in Grassmarket.

The University of Edinburgh was built on the site of Darnley's murder, Kirk-o'-Field. It was founded in 1583. Its eminent professors and its equally eminent graduates have placed Edinburgh among the foremost of universities. Together with other British universities, it has the right to elect representatives to parliament. On Lauriston Place is George Watson's School, the largest day school for boys in the kingdom. Leith, a close neighbor of Edinburgh, is the chief port of eastern Scotland. From it, ships sail to ports on the Baltic Sea.

The vicinity of Edinburgh has a number of points of great interest. Nine miles above Edinburgh is the famous Forth bridge, crossing the Firth of Forth from South Queensferry to North Queensferry. Opened in 1890, this cantilever bridge cost almost fifteen million dollars and many lives. It is over a mile and a half long and took seven years to build. A few miles beyond the bridge is Dunfermline, formerly the residence of the Scottish kings. In its church Robert Bruce is buried. At Linlithgow is another former residence of the Scottish royalty. Here Queen Mary was born. An hour's ride from Edinburgh are the picturesque ruins of Rosslyn Castle. The chapel of the castle, built in 1416, is one of the finest examples of Gothic architecture in Scotland. In it lie the remains of the lords of Rosslyn, who till 1685 were buried in complete armor.

Not far from Edinburgh is Craigmuller Castle. Queen Mary spent a great deal of time at this castle. The presence of her French guards in the village gained it the name of Little France. Mary's childhood bedroom is in the tower of the castle. It measured seven feet by five.

A former seat of Scottish royalty is the city of Perth. It was at one time the capital of Scotland. Then the kings were crowned at Scone, two miles away, until the removal of the famous Stone of Scone, on which the kings were seated as they were crowned. King Edward I, who removed the stone, brought it to Westminster, where it is still part of the coronation chair.

MACBETH

Eight miles northeast of Perth is Dunsinane, where Macbeth made his last stand and lost when "Birnam wood is come to Dunsinane" as was related by Shakespeare. The town is built on a hill on the top of which are the ruins of Macbeth's Castles.

On the border of the Highlands is Dunkeld, some fourteen miles from Perth. In this village is located Dunkeld House, with its beautiful grounds and an old cathedral.

From Dunkeld one usually goes to the beautiful Loch Tay, which is fifteen miles long. One of the islands in the lake contains the ruins of a priory built during the twelfth century by Alexander I.

Paul's Photos, Chicago

KENMORE, "MODEL VILLAGE" OF SCOTLAND
Viewed from the summit of the famous Black Rock, and showing the eastern
end of Loch Tay.

Loch Rannoch, nine and a half miles long and a mile wide, set off by picturesque Highland scenery, is situated in northwest Perthshire.

THE CAPITAL OF THE HIGHLANDS

Inverness, although strictly speaking not a Highland city, is called the "capital of the Highlands." It has over twenty-two thousand inhabitants. Inverness is famous for the annual *Northern Meeting* which is held here every September. It is a gala affair with bagpipe competitions, Highland sports, and dances.

Not far beyond Inverness is the field of Culloden with its heroic memories, where five thousand hungry, ill-armed Jacobites made a desperate stand under Prince Charlie against nine thousand English regulars under the Duke of Cumberland, April 16, 1746. Cumberland Stone marks the spot of the battle.

What has been called the "Kingdom of Fife" is almost a peninsula between the Firth of Forth and the Firth of Tay. One of its most interesting towns is St. Andrews, dubbed by someone "the Oxford of the North and the Monte Carlo of golf." The University of St. Andrews, the oldest in Scotland, was founded here in 1411. It is especially famous for its fine medical school. At its very gates, one of the first Protestants of Scotland, Patrick Hamilton, was burned alive. The famous museum here has a collection of Celtic relics. There is a legend that St. Rule, or Regulus, was instructed in a dream to bring the bones of St. Andrew to this religious center in the fourth century. The St. Rule's Tower dates back to the twelfth century. Not far from St. Andrews is the two-mile-long Tay bridge which crosses the Firth of Tay.

The bridge leads to the third largest city of Scotland, Dundee, which has a population of over 175,000. It is a prosperous city, being the site of a large linen and jute trade and also a center for whale fishing and other pursuits connected with the sea. University College, which is now part of St. Andrews' University, the town hall, St. Mary's Church (fifteenth century), Albert Institute, and Lochee and Baxter Parks are places of great interest to the visitor.

Going up the coast we are again in *Macbeth* country, for we reach Glamis, a civil parish with 985 people. The Glamis Castle is erroneously said to be the site of the murder of Malcolm II. It is also claimed as the place where George VI's Queen Elizabeth spent her childhood. It is believed that the castle contains a mysterious room, the secret of which is known only to the Earl and his heir.

ABERDEEN

Aberdeen ranks as the largest city in northeastern Scotland. It has a large harbor at the mouth of the Dee, near the mouth of the Don. Like Edinburgh, Aberdeen is divided into an old and new town. The old town is indeed old, having a history dating back to the ninth century. Aberdeen not only exports polished granite stones but has used a great deal of granite to beautify itself. It is also known for its large fishing and shipbuilding industries and paper manufacturing. Aberdeen University is located here. The university library has a great collection of books on Celtic literature and the Highlands.

The Dee valley contains some beautiful Highland scenery. Here is also located Balmoral Castle, the Scottish residence of the English king. Victoria was the first to take up residence here. She is still remembered with affection by the East Highlanders who refer to her as "her late gracious majesty." Many quaint fisher villages are to be found along the northeastern coast. Elgin, the center of a large agricultural district, is noted for its ancient cathedral which was founded in 1224. A fire partially destroyed it in 1270 and again in 1390. Not far away is the Pluscarden Priory, founded in 1230, and the ruins of a castle in which Edward I lived in 1296. Tourists may visit the Elgin Institute, a museum, hospital, an asylum and county and market buildings. Much of the surrounding country is of great historical interest. Here is some more *Macbeth* country with its Cawdor Castle. This neighborhood was the scene of much fighting in 1645 as well as a hundred years later during the Jacobite risings.

Let us turn for a few moments to the West Highland country. In Argyllshire is found one of the most picturesque Highland lochs, Loch Awe. Hemmed in by lofty mountains, and dotted with numerous wooded islands, Loch Awe presents an inspiring sight. At one end of the lake stands Kilchurn Castle, once the home of the Campbells. In the neighborhood are many other beautiful lochs, among them Loch Lomond, which we have mentioned in another connection.

A famous route from Glasgow into the West Highlands is worthy of description. This lovely water route starts at Glasgow, goes to Rothesay, then north to Loch Gilp. From Loch Gilp one goes through the Crinan Canal. Although only nine miles long, the canal has fifteen locks. It saves a seventy-mile trip around the Mull (the Scot name for cape) of Kintyre.

Staffa, a little island, lies in the same latitude as the "Giants' Causeway" in Ireland and presents the same natural phenomena. Here we find Fingal's Cave, one of the subjects of the beautiful music of Felix Mendelssohn. The cave is seventy feet wide and two hundred thirty feet long. In it are beautiful pointed hexagonal columns. Legend has it that these were laid as paving stones by the Giant Finn McCoul, but geologists explain it by volcanic action. Except during very high tide, one can go into the cave by boat. Other caves on the island present similar features.

ON THE ISLAND
OF STAFFA,
WEST COAST OF
SCOTLAND
Majestic columns of
black basalt rise
from the waves on
this uninhabited
but frequently vis-
ited beauty spot.

Paul's Photos, Chicago

From Oban, a tourist resort, one may visit beautiful sea lochs
that easily rival the fjords of Norway. The Argyllshire Highland gathering takes place at Oban each September. Here there
are Catholic and Protestant cathedrals.

THE MASSACRE OF GLENCOE

From Oban one easily reaches the glen of Glencoe. The wild
and somber scenery is in keeping with the memory of that terrible tragedy, the Massacre of Glencoe. A part of the mountains
which surround the glen are known as the three sisters, Faith,
Hope, and Charity. A few miles from Glencoe rises the highest
mountain in Great Britain, Ben Nevis, 4406 feet high. There is
an unpretentious hotel at the top whose rates are said to be in proportion to the altitude.

Sailing farther up Loch Linhe one comes to the Caledonian
Canal, the gateway to an all-water route from the Atlantic to
the North Sea. This sixty-mile chain of bodies of fresh and salt
water leads diagonally up to Inverness. Most of the route is made
up of natural bodies of water, but part of the way lies through
man-made canals. The locks are used continuously, for some of

the lakes comprising the route are above sea level. The highest, Loch Oich, is one hundred feet above the sea. The longest is Loch Ness, twenty miles in length.

Some of the finest but least frequented country in Scotland lies north of Inverness. In the regions of Ross and Cromarty, it is said, there is no spot more than ten miles from the sea, so heavily indented is this area. In Ross we find Loch Maree, one of the grandest sights in Scotland, hemmed in by precipitous mountains. From here let us go to some of the Scottish islands. The first of these islands is Skye, the largest of the Inner Hebrides Islands. The land is covered with moorland and mountains, many of which are snow-capped even in summer. The scenery here is very beautiful. The island is favored as a resort because of its mild climate. The traveler can find many historical associations here. Dr. Samuel Johnson and Boswell spent several days in this neighborhood. Prince Edward took refuge in a cave on the island.

THE FAR NORTH

The farther north one goes in Scotland the thinner the population gets until one reaches Sutherland and Caithness where the population is very sparse and the countryside very beautiful but not often visited. The Orkney and Shetland Islands are separated from the mainland of Caithness by an eight-mile strait, whose waters are noted for their terrible storms. The people are of Scandinavian and Lowland origin. The country is grim and barren, but fascinating. The Shetlands are even more isolated and forbidding. There are over a hundred Shetland Islands, but only about one-third of them are inhabited. Shetland sheep, cattle, and Shetland ponies are raised here. Both groups of islands are remarkable for their historical remains of very ancient date.

THE OUTER HEBRIDES

This group of five hundred islands contains some fine specimens of primitive architecture. The Standing Stones or *Temple of Callernish* have been called the most perfect primitive remains in the British Isles. In many parts of the islands little but Gaelic is spoken. Except for an occasional ship, many of the islands are severed from civilization in the winter months. Serving visitors is one of the primary occupations of the inhabitants of these islands. Agriculture, fishing, sheep raising, and the manufacture of woolen products are other industries.

Before leaving Scotland let us make a quick journey to the other end of the country, the border. Right near the border is the famous Gretna Green noted for the ease with which one can be married. The country is rich in the memories of these turbulent days when war was a constant visitor in this region. Now peace and quiet reign. There is no hurry or bustle. It is told that an old inhabitant of this country when asked whether he had the time to do something, replied, "Time? Oh aye, there's mair time than owt else, aboot here." Abbeys and churches of great antiquity abound in the border country. A good specimen of Scottish architecture at its best is Melrose Abbey. At St. Mary's Aisle, Sir Walter Scott lies buried. The entire country breathes the name of Scott, for this was the scene of his childhood days and formed a large part of the subject matter of his novels.

It is well that we take leave of Scotland by referring to Scott, for his spirit broods over this delightful and picturesque country, with its flourishing cities and sober citizenry. To the foreigner Scotland spells beautiful ruins, lovely lochs and picturesque mountains.

Courtesy The Art Institute of Chicago

THE CHANCEL, MELROSE ABBEY

Courtesy The Art Institute of Chicago

BLARNEY CASTLE, IRELAND

A BIT OF SOUTHERN IRELAND'S ROCKY SHORE

IRISHMEN are scattered all over the world, and wherever they have gone they have become vital, integral parts of their new surroundings. Yet few people are as intensely loyal to their Old-World homeland. A passionate devotion to "the ould sod" is the heritage of Irishmen, and in considering the Emerald Isle— its tragic history, its green beauty, its tender, violent people—a reason can be found for this loyalty. For it is comradeship in struggle, strong comradeship in a long, bitter struggle, that has knit the Irish together until every place name is a legend and every landmark a song.

GLIMPSES OF HIBERNIA

Ireland first crossed the main road of Western civilization in scattered references to Ierne and Hibernia in Greek and Roman works. These were largely sailors' tales carried home by the brave souls who dared to venture out into the stormy Atlantic at the risk of sailing off the edge of the world.

The first recorded inhabitants were the Scoti, a fierce Celtic tribe, who voyaged over the water to invade England and even

Gaul. Their government was a loosely organized alliance of tribal rulers under a more or less dominant king, himself a chief in the great central province of Meath. Perhaps the greatest force tending toward unity was the mysterious Druidic religion of the Celts.

ST. PATRICK'S SNAKES

In the late fourth century was born St. Patrick, Ireland's patron saint and one of her most famous leaders. He was not born in Ireland, however, but probably in Scotland. At the age of sixteen he was carried off to Ireland by pirates and spent six years of enforced servitude tending sheep in Ulster. Here, under the Irish skies, his religious faith increased and he resolved to spend his life in the service of the Church. When he at last managed to escape, he went to Gaul, where he entered a monastery near Cannes, preparing himself to enter a life of active service in the war against paganism.

And a more active life of devotion would be hard to imagine. During his years in Ireland, St. Patrick founded more than three hundred churches and personally baptized more than twelve thousand people. The banishment of snakes from the island is only the most famous of the stories of his exploits, for he took part repeatedly in contests of miracles against the Druidic priests, toppling idols, summoning thunderbolts, and defying flames.

St. Patrick came to Ireland when Christianity was a feeble spark glowing here and there where Roman influence had touched, but his work did not stop with his death. His followers went forth spreading the story of Christ, and for many years missionaries from Irish monasteries and schools led in the teaching of Christianity in Northern Europe.

Like most of northern Europe, Ireland fell under the terror of the Norse and Danish tribes sweeping westward from Scandinavia in their native galleys. Many of the Northmen were raiders, swooping down like hawks to harry the coast towns and leaving flames and fear behind them. It was in defense from these attacks that the many round towers which dot the shore were built. But some of the blond invaders settled in Ireland, in Limerick, Cork, Waterford, Dublin, and many other places. For a time they imposed foreign domination on the Irish, but before many generations had passed they became as Irish as the natives. And any incomplete sway of the Danes in Ireland was ended when in 1014 they were decisively overthrown by Brian Boru, one of ancient Ireland's kings.

THE NORMAN-ENGLISH FOOTHOLD

In the twelfth century, Ireland saw the beginning of English domination, and it is the struggle against this domination which makes up the greatest part of Irish history from that time until the present.

King Henry II of England received permission from Pope Hadrian IV to "subdue" Ireland. In the accomplishment of this subjugation he made use of Dermod MacMurrough, a deposed Irish king who was at that time at the English court. Dermod was seeking England's aid in regaining his power in Ireland, and with the blessing of King Henry he returned with a force under Richard, Earl of Pembroke, known as Strongbow, and reconquered the island. Strongbow judiciously married Dermod's daughter and succeeded him to the throne of Ireland. Thus the English gained their foothold in Ireland, but it was little more than a foothold. The Normans who represented England, like the colonizing Danes, adopted Irish ways of life, and, contrary to the intentions of Henry II, English influence in the island waned steadily until the accession of Henry VII in the fifteenth century.

The efforts of Henry VII, however, were successful in restoring English control to only a small area around Dublin, known then as "the Pale." His successor, the notorious Henry VIII, showed his wisdom in being satisfied with the direct rule of this small territory, and permitted the Irish living beyond the Pale to send representatives to Parliament. He showed his weakness in trying to force his Anglican church on the strongly Catholic Irish. The struggle between Catholic and Protestant, with the North of Ireland on the side of the Protestants, continued in the reigns of Edward VI and Queen Mary, herself a Catholic. For several centuries religious freedom was the chief bone of contention between England and Ireland.

Religious freedom was a sacred right to the Irish, and rebellion was almost constant. Queen Elizabeth, faced by an uprising under Shane O'Neill, instituted a strong policy of subjection by force and gave the conquered lands to Englishmen. The same

STONE MARKING
THE GRAVE OF
ST. PATRICK
This great boulder
at Downpatrick
marks what is be-
lieved to be the
resting place of Ire-
land's patron saint.

International News
Photo

violent conditions prevailed under James I and Charles I, though
they themselves were Catholics. Charles appointed the Earl of
Strafford Viceroy of Ireland, and Strafford began his "thorough
policy," which consisted of thoroughly demolishing Ireland. By
sheer force of arms he maintained a surface peace, but at his death
the spirit of revolution ran rampant.

DARK YEARS IN ERIN

Ireland was subdued also by Cromwell, upon his rise to
power. By far the greater part of the Irish people were still Catholics in spite of everything. But, since, according to law, Catholics were not permitted to own land, a handful of Protestants,
mostly English nobility who had never even put foot on Irish
soil, owned the land under a harsh system of "absentee landlord-
ism," keeping the Irish at starvation level by the exaction of huge
rentals. During the reign of the Catholic king, James II, there
was a short breathing spell, but with the coming of William and
Mary to England the English again set about to subdue the men
of Erin. The peasants lapsed into suffering as acute as any people
in the world have ever endured.

In the second half of the eighteenth century with the world-
wide spread of liberal ideas, England began to be more lenient in

her rule. The Relief Act of 1778 permitted nominal religious freedom and the holding of land by Catholics. The Irish Parliament was recognized as an independent body four years later, although it still consisted entirely of Protestants and scarcely represented the Irish people. William Pitt, the great prime minister, tried in vain to give the Irish genuine religious freedom and legislative equality by the Act of Union, but the Act proved in its administration to be merely another empty form, and the Irish rebelled under the leadership of Robert Emmet. In 1829 Catholics were allowed to sit in Parliament, but all Catholics were still forced to pay the tithe to the Anglican church.

The sufferings of the Irish were climaxed in 1846-7 with the failure of the potato crop. Potatoes were their staple food, and in the famine which fell on the island the Irish died by the thousands. Many more thousands were forced to emigrate—to the United States, to Canada, to Australia. The blow was extreme, and Ireland has never fully recovered from its devastation.

THE FIGHT FOR HOME RULE

With religious freedom at last achieved in some degree, the Irish, feeling that they were still far behind in an advancing world, continued to struggle for home rule. Gladstone's efforts to solve the problem were rejected. The Local Government Act and the Land Purchase Act were only partial solutions.

The Sinn Fein, spearhead of the Irish revolution, was fighting for a republic, and the hesitating efforts of the English to make their rule more liberal were far from what the revolutionaries were seeking. But when England entered the World War, the Irish turned their energies to help her. The majority of the people did not back the abortive Sinn Fein rebellion in 1916, and throughout the war soldiers from Erin fought side by side with men of Derby and Cornwall.

After the war the truce came to an end, and the Irish republicans renewed their battle under the leadership of Eamon de Valera, Arthur Griffith, and Michael Collins. The Sinn Fein was not to be satisfied by a more liberal rule on the part of England. They denounced all compromise measures as "English deceit."

At any rate, the moderates, believing that half a loaf is better than none, ratified a Provisional Government offered by England in their legislative Dail Eireann, and Griffith and Collins became its leaders. The irreconcilable De Valera, however, would be appeased by no such half-way measures and kept alive the spirit of republican rebellion. In 1922 the Provisional Government was supplanted by a permanent Irish Free State, excluding Northern Ireland, which was still a part of the United Kingdom. The next year the new Free State, under William Cosgrave, a moderate, was admitted to the League of Nations.

The separatists, still unsatisfied, continued to preach their republican doctrine, though De Valera's party, the Fianna Fail, refused to take any part in the government. When at last the members of the Fianna Fail agreed to enter official office, it was with the open declaration that they regarded the oath of office pledging loyalty to the British Crown as a mere "empty formula." They continued to muster strength, and in 1932 the fiery De Valera was elected president of the Irish Free State.

"COME BACK TO ERIN"

The shape of Ireland is something like a rough parallelogram. The island is separated from England by St. George's Channel and the Irish Sea, and from Scotland by the North Channel. North, west, and south, lies the great Atlantic.

Though none of the coast can be called smooth, it is true that the eastern shore of Ireland is less rugged than the western, where for uncounted ages the giant Atlantic has been beating with its mighty waves. The western coastline, where the mountains of Kerry and Connemara meet the sea, forms as intricate a pattern as a piece of Belfast lace. Donegal, Galway, Dingle, and Bantry are only the greatest of the innumerable succession of inlets and headlands that reach from Malin Head in the north to Mizen Head in the south.

The mountains of Erin are not as high as the Himalayas or the Rockies, or even the Alps. They are old mountains, green and low and wild, circling the seaward shores and forming a bulwark against the Atlantic. Through all the mountains, but especially in the north and west, are scattered many lakes, of which the largest is Lough Neagh in Northern Ireland. Most famous of them all are doubtless the Lakes of Killarney in County Kerry, in the south of Ireland.

The Shannon is probably the best-known river in the world, it is certainly the longest river in the British Isles and has the longest list of friends wherever ballads are sung. The Liffey,

OLD WEIR BRIDGE, KILLARNEY

Dublin's river, and the Boyne, emptying into the Irish Sea at Drogheda, are rivers with historical interest, along whose banks battle lines have been drawn up since the beginnings of Ireland.

The Irish weather is wet, a typical coastal climate. But the frequency of the rains which the island knows is the reason for the ever present green of the Emerald Isle. The shamrock is not the national emblem without reason in a land in which the entire landscape is "wearin' of the green."

COBH, THE JUMPING-OFF POINT

In the southwest corner of Ireland, in the county of Cork, the "pleasant water of the River Lee" joins the Atlantic. Here is the port of Cobh, in whose harbor can be seen great ships from around the world.

The harbor at Cobh is one of the greatest in the world. Its calm expanse, lying under the green Irish hills, is large enough to accommodate the whole British fleet. Cobh's other name, Queenstown, was given it in honor of the arrival of Queen Victoria in 1849. The city itself perches on the hillsides, looking down at the great harbor of which it is the nerve center.

Rising high over the city is St. Colman's Cathedral, its most imposing building. The headquarters of the Royal Cork Yacht Club are in Cobh; the Club is the oldest yachting organization in the world.

The sinking of the Lusitania in the World War took place not far from here, and there is a monument near the Town Hall commemorating the tragedy. Not far off are the graves of many of those who perished in the disaster.

"REBEL CORK"

Up the River Lee a few miles from Cobh, stands the city of Cork, "Rebel Cork" as its citizens proudly know it, on and around what was once the marsh of Corcaigh.

Like most Irish cities, Cork has important buildings identified with national leaders who addressed crowds from their windows, wrote articles in them, or were killed in or near them. The Victoria Hotel, in Patrick Street, recalls Parnell, Redmond and Cosgrave, who all delivered orations from its windows. In the Corn Market, in Anglesea Street, the arrest of Lord Mayor Terence MacSwiney took place, and thus began the hunger strike that lasted seventy-five days and ended in his death.

Patrick Street itself, Cork's chief thoroughfare, presents an odd appearance. It was the limit of the flames when in 1920 the Black and Tans of England burned half of the city, and while one side of the street is of the old Cork, an ancient Irish town, the other side of the street, which has been rebuilt, has a line of modern buildings. The only statue in Patrick Street is a monument to Father Theobald Mathew, the temperance crusader, whose influence cut the national consumption of whiskey to less than half of what it had been. Father Mathew also procured for the Catholics of Cork the only cemetery in which their priests could hold funeral services without securing permission from the Protestant Dean.

The Free Library and National Monument are on the Grand Parade, a broad avenue branching off from Patrick Street, the scene of many political gatherings.

Atop the old Court House, which collapsed in 1680, was a statue, so the story runs, of King James II, who lived in Ireland after he had been forced to flee from England. The head of James's statue was knocked off and the headless statue was given a new head, this time of King William III.

On the northern hills of the city is St. Mary's Cathedral and, nearby, the immortal Shandon Steeple, below which is the grave of the Father Prout who wrote the famous verses:

"The bells of Shandon
That sound so grand on
The pleasant waters of the River Lee."

FROM A SCHOOL TO CORK

Cork is a city built from a school. About 600 A.D. St. Finbarr, ending a wandering pilgrimage from the headwaters of the Lee, looked down from the hills around Corcaigh Marsh and decided that here was the place to found his school. With the spreading fame of the college grew the city, from a few rows of students' cottages near the monastery, to a community second only to Dublin in the Free State.

Perhaps the most beautiful of the buildings comprising University College is the Honan Chapel, with its lovely stained-glass windows. The chapel is one of the most nearly perfect examples of neo-Celtic building, and looks down at the winding Lee across peaceful green slopes. From the top of the college tower, Cork and its surrounding landscape present an unforgettable vista: the Muskerry Hills, the stately river, the college, and the city.

Of course there is Blarney Castle, whose miraculous Stone is a byword all over the world. Queen Elizabeth is usually credited with originating the legend that whoever kisses the Stone, high in the parapet, will not fail to gain marvelous powers of persuasion. Kissing the Blarney Stone used to be a rather difficult feat, since it necessitated hanging head-downwards over the edge of the parapet. Now, however, a platform has been constructed and all that need be done is to lie on one's back and tip the head back at a precarious angle.

The castle itself, formerly one of the seats of the MacCarthys, kings of Munster, is an impressively beautiful ruin, standing out like a great crag from the green hillside.

Along the coast to the east is the old city of Youghal. At one time Sir Walter Raleigh was mayor of this city, when Elizabeth had presented him with the forfeited lands of the Desmonds, who, with the MacCarthys, had been kings in Munster for centuries.

Here, Raleigh's garden is said to have produced the first potatoes grown in Ireland, brought by the gallant adventurer from the New World. Here, too, he is said to have smoked the first tobacco in Ireland.

During his stay in Ireland, Raleigh found the English poet Edmund Spenser, who had just completed three books of his long poem, *The Faerie Queene*, living in Kilcolman Castle close by. Raleigh, himself a poet, took Spenser to Queen Elizabeth, but Raleigh's favor at court was waning, and the pension the Queen granted to Spenser was disappointingly small.

A few miles north of Youghal is Lismore, where in 1627 Robert Boyle was born. At the age of thirteen he was sent to Florence to study the work of Galileo. His pioneer contributions to the sciences of physics and chemistry make Lismore a revered place for his sake as well as because of its charming castle, owned by the Duke of Devonshire. Its great trees and peaceful grounds are off the beaten path of pleasure seekers.

IT'S A ROCKY ROAD TO DUBLIN

Of course, like many old sayings, this is no longer literally true; Irish roads, at least the main ones, are fine highways now, but the old road to Dublin was a very rocky one indeed. The road along the course of Time, to the New Ireland, of which Dublin is at once the symbol and the culmination, has been full of obstacles, and traces of them are still evident everywhere in the capital of the Free State.

O'Connell Street is the busy artery of Dublin life. The English named it Sackville Street, but since the eclipse of English influence that name is rarely heard today. In the heart of O'Connell Street is the Nelson Column, the traditional meeting place of the city, from whose top the dispassionate figure of Lord Nelson has long looked down at scenes of peaceful activity and bloody strife alike.

The modernity of Dublin is in its people; its buildings are old. When they are destroyed, and it seems that every other important building in the city has at some time been either burned or demolished by gunfire, they are rebuilt from the original plans. Therefore, to outward appearances, Dublin is a picturesque city with its wounds so artfully healed that they are not apparent. Facing the Nelson Pillar is the Post Office. Here,

International News Photo

DUBLIN CASTLE, DUBLIN, IRELAND

in Easter Week, 1916, Pearse and Connolly ran up the flag of
the Irish Republic. Thus began their brief rebellion which saw
fourteen Irish leaders killed, and O'Connell Street in flames from
the Pillar to the Bridge. But the whole area has been reconstructed along the old lines and the new Post Office is, paradoxi-
cally, a fine old building.

South along O'Connell Street is the O'Connell Monument. It
is a tribute, as are the street and the bridge, to Ireland's beloved
liberator, Daniel O'Connell, who did more toward restoring the
rights of Catholics in Ireland than any other one man. The monument is just above the O'Connell Bridge, which crosses the Liffey
River with a span considerably wider than it is long.

ON THE BANKS OF OLD MAN LIFFEY

Running west out of O'Connell Street are the quays along
both the north and south banks of the Liffey. Here, among the
bookshops and markets, is the Old Dublin, quaint and romantic.
Most famous of these quays is Bachelor's Walk, the scene of massacre and peaceful meeting. West along the river is the great green
dome of the Four Courts building, a majestic, column-encircled
edifice, where the four principal courts meet in the four wings

opening off the great central hall under the dome. Also on the bank of "Old Man Liffey" is the Custom House, designed by Gandon, who also designed the Four Courts. The Custom House, seen across the water, is a really beautiful building, with its symmetrical façade, its colonnaded entrance, and its tower and graceful dome.

Directly across the river is the office of the Fianna Fail's newspaper, founded by De Valera. The building is the old Tivoli theater, and the theater itself is built where formerly stood the Conciliation Hall, in which Daniel O'Connell held his momentous weekly meetings. Beyond the building of the Four Courts is the famous St. Michan's Church, where Handel is believed to have rehearsed the "Messiah" before it was publicly played.

THE BANK TAKES OVER THE PROPERTY

South of the O'Connell Bridge is the Parnell Monument at the head of Westmoreland Street, which leads southward to College Green. Facing the west side of the Green is the Bank of Ireland, which was the House of Parliament until the Act of Union dissolved the Irish Parliament. Directly across from the Bank is Trinity College, which is now non-sectarian, but through the long stretch of Irish history was open only to Protestants. In the education of this minority group it did so well that among its great sons were Swift, Congreve, Burke, Goldsmith, Sheridan, and many others. Among its Nationalist students were Emmet, Moore, Hyde, Pearse, and Synge. Since 1801 the library of the college has had the right, by Act of Parliament, to receive a copy of every book published in the British Isles, and this oldest library in Ireland has in addition many priceless ancient manuscripts and books recording much of very early Irish learning. Probably the most prized of all these volumes is the Book of Kells, a beautiful copy of the four Gospels in Latin, believed to have been written by eighth-century monks. The workmanship, illustration, and illumination of the book are exquisite.

Most famous of all Irish theaters is the Abbey. Having fostered the genius of Yeats, Synge, Lady Gregory, and Sean O'-Casey, it is the center of the cultural development of the New Ireland. The Abbey Players and the plays which this group has introduced are internationally famous. Another theater engaged in brilliant experimentation is the Gate Theater.

CARDINAL NEWMAN'S DREAM

In St. Stephen's Green, one of the most famous places in all Dublin history, is located a part of Ireland's National University; the other two parts, in Cork and Galway, have already been discussed. The origin of this institution was the dream of John Henry Newman, later Cardinal Newman, of a great Catholic university for Ireland. In the Catholic university which, until the founding of the National University in 1908, was engaged in a constant struggle for survival, were educated an overwhelming number of the leaders of the present government including De Valera himself, and many literary leaders, prominent among whom is James Joyce. Across from the University College is Wesley College, where George Bernard Shaw received unwillingly what little "formal education" he acquired.

In Leinster House, formerly the residence of the dukes of Leinster, the Dail Eireann convenes in stormy session. This round Irish-Romanesque building is the home of Ireland's free government. The centuries of education and struggle which the Irish underwent in the attainment of their ideal are symbolized by the housing, in the same group of buildings, of the National Library and National Museum. In the Museum are such story-laden relics as the Tara Brooch, St. Patrick's Bell, and the Ardagh Chalice.

"I hate humanity," was Jonathan Swift's creed. One of the best-loved and most-hated men Ireland has ever produced, Swift, Dean of St. Patrick's, was active in his church and in political affairs. His satires, chiefly *Gulliver's Travels,* have taken their place among the classics of literature, because, like all really great satires, their main value is literary rather than satirical. St. Patrick's was a Gaelic church of no great proportions until it was rebuilt in the thirteenth century by the Normans.

Dublin Castle, a hodgepodge of feudal tower and rampart, Romanesque façade, and Renaissance hall, is the hub of Ireland's unhappy memories. Here was the focal center of the Pale, the emanation point of many of the cruelties which the Irish suffered from England. In Christ Church Cathedral; Phoenix Park, a city playground which is larger than New York's Central Park; Guinness brewery; hospitals, churches and famous birthplaces, Dublin offers ample reward to the thoughtful visitor.

KILKENNY

Southwest of Dublin is Kilkenny, the land of the chase. In a country of fine horses and daring horsemen, Kilkenny hunts are among the best, and in season the pink-coated hunters still follow the foxhounds across the green hills and glens of the country.

Long before the coming of the Normans, St. Canice had founded in Kilkenny the great monastery which bears his name. St. Canice Cathedral contains tombs inscribed with the date 1285. The cold architectural beauty of the Cathedral is softened by the gray-blue stone of which it is built. An impressive use of one of the county's products is seen in the marble floor of the choir. Another Cathedral, St. Mary's, has a tower two hundred feet high, overlooking the soft verdure of the Irish countryside and the winding River Nore which flows through it.

Kilkenny Castle was the seat of the royal family of Marshal before the Anglo-Norman invasion, when it passed into the hands of the Butler family, the earls of Ormond, who have held it through six centuries. Attempts to prevent assimilation of the Normans by the Irish led to the drastic Statute of Kilkenny, which, among other things, forbade Normans from admitting the Irish to their churches or listening to their minstrels and pipers. The edict declared that no Irishman living among the English could use the Irish tongue and that no Englishman could ride a horse, as the Irish did, without a saddle. In spite of these valiant efforts to prevent any mingling, the Butlers themselves married into the old ruling Irish families of the O'Briens and the MacCarthys.

Kilkenny Castle is a vast feudal pile, with massive, round corner towers and an array of chimneys. A great Mall before it recalls the days when the Ormonds made their capital one of the gayest centers in Ireland.

Across the Nore from the castle is the Kilkenny Grammar School, where Swift, Congreve, and Berkeley took their first steps along the path of education. Swift, the author of *Gulliver's Travels,* left Kilkenny, and must have received most of his inspiration from other sources. Congreve, before he left for Dublin to rejoin Swift in Trinity College, gave evidence of his poetic talent in a series of verses oddly entitled "Upon the Death of His Master's Magpie."

When Eamon de Valera was a prisoner in Lincoln jail, doing penance for his Sinn Fein activities, one of his jail-mates was former Mayor De Loughrey of Kilkenny. De Valera's fateful escape was made with a crude key fashioned by De Loughrey.

CASHEL OF THE KINGS

"Cashel of the Kings" is to southern Ireland what Tara is to Meath, farther north. It had been the seat of Irish kings a long time before St. Patrick came to convert King Aengus to Christianity in 445 A.D. Aengus is said to have had some difficulty in understanding the doctrine of the Trinity, how Three should be One and One be Three. St. Patrick picked up a little shamrock, with its three leaves on the one stem, and thus illustrated the Church's teaching to the satisfaction of the king.

From the plains around, the "Devil's Bit," a three-hundred-foot rock mass, rises at Cashel. It closely corresponds in size and shape to the great gap in the mountains to the north, and so the story that the "Divil" found the bite he had taken from the hills to be too much for him, and dropped it in his flight in the middle of the plain, seems plausible enough.

Here in Cashel is an amazingly preserved example of Irish architecture of pre-Gothic times. The chapel, which King Cormac MacCarthy erected in 1134, is finely ornamented in the Irish variation of Romanesque style.

To the south and west of Cashel is Tipperary, but the war spirit, which made the song about it ring in the hearts of those who sang it as they marched, is gone.

"BY KILLARNEY'S LAKES"

To the southwest, beyond Tipperary, is County Kerry in the tip of Ireland. Here are the Lakes of Killarney, believed by the Irish to be three of the Seven Wonders of the World.

Each visitor finds his own special delight among them. The wildness of the upper lake, the fern and arbutus and holly about the middle lake, the lower lake with the lovely island of Innisfallen, all have their devotees. From the ever changing waters of the lakes the rocks rise along the shores and arch lovingly in carved shapes over the water. The very skies of Killarney are somehow different, sunnier than those of the North, and seemingly responsive to every change the hours of the day and night bring. The whole landscape glows with changing colors, now blue, now rose, now soft purple or bright gold; the scenic effects are all wonders in themselves: Macgillycuddy's Reeks, the Purple Mountain of the Toomies, Muckross Abbey in graceful ruins, the Eagle's Nest, Colman's Eye, the Long Range, the Black Valley.

The well-known Kerry brogue is a rich tongue, musical and full of clean-cut images and apt figures. In the district about Dingle Bay and in other of the more remote parts of the county, Gaelic is still spoken almost exclusively, but when the Gaels turn to English, they create a new and startlingly picturesque language. It is said that after the defeat of the Spanish Armada large numbers of Spaniards escaped to the Kerry shore and inter-married with the Irish people. Certain it is that many of the Irish are dark-haired and many bear striking resemblance to the people of Barcelona and Madrid.

Limerick rises, a great sprawling city, on the Shannon. Like the rest of the country it is rich in history, but it has not stopped with that. Limerick was the capital of Danish power in Ireland. The oldest section of the city is on an island in the Shannon where the Danish settlement was located. But the Danes were driven from Limerick by the valiant Brian Boru.

In these days all of Limerick's early hardships are forgotten. The town is a busy modern city, third in size in the Free State. It has risen above the tragedies of its history to the prosaic business of supplying Ireland with ham and bacon, flour and butter, electricity and a thousand other things which are necessary, if not so poetic as views and beaches. Electricity is a great modernizing force in Ireland and comes from the Shannon Power Station three miles from Limerick at Ardnacrusha. Completed in 1929, the ambitious project consists of a seven-and-a-half-mile head-race which diverts half of the Shannon's flow through the generator turbines in a drop of a hundred feet.

POINTED TOWARD THE GRAND NATIONAL

Limerick is a great sports center. Its rowing clubs, which brighten the waters of the Shannon with their leaping shells, are known over the British Isles.

But to the man of Limerick, as to most Irishmen, horse racing is the prime sport. If Kildare can be said to be the greatest racing

town on the island, it is certain that Limerick is not far behind.
There are great racing families in Limerick, and in the green
fields of the surrounding countryside are stables vying with all
Ireland to produce the winner of the famed Grand National
Sweepstakes.

Far out in Galway Bay are the Islands of Aran, where life goes
on unchanged, as it has for hundreds of years. Here Synge laid
the scene of his play, *Riders to the Sea,* and here Lady Gregory
gained, in part, the knowledge of her people which has made her
a dominating force in Irish culture. Remote Galway is, in fact,
the center of the old Ireland which the new nationalistic literature
and art are extolling. In its University College are several chairs
in which all teaching is done in the Irish language, and in many
respects it is the most thoroughly Gaelic of the three colleges in
the National University.

"SHOES AND SHIPS AND SEALING WAX"

Belfast is the commercial capital of Northern Ireland. The
fact that Northern Ireland is a part of the United Kingdom and
therefore separate in many ways from the rest of the island, is not
an indication that she is traitorous or reactionary. The whole

ON THE ANTRIM COAST ROAD, IRELAND

International News Photo
PARLIAMENT BUILDINGS AT STORMONT, BELFAST, IRELAND

trouble with England started with the question of religious freedom. Since the Ulstermen were mostly Protestant, there was no
great question of persecution. Consequently, as they were not
excluded because of religion from the possession of land and
representation in the central British government, their other
grievances were not so acute as those of the Free State.

Belfast manufactures shoes and ships and sealing wax, but mostly ships. Her shipbuilding yards cover a hundred and forty acres of waterfront on Belfast Lough, and down her ways have slipped the *Majestic* and the ill-fated *Titanic*, to mention only two. On the south side of the Lough, across from antique Carrickfergus, Belfast's predecessor, is Bangor, home of the famous Royal Ulster Yacht Club. From this yachting center were issued the well-known racing challenges of the late Sir Thomas Lipton.

Ships are Belfast's most important product, but the city also claims the largest tobacco factory, the Gallaher plant; the largest spinning mill; and the largest rope works (Barbour's) in the world.

WIGS, GOWNS, AND SWORDS

At the opposite pole, in a way, from the Free State's Dail Eireann, is the Parliament of Northern Ireland. The members of the Dail wear the plainest clothes and conduct their sessions with the utmost simplicity. But in the Northern Parliament, which sends thirteen representatives to the British Parliament, ceremony is greatly in evidence. The speaker and clerks wear the traditional wigs and gowns, and the sergeant-at-arms bears a ceremonial sword, all in a manner to show the amity which exists between the assemblies of Belfast and Westminster.

The Parliament meets in one of the city's most beautiful buildings—a white edifice of classical design, set off by walks and beautiful scenery, at Stormont. The City Hall, a great Renaissance building of domes and window tiers, is an impressive structure, standing in its vast square. Queen's University is one of the pleasing sights in Belfast, with its dignified walks and shaded buildings. It is an autonomous university, the center of learning for all Northern Ireland.

THE PLAYGROUND OF THE GIANTS

On the northern coast of Ulster, near Bushmills, producer of famous Irish whiskey, is the land of the giants. Here is a weird collection of natural curiosities, so large and strange that it seems only natural that they should be attributed to huge men of past ages. Among such is the most famous of all the phenomena, the Giants' Causeway, composing a vast group of forty thousand

Courtesy The Art Institute of Chicago

HONEYCOMB, GIANTS' CAUSEWAY, ANTRIM COUNTY, IRELAND

basalt columns, six- and eight-sided crystals of some age-old lava flow. They stand close together and are truncated, extending more than two hundred yards into the sea toward Scotland. Here are to be seen the Giants' Amphitheater, Loom, Well, Wishing Chair, and Cannon. The straight black pillars marching in their solemn ranks are an imposing sight, and the mood of the place is so strong and definite that the mythical giants themselves seem to be not far away.

Of all the towns in Ireland, none recalls more historic memories than Derry, meaning the oak grove. The relics in its cathedral, its ruined castles and walls, speak of its ancient splendor, which dates back to as early as 550 A.D. Modern Derry, with its fine port and industries, contains many buildings of interest. The new Guild Hall, with its tall tower and stained glass windows; the great Craigavon bridge, with its double levels; Magee College; and the carillon and graceful spire of St. Eugene's Cathedral, all mark the progress of the second city of the North.

Retracing one's way into the Free State, toward either Cork or Dublin, one passes near Athlone, in the heart of the great central plain. Here is the vicinity of Lissoy, the birthplace of Oliver Goldsmith, creator of the *Vicar of Wakefield,* and Lissoy is the Auburn of the *Deserted Village.*

West of Dublin is Tara of the Kings, the ancient capital of central Ireland, where "the harp that once through Tara's halls" shed silver music for now-forgotten rulers. Nothing is left but long mounds where once were mighty walls. And there are the ghosts—one of them of Queen Maeve, who is Shakespeare's Queen Mab, the bringer of dreams and the fairies' midwife. Near to this ancient spot is Dunsany Castle, which was once the home of robber barons who robbed travelers crossing the plains of Meath. Now it is the home of Lord Dunsany, an Irish playwright whose fantastic work is a delight to all who love the theater.

Paul's Photos, Chicago

A BEAUTY SPOT IN ICELAND
A Rocky gorge near Thingvellir, with the "Justice Rock" in right foreground.

TWO HUNDRED and fifty miles from Greenland and six hundred miles west of Norway lies an industrious little island, where no crime, no illiteracy, and no poverty is to be found. A country without police, without a jail, without unemployment—that is Iceland!

Even before the time of Leif Ericsson, Iceland was a busy little country—sparsely settled, it is true, but destined to become one of the most perfect islands, both topographically and culturally, to be found anywhere in the entire world. Although some Irish monks settled here as early as the eighth century, Iceland is inhabited primarily by Scandinavians, and their religion is generally Protestant. Home rule was established in 1874, but in 1918 the island became a sovereign state under the crown of Denmark. In 1928 the Althing, or legislative body, voted to nullify the pact made with Denmark, and full independence was again established.

AN ISLAND OF MOUNTAINS AND HARBORS

Throughout its 40,000 square miles, Iceland is covered with rugged mountains of volcanic origin, most of them crowned with perpetual snow and ice. On the southeast the coastline is unbroken for miles, but in all other directions deep bays or fiords afford numerous wonderful, natural harbors.

While the climate of the island is not as extreme as the name might indicate, it is too cold for extensive agriculture. The summer sun produces a heavy growth of fruits and vegetables, but fishing is the main industry of Iceland. The leading agricultural product is grass, on which cattle and other live stock feed, making dairying an industry of considerable importance. Fishing furnishes occupation for at least ninety per cent of the nation. Naturally the Icelanders are a great seafaring nation. Manufactures are domestic and consist chiefly of mittens, stockings, and coarse woolens. Leading exports are wood, fish, feathers, woolens, and sulphur.

A COUNTRY WITHOUT POVERTY

What pleasure awaits the traveler when he reaches Iceland! Here he finds a verdant island, immaculately clean, with modern transportation and hotels, well educated people, and a bustle characteristic of any large, modern island. Icelanders do everything possible to make the visit of the traveler pleasant. Smartly dressed girls, as guides, conduct regular tours through the capital city of Reykjavik.

Iceland is not a land of snow and ice, as the name indicates. Indeed many parts of the United States have far more severe winters than does this little island. In fact, winters are often too mild to permit the practice of the favorite winter sport, skating; and snow is seldom deep enough to prevent the use of automobiles. One is impressed by the number of large automobiles, as the many unimproved roads make lighter cars impractical. Though the visitor may not be greatly impressed by Reykjavik's architectural beauty or grandeur of skyline, he readily recognizes its substantiality, so characteristic of the thriving nation. Plain little shops with unimpressive windows supply the native as well as the visitor with modern products from many countries.

Paul's Photos, Chicago

STREET IN REYKJAVIK, CAPITAL OF ICELAND

GOVERNMENT

In touring the city the visitor is invariably taken to the Parliament House, seat of the Althing, Iceland's legislative body. Originally, beginning in the year 930, the Althing met at Tingvellir, some thirty miles away. About nine centuries later the seat of government was transferred to its present site. Reykjavik owes its sensational growth to the fisheries developed nearby. It has gas, water, and electric systems; and a new harbor has been recently completed. The visitor will be taken to view the Art Gallery, the National Gallery, and Museum. The annual opening of the Althing is considered a gala occasion and is celebrated by a round of social functions.

Iceland possesses more hot springs than any other country of its size. Many of them have medicinal value. In some communities they are used for cooking, and even in the capital they are utilized for laundry purposes.

EVERYONE WORKS

The last serious crime in Iceland occurred in 1892. The country has not entirely succeeded in eliminating loafers and drunkards; but a short sentence in the "Working House" near Reykjavik is usually a sure cure, for inmates are sentenced to hard work and are temporarily deprived of the right to vote.

The traveler is forcibly impressed by the rapid progress shown here. At the beginning of the twentieth century practically no progress had been made. Now, however, hundreds of miles of new roads are in use, entire fleets of modern vessels have been added to Iceland's facilities for fishing, and many schools have been built. As the visitor leaves this charming island, he sails through sparkling blue waters and carries with him fond recollections of an industrious, progressive, and friendly people, living peaceably under an intelligent government.

Courtesy Press Bureau of the Ministry of Foreign Affairs, Oslo

THE MIDNIGHT SUN FROM NORTH CAPE, NORWAY

NORWAY is the most northerly of all the countries of the world inhabited by civilized people. Almost the entire upper half of this Scandinavian nation is the colorful, strange and magnificent "Land of the Midnight Sun," where the sun never sets during the short and lovely summer, and the long sunless winter is lighted up by the eerie beauty of the Northern Lights. The country extends almost 400 miles into the Arctic zone, yet the climate is extremely agreeable. The summer heat is never oppressive and the winters are rarely, if ever, as penetrating as those of the northern United States or Canada. No wonder, then, that Norway calls itself the ideal holiday land for both winter and summer sports.

HOME OF THE VIKINGS

Land of the Midnight Sun, of glaciers and mountains, of magnificent fiords and valleys, Norway was the home of the Vikings. In the year 872 Harald Haarfagre (Harold Fairhair) founded the kingdom of Norway by combining the many Viking tribes.

ONE MAN AND FOUR GRAVES

Harald's father, Halfdan the Black, is the subject of one of Norway's most interesting historical stories. In 860 Halfdan and many of his retinue were drowned in Lake Randsfiord. He was so beloved by his subjects that the four provinces of his kingdom all but battled for the honor of possessing his tomb. The situation became increasingly difficult until a Solomon of his people suggested that the dead man's body be divided up into four parts so that each province could bury a quarter of their dead ruler.

A few years after the formation of the united kingdom a few brave Norsemen headed westward into the unknown seas in their square-sailed and dragon-prowed galleys and discovered Iceland. A little more than a century later the Viking leader, Eric, called the Red, landed on the desolate shores of Greenland. From there, about the year 1000, his son Leif, is said to have sailed to the west and so discovered the North American continent. Thus was started one of history's greatest controversies.

Courtesy Press Bureau of the Ministry of Foreign Affairs, Oslo

FISHING HARBOR AT LOFOTEN

2

For the Italian is unwilling to have the laurels snatched from the brows of his compatriot Columbus and placed on the brow of this blond Viking.

These Norse Vikings were frequent though uninvited callers upon England. Whenever they felt like making a raid they boarded their vessels and swooped down upon the British Isles, as well as upon Western France, robbing and pillaging. But in 1066 the Vikings were set back when their King Harald III was slain by Anglo-Saxons, themselves of Viking descent, at Stamford Bridge in England.

In 1319 the direct line ran out and the crown was given to a Swede. Since that day to this Norway has not had a king born within her borders. In 1397 Norway, Sweden and Denmark came under one ruler. Although Sweden broke away about 125 years later, Norway and Denmark remained united until 1814.

A PAWN OF KINGS

In that year Denmark, as a punishment for its support of Napoleon, was forced by victorious European powers to give Norway to Sweden. But they had reckoned without the Norwegians, who were not at all used to being shunted about. They declared their independence and adopted a constitution. But five months later they were forced to join Sweden. Grumblingly they submitted but never were satisfied. Finally in 1905 their simmering discontent came to a boil over a really trivial dispute. The Storthing, as Norway's Parliament is called, proclaimed independence. But the big, blond and friendly Scandinavian is not one to bear a grudge. So Norway invited Sweden's king to name one of his sons as ruler of Norway. The king refused, and Charles, second son of Denmark's Crown Prince Frederick, accepted. Charles ascended the throne in 1905 as King Haakon VII.

Under his rule democracy steadily developed. The government is as liberal as that of the United States. Many social reforms which aim to protect the rights of all have been inaugurated. In the World War Norway was neutral, and since that time has been active in furthering the cause of international peace and friendship.

Norway is called "Norge" by its people. It is the northwestern part of the Scandinavian Peninsula. Extending in a northeasterly direction from the southern tip of the peninsula, there is a chain of mountains dividing it into the two countries of Norway and

Courtesy Press Bureau of the Ministry of Foreign Affairs, Oslo
LOGNEFJORD WITH HOTEL BALHOLM

Sweden. Norway, itself, is one of the most mountainous countries in Europe, though the ridges are not steep for they were worn
down millenniums ago by the glaciers of the great Ice Age. Actually, they are more like a group of elevated plateaus, intersected
everywhere by deep valleys.

The coastline is equally irregular. The cliff-lined shore contains numerous fiords, or indentations, and there are many thousands of rocky islands. Indeed, the country can boast of 12,000
miles of coastline, which is more than ten times the length of
Norway. The fiords penetrate far into the interior and are magnificent phenomena of nature. These long and narrow arms of the
mighty northern seas, bounded by high cliffs, surrounded by the
soft green of the forest in the south and the hard, stern wastes of
the north, are sublime manifestations of nature's grandeur.

LAND OF CONTRASTS

Geographically, Norway is truly a land of contrasts. During
the early summer while fruit trees are blooming in Hardanger,
the world's greatest skiers are meeting in international competition just fifty miles away. Oslo, capital of this kingdom on top
of the world, has all the brilliance and sophistication of a great
city. Yet on the thousands of islands there are idyllic fishing

Paul's Photos, Chicago

HOME OF THE REINDEER

Reindeer herds in the mountainous sections of Norway and Sweden are one of the sources of wealth of these countries.

hamlets where the men, master seamen like their forebears of old, still go down to the sea in frail boats. In the picturesque villages of the inland valleys the people still wear the colorful costumes of the peasantry. In the Land of the Midnight Sun the Lapps still wander with their herds of reindeer. Extensive and productive orchards stretch out at the foot of Europe's largest icefields. Miles above the Arctic Circle farmers produce valuable crops, yet Upper Norway lies in the same latitude as the uninhabitable Arctic wastes of North America and Siberia. The secret of Norway's climate is that warm waters and air currents come up from the south in the Gulf Stream to play upon its coasts.

The Norwegian summer is short, lasting from May to August. During this time there is no real night in the South; but a full twenty-four hours of daylight every day in the North. The crystal-clear air is perfumed by the pines that grow everywhere. It is then that vacationists swim and sail in the fiords. The heat of the Midnight Sun is so intense that the first hay is cut six weeks after the snows of winter have receded, and wild flowers bloom within two weeks of the end of the long night.

The months of the autumn are the halcyon days for the hunter. Norway's game ranges from the elk and reindeer and bear to the ptarmigan and duck. Autumn, too, is the season for the grand cross-country hikes and tours, for Nature is at her loveliest at this time.

But it is the winter season in which Norway's sport is at its best. The majestic waterfalls, so characteristic of this beautiful land, slowly freeze over. The mountains and valleys and forests become blanketed in a mantle of snow and a deathlike silence steals over the land. For weeks the snow falls, sets and hardens to become the world's finest skiing grounds. Then, with a joyous cry, the country becomes alive again. Everywhere is heard the soft, swishing sound of skis gliding over the snow, the merry call of the sleigh bells, the cheerful voices of a happy people who love the ice and snow.

The only drawback is the shortness of daylight. In the South midwinter night is seventeen and a half hours long. In the Far North the sun does not rise above the horizon for over two months and there is only a twilight at midday. The Northern Lights constantly play over this wintry landscape.

CHILDREN OF THE VIKINGS

The cities and towns are many and beautiful but it is the peasant villages that are most charming. The blond, strong peasant is a direct descendant of Viking culture. He is the backbone of his race. Rugged as his native hills, brave as his Viking ancestors, like all mountain and fisher folk he is an individualist who knows no master. Living in toylike villages that nestle at the water's edge of the fiords, or in the upland plateaus, the peasant has maintained his own civilization for many centuries.

There are two distinct types of this people—the farmer or forester of the inland regions and the fisherman of the coast. Fishing is the oldest of Norwegian industries and is still one of the most important. Norwegian fish are shipped to many foreign countries and Hammerfest, most northerly city in the world, is an important center for the manufacture of codliver oil. Whales, too, are hunted in the Arctic Ocean by these doughty men. The fishing season is in the first months of the year, and 100,000 hardy Norsemen heed the call of the sea, as did their Viking forefathers. Indeed, they often use the same kind of high-prowed, square-sailed boats in which the Vikings sailed fearlessly into uncharted waters. Many go out never to return, but the Norwegian is not afraid. He chooses to gamble with wind and water and he knows he cannot always win.

Courtesy Press Bureau of the Ministry of Foreign Affairs, Oslo

STATUESQUE YOUNG NORWEGIAN WOMEN CONTEMPLATING THE
QUIET BEAUTY OF HARDANGER FIORD

Courtesy Press Bureau of the Ministry of
Foreign Affairs, Oslo

PEASANTS WEARING THEIR NA-
TIONAL COSTUMES, IN SETERSDAL

The inland peasant is a farmer, cattleman and forester, for lumber is one of Norway's most valuable natural resources. In summer comes the saeter period, revealing one of the most charming aspects of the peasant life. This is the time when the herds are moved from their valley pasture where they forage during the long winter to the saeter or high pastures up on the mountains. The men are busy harvesting the valley crops, so the women and girls climb up to the little saeter buildings far above the treeline. Here they busy themselves with making the butter and cheese for use during the winter.

Everyone works in the peasant's home. But religion and education are not neglected. Schools are found everywhere and attendance is compulsory. Some of the village churches date from the eleventh to the fourteenth century. These are strange looking affairs, built of wood with high-pitched roofs rising in tiers. Nor are the Norwegians backward culturally, and Norwegian authors and artists have gained world-wide acclaim. Among Norway's great writers and artists are Henrik Ibsen, playwright of the nineteenth century, Knut Hamsun and Sigrid Undset, novelists, Gustav Vigeland, sculptor, and many others.

FORGOTTEN MEN OF THE ARCTIC WASTELANDS

But even the hardy Norwegian peasant has not been able to conquer the extreme northern tip of his land. Here, within the Arctic Circle, live tribes of people known to the world as Lapps (Swedish for "nomads"). The region is called Lapland, though it is not a political unit and extends across Norway, Sweden and Finland. Altogether there are only about 30,000 Lapps in the world. Smallest of all European peoples in stature, living on a land that barely supports them, they are healthy and contented. Many are nomads, and whole families live in small tents with their dogs, seldom bathing, and hardly ever taking off their clothes. Others live along the coasts, where they live by fishing, dwelling in rude huts of wood and clay. These strange people, rarely more than five feet in height, have decidedly Mongolian features. For this reason, and because of their language, it is believed that their original home was in Asia. For hundreds of years some have lived among the tall, blond and civilized Norwegians, yet they still maintain the appearance and semi-barbarous customs of their ancestors.

Lapland is the land of the reindeer, the only domesticated animal hardy enough to stand the frigid climate. The Lapps have huge herds, which supply meat and milk for both consumption and sale.

MODERN VIKINGS

It is only natural that Norway should have produced some of the greatest of Arctic explorers. The blood of the Vikings, the skilful seamanship, the love of ice and snow, all contribute to this. In earlier centuries these men of the North had plunged across the stormy North Atlantic to discover Iceland, Greenland, and America. In the last hundred years they have headed into new, unexplored lands in both the Arctic and Antarctic regions. Fridtjof Nansen was the first in this new era of discovery. In 1893 he touched the most northerly point ever reached by man. But Norway is proudest of that glorious adventurer—Roald Amundsen. He was the first man to reach the South Pole, in 1911. In 1926 he flew across the North Polar Continent from Spitsbergen, Norway, to Alaska. In 1928 he died a hero's death searching for the lost Italian polar airship.

Courtesy Press Bureau of Ministry of Foreign Affairs, Oslo

VIKING SHIP, OSLO
In boats like this early Norsemen sailed forth to explore
and conquer.

A TALE OF THREE CITIES

The cities of Norway have a setting of natural beauty that is unsurpassed anywhere in the world, for forests and fiords lie close upon the borders of human habitations. There are no ugly, straggling suburbs. Norwegians are neat people and they pride themselves upon their cleanliness.

Oslo, first of the nation's cities, lies at the head of Oslo Fiord and is surrounded by forest-covered hills. It was founded in 1047 and for 900 years has been the capital of the country. To-day, it is the headquarters of Norway's railway and steamship lines. It is a center of industry and trade, with over 300,000 people. But this ancient city is proud of its past and is eager to preserve all memories of it.

The outstanding place of interest in Oslo is the Folk Museum at Bygdö, a peninsula jutting out into Oslo Fiord. Here ancient timber houses from all parts of the country have been re-erected in a natural setting, showing to modern Norwegians how their ancestors lived from the earliest times. Here, too, are Norway's greatest historical treasures, the remains of two Viking ships— the Oseberg ship and the Gokstad ship.

Bergen (100,000 population) is Norway's second city. It is known as the City of Olav the Peaceful, an unusual name for a Viking chieftain. That gentleman was the founder of Bergen in 1070. The city stands magnificently on seven mountains and contains many historical buildings. First there is the Rosenkrantz Tower, built in the middle of the thirteenth century, which strikingly illustrates how people lived in a medieval fortification. Just back of this tower is the famous Royal Banqueting Hall of King Haakon Haakonsson, also built in the thirteenth century. Here the hearty Norsemen of old quaffed huge tankards of ale and devoured great roasts.

A stone's throw away is the Hanseatic block. These justly famed buildings were once the headquarters of the fifteenth-century German merchant and military organization called the Hansa. The merchants had their offices, salesrooms and living quarters in this block. The city has transformed one of the buildings into a Hanseatic Museum, so complete in every detail that it transports the visitor back to the life of five or six centuries ago.

Courtesy Press Bureau of the Ministry of Foreign Affairs, Oslo

HAAKON'S HALL IN BERGEN DATES BACK TO THE 13TH CENTURY

Trondheim (60,000 population) was once the capital of Norway and, in its magnificent Gothic Cathedral of St. Olav, the Norwegian kings still are crowned. It might well be called the "town that won't stay named" for in its history of a thousand years it has had at least four names. As late as 1930 all Norway was rocked by an argument over a new name but in the end everyone seemed contented with "Trondheim." It lies only three degrees south of the Arctic Circle yet has a surprisingly mild climate. Its river and fiord are seldom frozen and it is surrounded by a verdant forest.

Trondheim was founded in 997 A.D. by King Olav Trygvesson, who had once been a slave. It was Olav who began the conversion of his country to Christianity. But the Cathedral of St. Olav honors his successor, Olav Haraldsson, killed in battle in 1030. While alive this Olav was called the Fat, but shortly after his death he was found to have been a holy man and a martyr and was surnamed the Saint. Over his grave was erected one of the famous cathedrals of Europe. For many years Olav's body was enclosed in a beautiful silver casket, studded with precious stones, which rested above the altar. This disappeared in the sixteenth century, and legend has it that it was taken by the king then ruling and turned into coin to help finance his wars.

These three are Norway's greatest cities, but there are many others of much interest. For example, at Lillehammer a series of waterfalls extends right through the city. Here, too, is the famed Sandvigian collection of ancient Norse dwellings, all of which contain their original furnishings.

Courtesy Press Bureau of the Ministry of Foreign Affairs, Oslo

THE GOL CHURCH DATES BACK TO THE
12TH CENTURY

Courtesy Swedish Traffic Association, Stockholm

ENGELBREKT CHURCH IN STOCKHOLM

ROYAL PALACE OF STOCKHOLM
Erected 1690-1754 according to the plans of Nicodemus Tessin.

THE IMPRESSION which the traveler carries away with him from Sweden will depend on the guides to whom he gives a receptive ear, and on his own mental attunement. If he listens to those who glory in history and tradition, he will find a country rich in memories and relics of a thousand-year past. If his guide lays stress on the streamlined Sweden of today, he will return with an impression of a country which is vigorously forging to the front in industry, in applied arts and architecture, and in social and economic organization.

The guide devoted to tradition will emphasize the grandeur of the royal castles, and the great houses of Sweden's nobility; he will point to the picturesque little villages where farmers still attend church in heavily embroidered peasant costume, and where folk dances are performed at midsummer festivals; he will dwell on the famous museums and their array of hand-spun clothes, odd peasant-woven draperies, and highly decorated furniture of the Gustavian period.

The modernist, impatient of such sentimental preoccupation with the past, will lead the traveler to "functionalistic" coöperative apartments and office buildings, grain elevators, and factories, whose sleek lines bespeak twentieth-century efficiency. He will arouse interest in the new model workers' homes in the suburbs of Stockholm, and the many parks and athletic fields. The modernist will take the path to the shops where endless original designs in brass, ceramics, glass, textiles and furniture proclaim a vigorous activity in industrial arts.

Traditionalist and modernist alike may enjoy, however, the surpassing beauty and variety of scenery, for almost no section in Sweden is flat or dull. There are hills, mountains, watercourses, lakes, islands, forests and verdant fields, which are always interesting, and often magnificent. The late sun which lingers on far into the summer evenings paints the landscape with vibrant colors and leaves an afterglow into the night.

GOTHENBURG

The approach to Gothenburg—usually the tourist's first introduction to Sweden, is through a strange and bewildering maze of islets and skerries, many of them mere lumps of barren rock, others covered sparsely with pines that are gnarled and distorted from the impact of incessant winds. From the distance, the tall redbrick tower of the modern Masthuggs Church, stands high above the city, and within a short time, the great harbor of Gothenburg moves slowly into view with its floating docks, shipyards, and quays where vessels of every kind from ocean liners to fishing smacks are moored.

Courtesy Swedish Traffic Association, Stockholm
Photo by Heurlin
GIRLS FROM LEKSAND; INHABITANTS OF DALARNA STILL WEAR THEIR GAY OLD COSTUMES ON FESTIVE DAYS

Located at the mouth of the river Göta Alv, Gothenburg is an important sea-port on Sweden's Atlantic coast, and has a population of over 250,000. Now a busy commercial center, Gothenburg was originally a city of great military importance when it was founded by Gustavus Adolphus early in the seventeenth century. Remnants still exist of old fortifications built by Dutch architects, and an old moat, which together with the river once enclosed the city, still remains, though now the city spreads far beyond its confines.

Any account of Gothenburg is incomplete without a mention of "Trädgardsföreningen," a botanical garden and park located in the center of the city, which contains a profusion of magnificent flower beds and greenhouses, and of "Slottskogen," a large park located mainly on the hills to the south of the city proper, from which a wonderful view may be had of the city.

Courtesy Swedish Traffic Association, Stockholm   Photo by Gullers

THE WEST COAST

Both north and south of Gothenburg along the coast, are located many seaside resorts and watering places. The country is jagged and rocky, for the most part, with a cold, rugged, brutal beauty. Among the fiords of the Bohuslän coast north of Gothenburg, and on many of the larger of the multitudinous islands, are fishing villages to which tourists flock in the summer to enjoy the sailing, fishing, and refreshing salt-water swimming. In several places may be found *hällristningar*—strange inscriptions on rocks, carved by prehistoric dwellers more than 3,000 years ago.

From Gothenburg the traveler may journey to Stockholm, the capital of Sweden, located on the east side of the Scandinavian peninsula, by means of fast electric trains in six hours. However, if he has leisure, he will do well to spend three days on the trip and take the Göta Canal route. For centuries, the Swedes dreamt of the project of a water route which would connect Gothenburg with Stockholm, the two largest commercial centers of the country. Natural waterways were so located that only about a third of the way had to be artificially constructed. After thirty years, in 1832, the great project was finally completed, only to be rendered obsolete almost immediately by the advent of the railroads.

THE RIDDAR-
HOLM CHURCH
IN STOCKHOLM
The tomb of King
Magnus Ladulas,
who founded the
church about 1280,
as well as that of
King Karl Knutsson
(d. 1470), is now
preserved in the
aisle.

ENGINEER IN KNEE PANTS

One of the construction engineers was John Erickson, later famous as the inventor of the *Monitor,* the first modern type armored battleship which defeated the *Merrimac* in the famous Civil War battle. At the age of thirteen, young Erickson was a surveyor on the canal project, heading a crew of 600 men, though he had to climb on a box to peer through the surveying instruments.

Now the canal is mostly used as a tourist route, and a journey over it is a unique experience in water travel. In many places, the canal is so narrow that the boats seem to cut their way through the meadows and fields. Passengers may disembark and follow the boat on foot in many places while it traverses some of the sixty-five locks. The trip begins along Göta Alv, and proceeds to Trollhättan, scene of magnificent rapids and waterfalls.

THE CANAL ROUTE

From Trollhättan, the way proceeds through Lake Vänern, and then into the canal proper, through the fertile fields and meadows of Västergötland. In approximately the center of the Scandinavian Peninsula, the long narrow Lake Vättern is crossed. Stops may be made at Vadstena on the east shore of the lake, to inspect the fine old Renaissance castle, and the convent founded by Saint Bridget in the fourteenth century. The canal continues through Ostergötland, descending in a series of locks toward the Baltic Sea, past the idyllic towns of Hjo and Gränna and Vreta Abbey, where tombs of ancient Swedish kings may be seen; through a number of small birch-bordered lakes, and through the thriving industrial towns of Norrköping and Soderköping to the Baltic. From there, the route lies north through the lovely archipelago of the Baltic—as friendly and verdant as that of Bohuslän is cold and austere—to the coast town of Södertälje. Another short canal leads into Lake Mälaren, dotted with thousands of islands, to Stockholm.

VENICE OF THE NORTH

Swedish literature abounds in lyrical tributes to Stockholm. Named "Queen of Mälaren" and "Venice of the North," it is a city about which it is easy to become ecstatic. Much of its charm is derived from the many bodies of water which make up an integral part of the city. It is situated partly on Lake Mälaren, partly on the Baltic, and partly on thirteen islands scattered in both. Many of the streets follow bays and streams in the very heart of the city, and in the summer these are filled with numerous gaily

Courtesy Swedish Traffic Association, Stockholm

THE TOWN HALL, ON LAKE MALAREN

Erected in 1923 under the supervision of Prof. Ragnar Ostberg, this monumental edifice is one of the most artistic modern buildings in Europe.

colored craft of all kinds. Ferries compete with streetcars
and buses as means of transportation. Heavily laden lumber
schooners moor at the quay at Strandvägen, the most fashionable
street in the city directly opposite luxurious apartment houses.
Fishing boats bring their catch directly to one of the public markets located at another quay. There is a freshness and sparkling
charm about Stockholm, equalled by few cities in the world.

The oldest part of Stockholm is the so-called "City between
the Bridges" located on a small island. A few traces may be found
of structures erected as early as the thirteenth century, and many
of the houses were built in the seventeenth and eighteenth centuries. The outstanding building on the island is the royal palace
—a massive rectilinear building in Italian Renaissance style, erected in the latter part of the seventeenth century. With its severe,
angular structure, it is not out of harmony with some of the
modern architecture, despite its classic type of ornamentation.
In the "City between the Bridges" also stands the Riddarholm
Church, a high-vaulted cathedral, the Swedish equivalent of Westminster Abbey, rich with tombs and memories of Swedish kings
and heroes. A block away, stands the Assembly of the House of
Nobles, a good example of seventeenth-century Dutch Renaissance architecture.

HEROES AT THE CITY HALL

Stockholmers take a personal pride of possession in their City
Hall, and they have every right to do so. Designed by architect
Ragnar Ostberg, it took twenty years to build, cost a tremendous
amount of money, was the subject of plans which were changed
time and time again, and furnished a topic for constant newspaper
arguments by architects, critics, politicians, and indignant tax-
payers. One of the features which provoked much talk was the
plan to erect nude statues of famous Swedish men. Despite the
objection of moralists and others, the plan went through, and you
may now view August Strindberg in the nude, staring in anguish
at the ground before him in the formal garden outside the City
Hall, in the company of other distinguished Swedes, also in the
nude. Many Stockholmers literally own a portion of the building. At one stage in the construction, an appeal was made for
funds to lay a copper roof, and each donor of a copper plate has
his name inscribed on it. Surprisingly enough, the building turned

Courtesy Swedish Traffic Association, Stockholm

MODERN RESIDENTIAL SECTION OF STOCKHOLM

out to be an architectural masterpiece. A number of outstanding artists have had a hand in the interior decorations, which range in style from classical simplicity to oriental lushness.

A building of massive simplicity, constructed by Westman in the early part of the twentieth century, houses the law courts. Other stately edifices in the monumental style in vogue in the late nineteenth and early twentieth century are the University of Technology building, the Municipal Stadium, the Engelbrekt Church, and several of the schools.

THE NEW ARCHITECTURE

The newer Swedish architects, influenced by LeCorbusier's writings have made "functionalism" their slogan, and the buildings designed by this school contrast with the massiveness and pretentiousness of the buildings just mentioned, though they have in common with them, the fundamental simplicity of line and surface, which may be said to characterize Swedish architecture as a whole. The Municipal Library is a rigorously "functional" building, designed by Asplund, who became the high priest of the school during the 1930 exposition in Stockholm. The flour mills and silo of the co-operative union, and many of the co-operative apartment buildings are successful examples of "functionalism." There are many others. In fact, almost any random walk through Stockholm will reward the tourist interested in architecture.

Stockholm has a number of excellent museums, including the Nordic Museum with its fine historical collection, and the National Gallery which houses a representative group of Swedish and foreign masters. Of outstanding interest is Skansen, an outdoor museum on a wooded plateau just outside of Stockholm. It contains, in addition to a zoölogical garden, a group of old farm buildings, homesteads, and churches which have been transported from various parts of Sweden. They are completely equipped as they were hundreds of years ago, and enable visitors to study Swedish peasant life of long ago.

UPPSALA

From Stockholm it is only a short distance to Uppsala, the site of Uppsala University, founded by Gustavus Adolphus in the seventeenth century. "Domkyrkan" is an excellent example of Gothic cathedral architecture. Nearby are curious burial mounds and stones with runic inscriptions dating from the Viking period. The countryside surrounding Stockholm and Uppsala boasts a number of palaces erected by noble families during the seventeenth and eighteenth centuries, when Sweden was one of the most powerful and wealthy countries in Europe.

PEASANTS AND ARTISTS

In a northwesterly direction from Stockholm, lies the province of Dalecarlia, home of the most vivid historical lore in Sweden. In some of the villages near Lake Siljan the farmers still wear, at least on Sundays, the old-fashioned, bright-colored peasant costumes. At Mora, one may visit the former home of Anders Zorn, the world-famous etcher and painter, who immortalized the peasant types of the neighborhood and modeled the statue of Gustavus Vasa which now stands on a wooded hillock at Mora. Zorn also founded "Gammelgarden," a very fine local museum.

West of Dalecarlia is Värmland, a province of great natural beauty, with dark forests, broad valleys, rivers, and little winding lakes. Some of Sweden's greatest poets and authors, including

Tegner, Fröding, and Selma Lagerlöf, have written lovingly and vividly of this country. The beauty of the valley surrounding Lake Fryken, has been glowingly immortalized by Selma Lagerlöf, in *Gösta Berling* and *Morbacka*.

The northern part of Sweden, Norrland, is a land of tremendous forests; mountain ranges whose peaks are covered with perpetual snow; broad rivers and rushing torrents and waterfalls. Lumber camps are located far in the deep forests, and millions of logs are floated down the great rivers every year to the sawmills near the Baltic. The population is concentrated in the fertile river valleys, where farmers manage to eke out a living in spite of the shortness of the summer, and the early killing frost.

INDUSTRY IN THE ARCTIC

As one proceeds northward through Sweden, the summer nights become shorter and more luminous, until, north of the Arctic Circle, the sun stays above the horizon continuously for forty days and nights. This section, known as Lapland, is a wild, rugged, mountainous country, through which the nomad Lapps still roam, seeking grazing grounds for their herds of reindeer in the great forests. Yet, the modern traveler can reach these parts without inconvenience. An electric railway carries him directly from Stockholm, all the way through the arctic country, to Narvik on the Norwegian coast. The railroad reaches a number of tourist resorts situated on rivers and lakes. The main function of

THE MIDNIGHT SUN AT PORJUS, LAPLAND

Eight exposures made from 10:10 P.M. to 12:30 A.M.

Courtesy Swedish Traffic Association, Stockholm

the railroad, however, is to transport the great quantities of iron ore mined in Lapland. The largest mining town is Kiruna, over a hundred miles north of the Arctic Circle, with a population of 12,000.

SOUTHERN SWEDEN

From Stockholm, the traveler whose taste runs less to the grand sweep of desolate mountains and dark forests, and more to the intimate beauty of cultivated land, will turn south rather than north. And the further south he journeys, the more densely populated and verdant the country. The southernmost province, Scania, is rich farm land, with fertile plains divided by rows of willow trees, and dotted with small villages and white-towered churches. Many landmarks still remain of the early days when Scania was under the domination of Denmark. They can be found in the quaint old university town of Lund, with its stately romanesque cathedral, in Hälsingborg on the coast, immediately opposite Elsinore in Denmark, in the picturesque towns of Fasterbo and Ystad, now popular summer resorts with modern golf links. Near the idyllic village of Bostad, are the Lugnaro mounds, burial grounds of the Viking period.

The largest city of southern Sweden, with a population of 130,000, is Malmö, located on the sound separating Denmark and Sweden. From Trälleborg on the southern tip, direct connection by railway ferry is made with Sassnitz in Germany. Trains move directly onto the ferry which makes the trip in four hours.

CITY OF RUINS AND ROSES

The two large islands in the Baltic, Oland and Gottland, are both rich in historical interest. The latter was once of great commercial importance when, as a member of the Hanseatic League during the twelfth and thirteenth centuries, it controlled the trade on the Baltic. Its principal city, Visby, was once one of the richest in northern Europe. Sacked by the Danish King Valdemar IV in 1362, it was never completely rebuilt. Beautifully situated on rocky terraces sloping toward the sea, Visby is still surrounded by the thirteenth-century town wall, two and one-half miles in length with thirty-seven square towers. The ruins are overgrown with wild roses, and a melancholy peace rests over the city that

Courtesy Swedish Traffic Association, Stockholm

VISBY, "CITY OF RUINS AND ROSES"
The city wall of this old Hanseatic stronghold is one of the best preserved in Europe.

was once the "Queen of the Baltic" and now is known as "The City of Ruins and Roses."

The island of Oland, too, abounds in historical tradition which goes back as far as the days of the Vikings. On a high terrace above the main city, Borgholm, lie the magnificent ruins of a medieval castle, its massive towers, ramparts, and moat still intact.

Courtesy Royal Danish Consulate, Chicago

THE CITY HALL OF COPENHAGEN

Courtesy Royal Danish Consulate, Chicago

THE ROYAL CASTLE AT COPENHAGEN, SEEN FROM THE MARBLE BRIDGE

THE PEOPLE of Denmark today look back for inspiration to their Viking ancestors, who, for hundreds of years before the Roman legions invaded northern Europe, were seafaring adventurers, piloting their tiny ships across uncharted seas, making the Danes a power to be reckoned with on the waterways of the world.

Today, however, the Danish nation is respected for achievements more in keeping with its place in a modern civilized world. Among the leaders in social, democratic, and scientific movements Denmark ranks high. The adventurous spirit of the old Vikings has turned to pioneer work in social insurance, in agricultural conservation, and in education. As a result, the citizens of the picturesque, sea-encircled kingdom lead enviably secure lives, free to enjoy the diverse recreations offered by their bright beaches, beautiful forests, and island resorts. The oldest kingdom in Europe, Denmark is proud of the record of constant improvement and accomplishment which has made it a recognized leader in many fields among the enlightened nations of the world.

[131]

ANCIENT VIKINGS

The earliest inhabitants of Denmark were the Germanic tribes of the Cimbri. They were overcome early in the Christian era by invasions of Angles, Saxons, and Jutes, who overran the entire country. There are sparse records of a unity in Denmark as early as the eighth century, but the first king to achieve any marked historical prominence was pagan Sweyn I, about 985 A.D. His son was the famous Canute I who led the conquest of England. It was during these two reigns that Denmark was converted to Christianity, largely by Bishop Absalon, the founder of Copenhagen. He was a man of outstanding talents as a fighter, organizer, and leader; and when he learned that he had been named bishop, he firmly declined the honor. However, in the face of threatened excommunication if he continued to refuse, he consented to accept. The story of his heroic conversion of the Danes and Wends by physical force and strength of personality is an amazing epoch in church history.

In the latter half of the nineteenth century Denmark was ruled by Christian IX, facetiously dubbed "the father-in-law of Europe" because of the many marriages of his children into the ruling families of Europe. He was succeeded by Frederik VIII, whose brief rule was terminated by his death in 1912. Since that time Denmark's peaceful and progressive history has been under the leadership of her present king, Christian X.

SCULPTURED BY THE SEA

The features of Denmark have been shaped by the seas which nearly surround it. The North Sea to the westward, the Skagerrak and Kattegat to the north, and the Baltic Sea on the east have all carved the land; so that, although Denmark is only about half the size of the state of South Carolina, its total coastline is much longer and so irregular as to be difficult to compute.

The country is divided physically into two parts: the peninsula of Jutland, which joins the mainland of Europe and comprises more than two-thirds of the total area, and the many islands. There are some five hundred of these; the largest are Zealand, on which the capital, Copenhagen, is located, Fyn, Laaland, and Bornholm.

With the exception of Bornholm, which is a beautiful craggy island in the Baltic, Denmark is a low-lying country of fertile

Courtesy Royal Danish Consulate, Chicago

KOGE, OLD PROVINCIAL CITY OF DENMARK

fields, heaths, woodlands, and peat bogs, everywhere fringed by
white sandy beaches. The entire landscape is sprinkled with innumerable lakes, fiords, belts, and sounds. The largest of these is
the great Limfiord in the north, which cuts across almost the
entire breadth of Jutland.

"THE CITY OF BEAUTIFUL TOWERS"

Copenhagen, Denmark's capital, is the nerve center of Danish
life. The name itself means "port of merchants," and since the
days of Frederick II Copenhagen has held a place as one of the
leading ports of Northern Europe.

The reason for the nickname, the "city of beautiful towers,"
becomes clear as Copenhagen is approached from the waters of the
sound. From the harbor can be seen towers of every description,

Courtesy Royal Danish Consulate, Chicago

THORVALDSEN MUSEUM IN COPENHAGEN
This museum contains a complete collection, in originals and models, of the works
of the renowned sculptor.

rising above the level of the rooftops in all directions. Here one beholds the unusual spire of the Church of Our Savior (Vor Frelsers Kirke) with its spiral staircase winding up the outside of the spire. Over there is the Nikolai Church with its magnificent and massive tower, and there, the Exchange building (Brsen) a fine example of Renaissance architecture, rearing its strange spire of twisted dragon tails. Just beyond the Exchange spire is the elaborate tower of Christiansborg Palace, where the Rigsdag, the Danish parliament, holds its sessions. To the west rises the tall peaked tower of the Raadhus, the City Hall, in its great open square, and away to the east can be seen the immense copper dome of Frederik's Church. Towers everywhere, raising the gleaming green of their copper heads over the city, make Copenhagen's skyline as interesting and as typically Old World as it is different from the Western skylines.

A CITY OF CONTRASTS

But Copenhagen is not always representative of the Old. Blended with sights reminiscent of the past are scenes that are

completely modern. The city abounds with such historic buildings as the famous Round Tower, erected as an observatory by
King Christian IV and ascended by a winding ramp. It was to
the top of this ramp, according to an old legend, that the Russian tsar, Peter the Great, drove in his imperial carriage. One
can see the changing of the guard at noon before Amaliensborg
Palace, the Royal residence, a traditional and changeless ceremony,
with the band playing and the magnificent sentries themselves
marching stiffly under their immense beaver caps. Remains of
the underground stronghold built eight centuries ago in defense
against the marauding Wends by Bishop Absalon can still be seen
beneath the Christiansborg Palace.

But on the other hand, whole blocks of coöperative apartment buildings, with simple and artistic lines, exemplify the finest
of modern architecture. The recently erected Grundtvig Memorial Church is one of the most striking structures of the world,
designed to resemble the pipes of a vast organ and constructed
with yellow brick. To harmonize with the plan of this unique
structure, all nearby houses have been redecorated.

A CITY OF COLOR

Wandering through the streets of the city, one is everywhere
greeted by color—gay reds, blues, bright yellows. Past the Brsen
and Christiansborg Palace is the Thorvaldsen Museum, in which
are the works and the tomb of the noted Danish sculptor, Bertel
Thorvaldsen. Beyond this is Gammel Strand, with its picturesque
fish market, where the Skovshoved fishwives, wearing bonnets like
stiff flour sacks, display their wares along the quay. Another
colorful market is Grntorvet, the vegetable market, swarming
with farmers and their produce—fruit, vegetables, and flowers;
and alive with the buzz of bargaining housewives. The market
is crowded and overflows into nearby streets until 9 A.M. when it
is cleared until the next morning. In the great public square at
the foot of Stergade is the Royal Theater and its annex, the
"starling box," which houses the State Broadcasting Institution.
In the theater are presented opera, ballet, and legitimate dramatic
productions which make the state-owned institution one of the
bright spots of Danish culture.

Another color evident in Copenhagen is the green of its parks
and gardens. Continuing north along the Bredgade, past Amaliensborg Palace and the various legations and embassies clustered

HANS CHRISTIAN ANDERSEN'S TOMBSTONE

around it, the visitor enters the Langelinie Promenade. Here is the Gefion fountain, the most famous of Copenhagen's many fountains, named for a mythical goddess who was granted by the king of the gods as much land as she could plow in a single night. Transforming her four sons into oxen, she managed to plow around the entire island of Zealand, which then became, and in a large measure still is, the focus of Danish life. North of the fountain is the Yacht Club with the charming statue of the Little Mermaid (Havfrue) before it. Close at hand is the ancient Citadel with its moat and green park around it. This is the most northerly of the chain of parks which encircles the city along the old line of defense fortifications, moats and ramparts. To its west lies the green expanse of the Ostre Anlaeg in which is located the Kunstmuseum, the state museum of art with its fine collection of Dutch paintings of the seventeenth century as well as other treasures. The other two links in the chain of parks are the Botanical Gardens and the King's Garden. In King's Garden is Rosenborg Castle, and also one of the several statues of Hans Christian Andersen, loved throughout the world as the weaver of children's fairy tales.

DEMOCRACY ON TWO WHEELS

Everywhere in Copenhagen people are on bicycles. Every new street, every open square is a reminder of this. Everyone, apparently, from the most dignified magistrate to the smallest schoolboy, rides a bicycle. Actually, bicycles outnumber cars twenty to one, according to records. The throngs of cyclists on the street reflect the democratic feeling that comes naturally with this sort of association and the general attitude toward exercise in promoting good health. Both are important elements in Danish life.

Facilities for recreation exist in Copenhagen both for the Danes in their moments of leisure, and for visitors from abroad. Pleasant sidewalk cafes dot the Raadhusplads and extend into Vestergade and other streets in the neighborhood. Nowhere else in northern Europe is the delightful custom of eating and drinking in the open air followed to the extent that it is in Copenhagen. The center of recreational life in the city, however, is the Tivoli,

Courtesy Royal Danish Consulate, Chicago

"AFTER OFFICE HOURS"
Bicycles outnumber automobiles twenty to one in Copenhagen.

where an overwhelming variety of amusements is available. Among its features are excellent symphonic concerts, fireworks, many dancing places, a pantomime theater, and an amusement park.

The cathedral of Roskilde, not far from Copenhagen contains the tombs of Danish royalty, from the recent past back to King Harald Bluetooth, the early ruler whose name is associated with many of the antique runic stones scattered throughout Jutland. Only a short distance from Roskilde is Lejre, famous as the scene of the old Anglo-Saxon epic, *Beowulf*. But the dismal swamps of Grendel are far removed from the pleasant fields of modern Zealand.

The thirty-five miles of coast northward from Copenhagen along the sound has been called "Denmark's Riviera." The attractive beaches extending shoreward to forests of pine and beech are certainly some of the most pleasing scenes to be found in the country.

At the northern entrance to the sound is Elinore (Helsingör) and Kronborg Castle, which Shakespeare made the scene of his *Hamlet*. The castle itself is a huge impressive building, vastly heightened in interest by the almost tangible presence of Hamlet and Polonius and Ophelia in the stone halls and upon the parapets.

Cannon exhibited on the platforms of the castle are a reminder of the days when Elsinore controlled the shipping through the narrow neck of the sound, and exacted a toll from all passing ships. Also on display in Kronberg Castle are models of scientific and engineering devices made by Danish experimenters, including a complete model of a Diesel engine, in the design of which Denmark is one of the leaders.

NATURE ON ISLAND AND PENINSULA

The island of Funen and its neighboring small islands, lying between Zealand and Jutland, is outstanding for the fertility of its land and the mildness of its climate. On Funen is the town of Odense, the birthplace of Hans Christian Andersen; and the placid and good-natured charm of his fairy tales seems to pervade the entire atmosphere of the island.

Jutland is the bulwark of Denmark against the pounding breakers of the North Sea. Always Jutland suffered from inundations, shifting sand spits, and restless dunes. But the perseverance

Courtesy Royal Danish Consulate, Chicago

KRONBERG CASTLE IN HELSINGOR
This seaport is also known by the name of Elsinore, famed as the scene of
Shakespeare's *Hamlet*.

of the Danish people has long controlled the ravages of the sea by a dike system, and about eighty years ago the dunes were covered with plantations and forests to prevent them from shifting. There is little waste land in Denmark, about ninety percent of the land being made productive by the thrifty Danes.

The only possible rival to the unique place Bornholm holds in the Danish scene is the little island of Moen, located just south of Zealand. Impressive though they are, the chalk cliffs of Moen are scarcely comparable to the rugged granite crags of Bornholm. Ronne, the capital, is a village of gaily colored houses painted in amazing reds, blues, corals, yellows. The cliffs of the island serve as background for the peculiar round churches. These massive towers are reminders of the days when protection, vital against pirate raids, was combined with religious worship in church-fortresses.

Courtesy Finnish Central Chamber of Commerce. Helsingfors

RAILWAY STATION IN HELSINGFORS, FINLAND

Courtesy Finnish Central Chamber of Commerce, Helsingfors

TYPICAL FINNISH LAKE SCENERY

SITUATED far up in the northeastern corner of Europe, Finland is one of the most romantic as well as one of the most forgotten countries in the world. Its very solitude lends charm to its virgin landscape, and the invigorating climate gives health and strength to the inhabitants. The exhausted city dweller, the curious naturalist, the enthusiastic hiker and sportsman, and especially the angler—everyone will find Finland richly remunerative in the quest for romance, beauty, and culture. Not only is Finland a country of vast forests, numerous lakes, and tidy agricultural communities; but its cities and towns are modern, prosperous, and noted for their cleanliness.

CENTURIES OF STRUGGLE FOR INDEPENDENCE

Life was hard for the early Finnish tribes that settled in prehistoric times amid the wild forests that covered most of northern Europe. To obtain their livelihood, they cleared with utmost difficulty sufficient land to cultivate their fields, and the poor soil and a rigid climate demanded a sturdy character of the settlers.

Courtesy Finnish Central Chamber of
Commerce, Helsingfors

MEDIEVAL CASTLE OF VIBORG,
FINLAND
The statue of its founder, Tyrqils Knutsson
is in left foreground.

Thus the Finns early developed a strain of stubborn determination which was to lead them to ultimate independence from foreign domination.

Swedish crusaders converted them to Christianity in the twelfth century and shortly afterward the country was annexed by Sweden. The Swedish rule lasted for seven hundred years, during which time Finnish soldiers fought in all of Sweden's wars. Thus, by the time Finland passed into Russia's grip in 1809, it had become not only thoroughly westernized, but also it was conscious of its own nationality. Russian domination had very little effect on Finnish thought and culture, and in 1917, after various encroachments on their liberty by the tsars, the Finns declared their independence. Foreign countries, including the Union of Soviet Socialist Republics, recognized the new nation, and Finland was now enabled to give free expression to its national culture molded during its long history.

A LAND OF SIXTY THOUSAND LAKES

Although Finland is popularly styled "the Land of a Thousand Lakes," in reality it has sixty thousand lakes and some forty thousand islands. The lakes are of varying sizes—Ladoga, the largest lake in Europe, is located between Finland and Russia—and their crystalline surface is dotted with dozens of islands of odd shapes. More than half of the country is covered with forests, mostly of firs, pines and birches, and everywhere, as far as the eye can reach, the landscape stretches out in a vast, green, and sometimes gently rolling expanse. The air is clear and rich with the scent of flowers and timbers. No smoke obscures the view, whether in urban or rural communities. Imagine this virgin summer vista of lakes, islands, and forests bathed in almost continuous

STEAM BATHS
AT HELSINGFORS

Probably the nation-
al custom of taking
sauna (steam) baths
contributes to the
health and strength
of Finnish athletes.

Courtesy Finnish Central
Chamber of Commerce,
Helsingfors

sunlight! For during June and July the sun sets for scarcely an
hour, and in this short season it drenches the air with warmth,
bringing forth a wealth of flowers in the fields and wild forests.

While the warm summer days make us forget the northern
location of Finland, we would get a taste of its winter if we
stayed there from October to April. During this time the hours
of daylight are few, and an abundance of snow and ice challenges
the endurance and good humor of the inhabitants. But communication is not interrupted, for the deep snow permits one to slide
all over the landscape on skis.

It is no wonder that such a healthful climate should produce a
hardy race of people. In sports, Finland has more world's records
than countries with a population ten times its own. It ranks
especially high in track athletes, of whom Nurmi is the most
famous, and, in fact, some people remember Finland only for its
records in the Olympic Games.

MODERN CITIES

Finland is by no means solely an agricultural country. Indeed,
the visitor is surprised to find modern and prosperous cities and
towns with the comforts and pleasures of any large American city.
The settlements are connected with one another by fine highways
and railways, which are owned by the state, as in most European
countries. Cities are not very large, but they are spotlessly clean
and present a strikingly modern architecture.

Courtesy Finnish Central Chamber of Commerce, Helsingfors

HARBOR AND MARKET PLACE OF HELSINGFORS, FINLAND

"The White City of the North" is the descriptive appellation for Helsinki (Helsingfors), the capital of Finland, and incidentally, the northernmost capital in the world. The light-colored stucco and red granite buildings, the broad clean streets, and the sun-washed air impart a whiteness to the city, which might almost suggest a southern climate were it not for the long winters.

Helsinki is a relatively new city, its buildings dating for the most part from the nineteenth century. There is little evidence of old Helsinki, except for the large Senate Square, where a few impressive buildings of the early nineteenth century still stand. The State University and the State Council Building are located here, and so is the *Suurkirkko*, a beautiful domed church, with a stately flight of steps leading to it. But most of the buildings were erected during the last seventy years, and it is the modern architecture that interests us most in this city.

There are few cities in the world that can boast of such a splendid building as the monumental Railway Station in Helsinki. Designed and built by the famous architect Eliel Saarinen, it has an austere and powerful simplicity, with its bold broad arch over the main entrance, and its gigantic tower, all constructed of red granite. Equally imposing is the huge new Diet Building of pink-white granite in severe, geometric proportions. Erected on a large mound of granite, it appears as if it were a natural outgrowth of the landscape. Immediately beyond the Diet is an edifice of singular beauty, the National Museum, interesting for its unique architectural style—purely Finnish, perhaps—as well as for the fine exhibits of Finnish civilization since prehistoric times.

Helsinki is practically surrounded by water, for it is built on a peninsula, and harbors built on three sides of the city lead almost into the town center. The Market Place, located on paved squares bordering on the South Harbor, is a busy spot. Here most of the day's food shopping is done, and here, too, passenger steamers from Denmark, Sweden, Germany, and England make port and unload. Facing the market and the water front are several important buildings, including the temporary Town Hall, the Swedish Legation, and the residence of the President of Finland.

TOWNS OF MEDIEVAL BACKGROUND

While Helsinki impresses us as being a modern city, there are many spots which reflect the long past of the country. One of the most interesting towns is Viipuri, until recently better known under its Swedish name of Viborg. Its thirteenth-century castle looms up on a steep hill, facing a bay of the Gulf of Finland. Parts of the wall surrounding the old town of the thirteenth century still stand; and the quaint Round Tower, which defended the wall on the landward side, is now a restaurant. Six miles down the bay from Viipuri is the port Uuras, the largest timber-exporting center in the northern countries.

LUMBER, LUMBER, AND MORE LUMBER

It is natural that lumbering should constitute the main industry of Finland. Witness the endless stretches of forests; consider also the numberless lakes, many of them connected by canals, thus facilitating the transport of logs. Everywhere we see small lumber-craft plowing across lakes, or endless rows of long log-rafts gliding and bobbing down the rapids. Finland exports in large quantities lumber and its by-products, such as paper, cellulose, and cardboard.

Courtesy Finnish Central Chamber of Commerce. Helsingfors

FARM LANDS IN SOUTHERN FINLAND

Next to lumbering, the dairy industry is the most important. The immaculate dairy plants, the surrounding fields, and the pastures with thriving cattle harmonize in their beautiful simplicity with the untouched appearance of the landscape. Butter, cheese and other dairy products, are exported in large quantities.

FINLAND—THE HOME OF SIBELIUS

This country of harmony and peace produced the genius of Jan Sibelius, whose works are known to concert-goers throughout the world. Here he writes the exquisite musical masterpieces which reflect the environment cherished by the nature-loving composer.

In other cultural aspects, too, Finland is outstanding. It is, for instance, claimed that in Finland more books are bought in proportion to the population than in any other country in the world. This was the first European country to grant equal suffrage and rights to men and women. There are three state universities in Finland, besides privately endowed institutions, and the general educational system is of recognized excellence.

The unique trait of the Finns is their sound financial policy. Although internal resources are relatively poor and the trade balance is unfavorable, Finns have paid their debt to the United

States and other countries. No other European state seems to have such a distinctive record, and of this unique performance the Finnish people are highly proud.

MORE HIGHLIGHTS OF FINLAND

It is impossible to mention here all the attractions that the country offers, but, once in Finland, the visitor should not fail to visit Valamo (or Valaamsky), a Greek-Orthodox monastery of old Russia, now within the boundaries of Finland. When taking a steamer to the island on which Valamo stands, a traveler may be startled by the unusual looks of the ship's crew, usually composed of long-bearded Russian monks from the monastery. One should not fail either to see the well-preserved medieval castle "Olavinlinna" in Savonlinna; but, above all, one should take a trip to the Arctic coast into the country of the Lapps.

As we travel north, we will want to stop occasionally to make a big catch of salmon and trout, or, perhaps, to take a ride right on the rapids in a long narrow boat guided by an expert steersman. Finally, we reach the "Great Arctic Highway," the only motor road to the Arctic Ocean. We pass through Lapp villages with their staring inhabitants and their reindeer. Not far from the Arctic coast is situated Yläluostari, the northernmost monastery in the world.

CASTLE OLAVIN-LINNA, SAVON-LINNA, FINLAND

One of the most beautiful medieval castles in the Northern Countries.

Courtesy Finnish Central Chamber of Commerce, Helsingfors

We have seen how Finland combines natural beauty with modern culture, and it is conceivable that such a setting would furnish an admirable playground for travelers. One can indulge in all sports imaginable—fishing, swimming, hiking, and boating in the summer; skiing in the winter; also such city sports as tennis, golf and, if you will, dancing. The cost of living and traveling is low in Finland; in fact, lower than anywhere else in Europe.

Yet the real enchantment, the poetry of Finland which one will never forget, is the "white night" of the North. For even after the sun sets, the sky remains a silvery white, and the landscape appears bewitched in its phosphorescent luminosity, as though an invisible moon poured forth silver rays of light. In such an environment a traveler forgets everything around him, and may take his own prosaic self for a character in fairyland.

INTERIOR OF
600 - YEAR - OLD
CHURCH AT
LOHJA, FINLAND

Courtesy Finnish Central
Chamber of Commerce,
Helsingfors

TODAY THE PRESIDENT of the Estonian Republic occupies the palace built at Tallinn, its capital city, for his wife Catherine in 1718 by Peter the Great, Russia's most aggressive and progressive tsar. It is an ideal "White House," large and commodious, bright and friendly in appearance, shining in the northern sun, with stucco-covered profile, graceful window frames, and light green roof. The palace is surrounded by shady linden trees, and from its front entrance a wide promenade leads down to the sea. Near Catherine's palace, but well within the quiet forest, Peter built for himself, at the foot of a great limestone rock, a small Dutch house of five rooms. It is simple, comfortable and "homey". The great tsar's little retreat is carefully preserved as it was when he occupied it, and is visited as one of the many sights worth while in old Tallinn.

CHARMING MEDIEVAL CITIES

King Valdemar II of Denmark founded Tallinn in 1219, and that city has been fought for and held successively by Danes, Germans, Swedes and Russians, each of whom added some characteristic features. The result is that Tallinn is one of the quaintest and most interesting medieval cities in Europe. Three churches, the castle, a number of houses, and part of the town walls and towers date back to the earliest period, that of Danish domination. The streets run in every direction, up hill and down dale, with many curves and angles. Ancient archways suddenly confront one, and these may be openings into other quaint streets and squares centuries old. Tallinn, before it was renamed by the republic, was known as Reval, and was an important Baltic seaport through which Russia sent her exports to Western Europe.

Narva, on the frontier facing Russia, has an eventful past and a wealth of antiquities. Its fortress was built in the thirteenth century. Danes, Germans and Russians have left examples of their architecture in castles, government buildings and churches. Estonia has an area about half that of the State of Indiana and a population of 1,250,000. Agriculture, timbering and dairying are the chief pursuits of its people. Estonian vodka sells at a premium over domestic brands in other European countries.

2

LATVIA

Photo by Krautcs, Riga, Latvia

LATVIAN GIRLS IN OUT-DOOR DANCE

O F THE three Baltic republics lying on the eastern shores of the Baltic Sea, Latvia, an independent country since 1918, is the largest. All three of these small republics were formally recognized as such by action of the Supreme Council of the Allied Powers, January 21, 1921. Although young politically, the Letts, as the natives of Latvia are called, nevertheless have a colorful history and traditions of their own.

Along with the Lithuanians, ancient Prussians, and some other tribes that have ceased to exist, the Letts formed a Baltic branch of the Indo-European family of nations. Their language, the best proof of their ancient origin, is similar to Sanskrit and is of interest to philologists. Originally these people lived on the upper and middle Vistula, later, at the beginning of the Christian Era, making their way to the shores of the Baltic. The tribes of the Letts lived in comparative peace for many years, carrying on commerce with the Arabs, Romans, and Scandinavians. In the thirteenth century Germany succeeded in subjugating this territory, but five hundred years later the Russians grew more powerful and drove out the Germans. These wars brought hardships to the Letts, but in return prevented the invaders from forcing them to adopt a different culture and to change their age-old customs.

A FARMING COUNTRY

As one would expect, Latvia is essentially a farming nation, approximately two-thirds of the population taking their living from the soil. Timber, butter, flax, small grains, meat, and liquors form the greatest part of the exports. Imports from other nations consist chiefly of coal, machinery, woolen and cotton yarns.

Education is compulsory for children between the ages of seven and sixteen years, and illiteracy is practically unknown. Many theaters, opera houses, and museums, as well as numerous libraries, make Latvia a genuine center of learning. As a country of only two million inhabitants, Latvia may well be proud of her educational and artistic achievements.

TOURISTS' COUNTRY

Riga, the stately capital of Latvia, is the gate through which travelers enter the country. It is one of the most modern cities in Europe, yet with a certain old German air persisting to this day. Here the traveler may visit many historic edifices. The castle, built in the sixteenth century, is still used as the residence

Photo by Krautes, Riga, Latvia

FARMING IN LATVIA

Photo by Krautcs, Riga, Latvia

SKYLINE OF RIGA, LATVIA

of the President. Fine cathedrals, such as St. Mary's, St. Peter's, and St. John's, each with a fascinating history, make Riga a religious center and a travelers' mecca. Other interesting buildings are the Powder Tower, preserving part of the city wall, rebuilt by the Swedes. The principal industry of Latvia is the manufacture of wood products. Except for the fact that there is little air travel, the country offers unexcelled transportation. Dependable train and bus service cover Latvia completely and link her with international lines to every European center.

An outstanding feature of Latvia is the number of resorts to be found there. Kemeri, the most famous, is known for its curative waters. Numerous baths and mud compresses annually attract throngs of patients seeking relief from varied ailments. Seaside and summer resorts supply recreation in bathing, hiking, and exploring. Hunting, sailing, and fishing round out a list of sports for the outdoor enthusiast and make Latvia an ideal spot for complete relaxation and enjoyment.

Black Star photo. By Dr. Wolffe

"GIVE US THIS DAY OUR DAILY BREAD"

WHEN A TRAVELER comes to Lithuania, he comes to a battlefield of many a war old and new. The country is quiet, but it is a stillness of the brooding kind; in the sad air the cannon rumble of the yesteryears seems to echo with a ghostlike muffled sound.

The Teutons were the first to invade Samogitia, as early Lithuania was known. Then, united with Poland, in the eighteenth century Lithuania was divided between Russia and Prussia. But the Lithuanians would not be amalgamated. Despite force and persuasion, their language persisted and their old customs remained. With the close of the World War, Lithuania became independent. Her forests ravaged, her countryside in ashes, Lithuania prepared, after centuries of bondage, to establish her culture and preserve her newly gained liberties.

Nestled in a little valley, under wooded hills where stand the Crusaders' ruined castles, is Kaunas, the capital. Down the middle of her cobbled streets run tree-shaded walks where her inhabitants pass: bearded Jews to their shops or the market; tall, White

Russians in their sheepskin coats; stocky Lithuanians; cassocked priests; and barefooted, or heavy-booted, peasant women, heads covered with white kerchiefs.

Significant of the new day in Kaunas is the municipal electric plant. The handsome, red-brick Gedimine University is also one of its show places. With its ever burning flame, the modern War Memorial is a reminder of Lithuania's war-torn days. Even more so is the red-brick, fifteenth-century Lithuanian-Gothic church of St. Vytautas, used, during the German occupation, as a store, but now restored to its parishoners.

KLAIPEDA

Founded on the shores of the Baltic in the eleventh century by the Teutonic Order is the city Klaipeda. Commercially important, Klaipeda has been burned many times; the marks of the fires are still to be seen on the ornate and grandiose sixteenth-century German houses. German Klaipeda, with its paved, scrupulously clean streets, houses of brick instead of wood, and its general air of modernity and bustle, is a striking contrast to cities in Russianized Lithuania.

It is from Klaipeda that the world gets most of its amber, which is found mainly on the shores of the Baltic sea. Trade in amber is one of Klaipeda's chief occupations and there are many craftsmen who painstakingly prepare amber and carve it as did their ancestors.

There are new government buildings in Kaunas; there are new office and commercial buildings; there is the Casino of Klaipeda. All these indicate vast changes in the old land, reflecting changes in the people.

Homer Smith photo, Chicago

HISTORIC WARSAW, CAPITAL OF POLAND
View of Château Square showing the old cathedral and château.

POLAND ENJOYS THE DISTINCTION of being one of the most interesting, most varied nations in all Europe. Picturesque, dramatic, and impressive, it has been a favorite destination of travelers. Here stately medieval cathedrals rear their heads; baronial castles create a photographer's paradise; treasures of art and architecture, ruins of fortresses, and ancient city walls, long Christianity's protection against the hordes of Asiatic invaders, offer the traveler a beauty of scenery never to be forgotten.

Poland was originally inhabited by a Slavic race, split up into nearly a thousand communities and ruled over by Mieczyslaw I. Under him Christianity became the official religion of the people. He was succeeded by Boleslaus the Great, whose initiative was shown in binding together these separated communities and by enlarging the territory. At this time great distinctions were made in Poland between the peasantry and nobility, distinctions destined to have a far-reaching effect in the history of the country. During the next few hundred years Poland was engaged in wars against the Danes, Hungarians, Russians, and Prussians in order to maintain her independence. Then adding to her troubles, the Tatar invasions of the thirteenth century brought about a division into independent municipalities. Commerce and industry suffered so much from Tatar ravages that German artisans and traders were invited to enter Poland. These civilized immigrants, who did much to improve Polish commerce, were finally absorbed into the population. The Teutonic Order of Knights was encouraged to settle in what is now East Prussia in order to protect that district from the endless raids of Prussian invaders. This Order threatened to conquer all of Poland until its defeat by Wladislaus I in 1332.

Casimir the Great (1333-1370) laid the foundations for a strong Polish nation. Louis of Hungary succeeded to the throne in 1370, and at his death, twelve years later, civil war broke out. Poland and Lithuania were united under one crown late in the fourteenth century when Jagiello became king. As Wladislaus II, this ruler contributed much to Polish stability. His successors reduced Prussia to the position of a subject province; but in the meantime Poland's territories extended as far south as Moldavia, and conflicts with the Turks were inevitable.

DECLINE AND RESURRECTION

After a period of relative greatness, wars were fought with Sweden, Russia, and Turkey which forecast Poland's doom. The Thirteen Years' War with Russia (1655-1667), with intermittent struggles with Sweden, hastened the decline. Foreign intrigue found a fertile field in the chaotic political conditions which prevailed. The story of corruption and dissolution was relieved by the great victory of John Sobieski over the Turks at Vienna in 1683. When the war with Turkey ended at the close of the century, Russia was the chief enemy of Polish independence. The unfortunate country became the principal victim of the Great Northern War (1700-1720), and in 1772 Russia, Prussia, and Austria signed treaties to divide much of Poland among them. About 82,000 square miles of territory went to these despoilers. The small Polish army was unable to cope with the powerful countries which were determined to add to their territories. Successive partitions followed in 1793 and 1795, leaving Poland little more than a memory. When the Poles tried to throw off the yoke of Russia in 1830, they lost their freedom completely and Russian became the language of the courts and schools.

In 1915 Russia was violently expelled from Poland by Germany, and in the Treaty of Versailles (1919) the freedom of Poland was finally established for the first time since 1795, although there remained some dispute over the boundary with Lithuania. Pilsudski became the virtual dictator of Poland in 1926 and remained so until his death in 1935. So we find Poland, territorially intact, but occupying an unenviable position as a buffer nation between Germany and Russia.

LAND AND PRODUCTS

Topographically, Poland is an enormous plain with the Carpathian Mountains in the south. It is drained by several large rivers: the Vistula, Niemen, and Dvina, which flow into the Baltic Sea; and the Dnieper, Dniester, South Bug, and Pripyat, which empty into the Black Sea. Lying in north central Europe, Poland is bounded by Germany on the west, Russia on the east, Latvia, Lithuania, and East Prussia on the north, and Czechoslovakia and Rumania on the south. The seaport of greatest importance is Gdynia, a city of some 50,000, lying on the Baltic Sea, not far from Danzig.

Homer Smith photo. Chicago

WINTER SPORTS IN POLAND
Skiing at the winter resort town of Zakophane.

By far the most important occupation of Poland is agriculture in which about two-thirds of the people are engaged. Wheat, barley, rye, oats, potatoes, and sugar beets are the principal agricultural products. Dairying and stock raising also are prominent occupations. Poland is rich in coal, salt, and oil. One of its larger salt mines, at Wieliczka, has a complete city carved out underground by the miners, with streets, a chapel, a ballroom, and other features of a regular city. The largest industrial city is Lodz, which is so important as a textile center that it is sometimes called the "Polish Manchester." Lumbering is carried on with much the same methods used in Maine. The logs are floated down the Wilja River to a spot a mile below Wilno, where rafts and lumberyards line the riverbank.

PORTS, TRAVEL FACILITIES, AND RECREATION

From the time the traveler first sets foot on Polish soil at Gdynia, he is pleasantly surprised by the latest facilities and comforts for travel. Scarcely a decade ago Gdynia was only a fishing village, set in the midst of dunes and scrub pine. Today wide boulevards stretch across the city, flanked with banks, hotels, theaters, and shops. With a thoroughly modern harbor, Gdynia, though the youngest city in Europe, has already outstripped other world ports in the enterprise of shipping. In contrast to the modern city of Gdynia is Poland's former outlet to the Baltic Sea, the Free City of Danzig, ancient seaport of the Hanseatic League, whose old, stone streets hold great charm for the visitor. Gdynia, however, is a logical distribution center. From it radiates every modern means of transportation reaching all of Central Europe, Russia, and the countries east, south, and west. Gdynia, then, might be likened to an enormous bay window opening upon the sea and comprising a great gateway to a continent.

Poland's many railways form an intricate network between places of interest. They hold an enviable record for safety and convenience. Regular travel by air is maintained between the leading Polish cities and Berlin, Bucharest, Saloniki, and Moscow. London is less than thirteen hours away by air, and one can leave Paris at dawn and lunch in Warsaw. First-class hotels and restaurants are established in all the larger cities and resorts. Noteworthy is the excellence of food served in these famous dining places, and Polish skill in the culinary arts is widely recognized.

Especially endearing to the traveler is the simple, unaffected hospitality enjoyed in Poland, where every visitor is considered an honored guest of the nation. For hunting the wild boar or giant wolf, for tobogganing and skiing at Zakophane and Krynica, for vacationing near Gdynia, or indulging in the night life of Warsaw, Poland bows to no nation for more complete possibilities in sports and recreation.

Though subjected to the ravages of war, the curse of innumerable invasions and conquests, Poland has retained many vestiges of its medieval culture. Ruins of castles attest the power, wealth, and civilization which prevailed in Poland during the early Middle Ages. Grand palaces of the Polish nobility have been preserved and still hold within their walls priceless treasures of furniture, painting, sculpture, and tapestries. The theater in Poland ranks high and has an outstanding reputation in the production and presentation of the drama. Plays later scoring international success frequently have had their première in Warsaw. Polish cabarets are celebrated for their color and brilliancy.

PROMINENT CITIES

Bridging the medieval and the modern stands Warsaw, the capital city of Poland. From the sixteenth century on, it served as the place of coronation of kings. Wandering through its crooked side streets or busy market places, one sees the old, varicolored houses like veritable gems in a unique setting. One finds here world-renowned wine cellars with vintages that date back to 1606. Brilliant cafés, music halls, and theaters have earned for Warsaw its title as the "Little Paris of the North."

For ten centuries Krakow has held an important place in Polish industry and commerce. From the thirteenth to the sixteenth century it served as the capital city of the Poles. Its medieval character is especially evident in the appearance of its streets and buildings; and vestiges of its old city walls recall the days of its legendary founding by Prince Krakus. Every day at high noon in this beautiful city, the clear note of a bugle rings out from the tower of the Church of St. Mary. The note is suddenly interrupted—the famous "broken note"—in memory of the heroic bugler who from that very tower warned the people of Krakow of the approach of the Tatars, and who fell, his throat pierced by an arrow from an enemy's bow.

Black Star photo. By Henryka Poddesbskiego
SUMMER PALACE OF LAST POLISH KING, IN WARSAW

Splendid museums offer not only the best of Poland's art, but also many works by such great masters as Leonardo da Vinci, Titian, and Rembrandt. Towering over the city is magnificent Wawel Castle, surrounded with the atmosphere of an age-old civilization. Within its walls is a priceless collection of old Dutch tapestries. In the crypt of the adjacent cathedral are the tombs of many Polish kings and national heroes. The university at Krakow was founded in 1364 and has long been a center of culture and learning. There are many fine churches, including the splendid Gothic cathedral of St. Stanislaw, built in 1359. The location of Krakow commands extensive trade from the surrounding country. Only eight miles to the southeast are the great salt mines of Wieliczka.

Standing for a thousand years and vying in interest with Warsaw and Krakow is Poznan, with a history as fascinating as it is varied. Likewise important in commerce and culture is the city of Wilno, with its famous Gothic church of St. Anne, which so pleased Napoleon that he considered transferring it to Paris. Ancient Jewish cities, such as Kazimierz, on the Vistula, and Gora Kalwarya, reveal a medievalism scarcely touched by modern civilization.

THE STRENGTH OF POLAND

To know Poland, one must know the peasantry. In the different regions, one observes strong differences of tradition, types of people, customs, and dress. For example, the mountaineers are taller and have bolder features than have the plainsmen. The women of Lowicz wear loose skirts of striped green, yellow, and red fabric, symbolical of the fields so loved by the common people. A peasant wedding or a Corpus Christi procession is a brilliant affair that any tourist would gladly travel miles to see. Although the various sections of Poland differ in dress, customs, and traditions, the traveler is strongly impressed by the fact that, in spite of these differences, a common love of liberty has welded them into an inseparable nation, which even generations of oppression could not destroy.

Courtesy German Railroads Information Office, N. Y.

PLOENLEIN WITH SIEBER'S TOWER AND KOBOLDZELL GATE
IN ROTHENBURG

PICTURESQUE PARTENKIRCHEN IN THE BAVARIAN ALPS
In the background is the Wetterstein group of peaks, with the famous "Dreitorspitze."

GERMANY has been rightly named the Crossroads of Europe. For the past 2,000 years invading hordes, armies and merchants, have crossed from one side of Germany to the other. The map of Europe reveals at first glance the reason for this. Germany lies between the Mediterranean and Scandinavian lands, with Poland and Russia to the east, and France and Spain to the west. The invading Huns, who caused the fall of the Roman Empire, swept across the country in remote times. The merchants of Italy imported goods from the Near East and sent them up over the Brenner Pass through Germany to North Europe long before Germany could be considered a civilized country. When trade was established with Russia and goods moved east and west across Europe, Leipzig became the market where furs from the remote wastes of barbaric Asia were traded for the finished goods of Europe. Russian, Swedish and Danish armies have marched down through Germany from the north and east; French and Spanish armies have invaded from the west. Thus Germany can justly be called the middle of Europe, the Crossroads of the Continent.

The earliest writings which we have about the Germans are those of Tacitus. At the time of the Roman Empire the civilization of the Mediterranean barely touched the great dark forests where the Germans dwelt. Tacitus found them a brave and hearty people living under crude but sound laws. Many of their practices would certainly be condemned today as ignorant and brutal, yet it is interesting to note that Tacitus found much to admire in the life of the Germans, and we have a feeling that he would have liked to see some of the simple but wise customs of the Germans followed in Rome.

THE AGE OF CHARLEMAGNE

In the age of Charlemagne, Germany was for the first time organized under one leader. The great empire which Charlemagne developed can not be compared with the highly specialized National States of today, for feudal conditions developed soon after his death. The central organization of his time did, however, leave a tradition, and during the centuries which followed attempts were made to draw the country together. The great Hohenstaufen family achieved some degree of unity in Germany, as did the Hapsburgs, who ruled from Vienna. One of these attempts was made in the seventeenth century when the Thirty Years' War brought soldiers from all over Europe into Germany and left the country scarred by war and without hope for the future. During the century that followed, powerful states were organized in France, England, Sweden and Russia. Germany seemed to lag behind. The one great hope of Germany eventually arose in Prussia, under Frederick the Great. Although he ruled only part of Germany, his wars were victorious and made him the hero of all Germany. After his death the will to unite developed in the hearts of patriots all over the land and Prussia was looked upon as the logical center for that unification.

Sad days were to follow, however, and the German dream of the powerful unified state seemed for many years to sink into the background. The Revolutionary armies of France under the leadership of Napoleon conquered Germany. Germany's resistance to the invader was weak and disorganized. Thus the dream of a great Germany was followed by the bitter humility of defeat. Their land was laughingly referred to as "The Empire in the Air," and the Germans were looked upon as a gentle people, capable of poetry and philosophy, but utterly impractical in matters of government.

Courtesy German Railroads Information Office, N. Y.

TYPICAL RHINE SCENE NEAR CAUB, GERMANY
It was here that Blücher crossed the Rhine in the winter of 1813-14 during his campaign against Napoleon. (Gutenfels Castle at left.)

The following century was to show how wrong this estimate was. Under the leadership of Bismarck, the Iron Chancellor, Germany was welded into a centralized state with the King of Prussia as Emperor. German leadership was respected by all the other nations of the continent and the great German army was a model for the world.

WORLD WAR CATACLYSM

The World War caused the downfall of the German monarchy and the establishment of the republic. The years which followed the war were hard indeed. The country was in debt. Markets for Germany's goods were gone, and the re-establishment of the former business leadership among the nations seemed hopeless. During these years the dogged determination of the people to fight their way back won the respect of all the world. A new Germany has been created since the war. It is a monument to a people who would not accept defeat.

In 1933, as the result of a coup d'état, the republic fell and a one-party government was established by the National Socialists. Since they have come into power, there has been unceasing work on their part to improve and replace buildings, roads and bridges all over the land. Thus Germany is not only a land with a romantic past and an up-to-date present, but it also promises a thrilling and interesting future.

By traveling in Germany it is possible to study every period through which the country has developed. The great Gothic cathedrals and quaint medieval towns take us back to the days of knighthood. The many German palaces which dot the country remind us of the days of powdered wigs and courtly manners. Massive buildings and huge museums recall the glorious nineteenth century. Modern office buildings and great hotels tell us the story of Germany's struggle to recover from the war. The new express highways, exhibition grounds and public buildings of the National Socialist State tell the story of a pulsating life and hope for the future. To travel in Germany is to see history.

BIRTHPLACE OF GREAT MUSIC

Yet there is more to Germany than history—much more. Germany's contribution to the culture of the world has been, in some ways, without parallel. No country has produced so much great music. The immortal works of Schultz, Händel, Bach, Haydn, Beethoven, Mozart, Schubert, Weber, Schumann, Wagner, Brahms, Bruckner, Hugo Wolf and Richard Strauss are familiar to all music lovers and appreciated by all mankind. The performances given in the opera houses and concert halls of Berlin, Dresden, Leipzig, Frankfurt-am-Main, Wiesbaden, Hamburg, Cologne, Düsseldorf, Hanover and many other cities are worthy of the masters. Exceptionally good are the concerts of the great Berlin Philharmonic Orchestra, the Berlin Sing Akademie, and the Leipzig Gewandhaus.

German music has a deep hold on the people. Not only do they attend superb performances of the masters. They listen to classical and semi-classical music as they sip their coffee or drink their beer in restaurants and garden cafés. They also organize hundreds of little choral societies and string quartets which perform without audience. These organizations mean as much to the Germans as do social clubs to the English and Americans.

In the field of art, Germany does not rank first, although the works of Albrecht Dürer, Hans Holbein and many others are considered masterpieces of universal standing. Surely one should never forget the great scientific and intellectual contribution which Germany has made. Results in these fields are to be found in every phase of our civilization. The universities are the guardians of this great tradition. Although it is not possible to hear the lectures of Kant, Hegel, von Ranke and Helmholz, it is an inspiration to visit the buildings in which they taught, and to study the policies which govern the academic life of Germany. One should also be on the lookout at every turn for the memorials and museums erected to Germany's poets and dramatists. It is only through an understanding of contributions of men like Fichte, Schiller, Herder, Goethe, Lessing, Heinrich Heine and many others that one can appreciate the German outlook on life. After visiting a museum such as the Goethe House in Weimar, one has the feeling that the great poet is closer as a human being.

PRIMITIVE AND MODERN INDUSTRY

There are also many chances to observe the commercial, financial and industrial life of Germany. One can see the most primitive forms of production in the Black Forest and the most modern industrial establishments at, for instance, the Krupp Works at Essen, or an ancient market such as the one in Nüernberg and the modern cotton market in Bremen. The economic history of modern times could be compiled by simply taking photographs in different parts of Germany.

Finally there is the field of sport. The oldest sport of the race still exists and flourishes in Germany. From the days of Tacitus to the present, the Germans have had a great love for hunting. Deer, roe, stag, fox, snipe, mountain cock and partridge dwell within the limits of Germany in large numbers. For many, Germany is one huge, intricate hunting map. The rules which cover the conservation of game have been wisely made and are strictly enforced so that even today a considerable percentage of the nation's meat is derived from wild game. It amazes one to think that in this thickly populated country there are tracts of land where wild life exists. One of the most accessible hunting grounds is the Lueneburger Heide south of Hamburg. The care-

Courtesy German Railroads Information Office, N. Y.

DEUTSCHLAND HALL, BERLIN'S GIGANTIC SPORTS PALACE

fully planted and carefully guarded trees make it a place which is new and different to the eyes of a traveler from America. Yet there is a great charm in the parklike forests of Germany, enhanced by the existence of wild life in them.

After the war, the youth of Germany, put on stout hiking shoes and went out to see their native land afoot. They established routes and camps throughout all of picturesque Germany. What started as a fad, a mere reaction to the restrictions of prewar German family life, has grown to be one of the most important movements in the German sports world. The influence of this movement has been great, for thousands of foreign students have hiked the paths of Germany side by side with German youth. The spirit of comradeship and the will to mutual understanding built up in this way has been an effective means of bringing nations closer to one another.

Germany is an ideal winter playground. The charm of the German mountains has drawn skating, tobogganing and skiing fans from all over the world. The Germans themselves have taken to these sports with the enthusiasm and thoroughness for which they are justly noted. Bavaria provides hotels for every purse and skiing grounds for the beginner as well as the experienced sportsman. The gay and carefree life at Garmisch, Oberstdorf and many other Bavarian towns is found in few other places in the world.

A COUNTRY OF DIFFERENT COUNTRIES

Germany has more interesting cities and towns than any other country in Europe. The reason for this is that before the unification of Germany, there were a number of independent states. Each state had its capital, and these capitals competed with one another in erecting buildings, fostering the arts, and developing industry and commerce. In addition to the capitals there were the great free cities of the Holy Roman Empire, which owed allegiance only to the empire. Whereas in France the citizens of

A STREET IN AUGSBURG, GERMANY

Lyons looked upon Paris as the center of national life, in Germany the citizens of the free cities and local capitals concentrated their pride and allegiance on their own municipalities. Furthermore, the lack of unity in Germany led to separate cultural development in different parts of the country. Even today it is hard for a citizen of Hanover to understand the dialect of the uneducated class in Berlin or Munich.

UP-TO-DATE BERLIN

Everyone likes big cities. Not everyone likes to live in them, but for a visit, the bigger the city, the better the visit. Berlin, the capital of Germany as well as the capital of the great state of Prussia, is a big city in every sense of the word. It is the third largest city in the world and it moves at a pace which would make it comparable to the most up-to-date, fast-moving city of the Western Hemisphere. Although there is much in Berlin to remind the visitor of its past, the most striking thing about the city is that it lives entirely in the present.

It cannot be said that nature has bestowed special favors on Berlin. The city is built on a fairly uninteresting piece of land on the banks of the Spree River. Yet man has given it a magnificence and grandeur which make it unique among the cities of the world.

The heart of Berlin is a street which stretches from the King's palace to the Brandenburg Gate, the famous Unter den Linden. This street, with a wide parkway in the middle, modern office buildings on either side, government buildings at one end and the Tiergarten at the other, ranks with Fifth Avenue, the Champs Elysées and the Strand. Fashionable Berlin and visitors from all over the world crowd its sidewalks. A number of great restaurants are situated on it and the coffee houses seem never to be empty.

The Brandenburg Gate was fashioned after the Propylaea. A famous statue of Victory stands on the top of it, reminding one of the wars which have ravished the continent of Europe. It was taken to Paris in 1806 by Napoleon and then recaptured and returned to Berlin by the Germans during the Franco-Prussian War in 1870. Although it has ceased to be a prize of war, yet it is a stern reminder that even victory can be fickle.

THE FAMOUS
DOM IN BERLIN
This cathedral in
the Italian Renais-
sance style domi-
nates the Lustgarten
and its surroundings.

Paul's Photos, Chicago

Beyond the Brandenburg Gate is the Tiergarten where the kings of Prussia formerly indulged in the hunt. The Tiergarten is now one of the loveliest city parks in the world, and it is amazing to think that here in the center of what is now the great city, wild game once roamed and the call of the hunt was heard. As one enters the Tiergarten, the Reichstag Building and the Kroll Opera House are seen at the right. The Reichstag Building was mysteriously burned in 1933 and since then the German Parliament, or Reichstag, has met in the Opera House.

An interesting sight in the Tiergarten is the Avenue of Victory built by William II. Statues of his illustrious ancestors line this avenue, each one with the busts of two eminent contemporaries. The Berliners, never lacking in wit, have named this famous Sieges Allee "The Avenue of Dolls." Yet even though these statues are not great, they have found a use. School teachers are able to lead their classes along the avenue and teach them the chronological history of Prussian monarchy with great ease.

Beyond the Tiergarten is the famous Zoo district. Here on the Kurfürsten Damm the night life of Berlin scintillates in many smart coffee houses, cabarets, and night clubs. Starting in the afternoon at coffee time, the best dressed people of the city gather for pleasant social intercourse. Great restaurants, famous for their wines as well as for their food, are located in this district. Surely the Zoo area is a sight never to be forgotten, particularly when seen on a rainy night, when the many gay lights are reflected on the shiny asphalt.

At the east end of the Unter den Linden is a magnificent grouping of royal and official buildings. Dominating, and in the center, is the great Cathedral of Berlin, built at the expense of $3,000,000. The baroque architecture of the Cathedral suggests the solemn and magnificent Lutheran service and the great religious music of Bach and Händel. Here is a state church, a national shrine, a modern one, to be sure, but fully in keeping with the spirit of the great Lutheran Church of Prussia.

A shrine to another god is found in the Arsenal. In it are the trophies of the Prussian and German armies. Freiherr von Richthoven's airplane stands near the uniform of Frederick the Great, two symbols of the pride and glory of Prussian arms. A history of the soldiers of European wars could be written around the uniforms of nobility, and war conditions in the past are strikingly revealed in the equipment of the troops. Dominating the whole scene is a row of heroic-size statues of Prussia's great military leaders. These are the men who have made it possible for all but two of Prussia's kings to boast that they added lands to their domains. Modern Germany, unified and free of oppression, has been their gift to a nation.

The Royal Guard House standing nearby is a shrine to Germany's fallen dead. The impressive ceremony of changing the guard is a symbol of loyalty and a daily reminder of the heroism and devotion displayed in the last war.

THE UNIVERSITY

The great University of Berlin surrounds an imposing square. Lists of the prominent men who have lectured at that university contain the names of many who have made significant contributions to their land and the world. The building itself is interesting as it represents the typical German university, a place for lectures and seminars with no provision for sports or social

life. The students in a large city school such as this are forced
to find their recreation in organizations not connected with the
university. A change in this situation is slowly being made since
the German government has recognized the advantages of our
system. Across from the University is the unimposing, yet justly
famous, State Opera House. Here the greatest singers of Germany
are brought to perform before select audiences. Here Germany's
loved composer, Richard Strauss, occasionally conducts one of his
own masterpieces. A performance of the Berlin State Opera is a
treat which has few equals.

PALACE AND CATHEDRAL

The palace of William I is close to the Opera House. It seems
to express the character of that gentle and beloved monarch, a
man who loved the people of his country and did not wish to
live apart from them in the enormous palace on the other side of
the bridge. It is said that it was his custom to spend some time
each day sitting before a window in his palace and watching
the people as they walked up and down Berlin's great thoroughfare.

On the other side of the bridge the Protestant Cathedral,
which has been described, the palace of William II, and the Old
Museum stand around the huge square known as the Lustgarten.
This square is often the scene of impressive public functions.
In the past it has witnessed party demonstrations and even revolutionary mobs. The palace itself is both large and impressive.
Various types of interior decoration are represented in it, and
one comes upon furniture which is indeed exquisite. Perhaps the
most interesting room in the palace is the one in which the Kaiser
renounced the throne of Germany.

The Old Museum and the National Gallery contain works of
great value. It is possible to walk miles through these museums,
yet perhaps the most important and interesting objects are the
paintings by the old German masters and the amazingly fine reconstruction of the Altar of Pergamon. The restrained and careful way this great masterpiece of antiquity has been set up and
the beautiful building which encloses it make it a delight to the
eye. Many people who have never felt close to the Greek Age
have found in this reconstruction a new and really exciting approach to classic art.

In addition to the more familiar and official side of Berlin, one should certainly visit its great retail center, Leipziger Strasse. The stores on this street are known all over the world for the quality of the merchandise they carry and the beauty of their displays. Here one can find examples of artistic skill devoted to things of everyday life. The finest porcelain, linens and dyed materials to be seen anywhere on the continent are on display on the Leipziger Strasse. Many a connoisseur has found hours of delight in going through the surprisingly large stocks of these stores.

Wilhelm Strasse, which emerges from Unter den Linden is the capital's street of officialdom. Here the British Embassy, the Home Office, the Ministry of Justice, the Foreign Office, the Chancellory and the residence of the Chancellor are to be found in but a few city blocks. It has often been the case that in referring to official opinion in Germany, newspapers have stated that "Wilhelm Strasse thinks this way," or that "Wilhelm Strasse thinks that way." For many years the world of international affairs has been accustomed to listen carefully for any hint of what Wilhelm Strasse has to say about any given subject, for behind these decisions is the power of a great state.

Charlottenburg is the most important residential area of Berlin. Most of it was built before the war and the heavy, ornate architecture seems to weigh down upon this otherwise lovely section of the city. A fine municipal opera is located in Charlottenburg and amazingly enough operates in competition with the state opera in the center of Berlin. This, however, seems to be a friendly competition since Berlin has so many music lovers that neither of the great opera companies lacks patronage.

HOHENZOLLERN RETREAT

Around Berlin there are many lovely suburbs. Lakes, woods and small hills make this area one of the most enchanting metropolitan districts in the world. In the summer these lakes have the gay regatta-like appearance of a summer resort, and many a weary traveler has found real recreation in visiting them. Certainly the most interesting suburb of the city is Potsdam. Here since the time of the Great Elector in the sixteen hundreds to the days of the recent war, the Hohenzollerns have had a city of their own. Away from Berlin where even the magnificence of royalty is submerged in the massive life of the city, Potsdam presents what one might call the essence of the Hohenzollern tradition. The oldest palace stands in the city itself. It was built by the Great Elector in 1660 and reconstructed nearly a century later by Frederick the Great. It is a noble mansion in the classic style showing the creative ability and good taste of Frederick. At the time of the invasions of Napoleon's armies, the silver furniture in the library was painted black in order to masquerade it as common stuff. The Corsican, however, did not allow anything to be disturbed in the palace with the exception of some of the paintings and Frederick's desk.

SANS SOUCI

Few palaces in Europe rank with the small summer residence, Sans Souci. That exquisite château was the favorite dwelling of Frederick the Great and has never since been occupied. The room in which Voltaire lived when he and the great king worked together over the problems of poetry, philosophy and the future of the world has been left just as it was when he used it. Typical of the age, Sans Souci was built in the French Rococo style and is considered a masterpiece of its type. It seems to stand as a monument to that strange monarch whose military ability was rivaled only by his taste for poetry, philosophy and art. Its size suggests the impressive scale of his living.

Courtesy The Art Institute of Chicago

CHARLOTTENHOF, POTSDAM, GERMANY

Paul's Photos, Chicago

SANS SOUCI PALACE IN GERMANY
One of the magnificent show places of Europe, the Palace is reached by a long series of
steps rising from a beautifully landscaped lagoon.

Although Potsdam has many buildings, perhaps the only other
one of great interest is the New Palace which was also built by
Frederick the Great. It cost him 9,000,000 gold marks and was
a heavy drain on the treasury at that time. On the cupola are
three naked female figures. These are believed to represent the
three women who caused him the greatest amount of trouble—
Catherine the Great of Russia, Maria Theresa of Austria, and
Madame de Pompadour. Upon their heads they support the Prussian crown.

HANSA CITIES

The Middle Ages and early modern times have left their stamp
upon some of the most important cities of Germany. Bremen,
Hamburg, and Lübeck represent this group well. What has
characterized these great trading cities? In the first place, they
have been free cities, and local pride and self-government runs
back through the centuries. These are deeply ingrained in the
people. Then, too, the cities were in the past one stupendous ware-

Courtesy German Railroads Information Office, N. Y.

CITY HALL IN HAMBURG
The building is of sandstone in the style of the German Renaissance, and the tower
is 367 feet high.

X—12

house for northern Europe, and the tradition of sterling honesty in business transactions has been built up and maintained in modern times. The Bourses of Hamburg and Bremen are said to have a higher reputation than the Berlin Bourse. Years of dealing in rice, tobacco, cotton, coffee, bananas, oranges, wine, tea and petroleum have built up a world outlook in the citizenry of these ports. The Hansa youth consider foreign apprenticeship an experience for which nothing else can be supplemented. Institutions for the study of foreign countries and the maintenance of pleasant commercial relations with the world have been established in Hamburg and Bremen and exist even to the present day.

PORT OF HAMBURG

The most important of these cities is Hamburg. Essentially Hamburg is a modern city. The port is the greatest on the continent and anyone interested in ships can find here commercial fleets come from the corners of the globe. The ships which serve the city must come up the river. An intricate system has been developed for handling the traffic in this great stream so that one of the most profitable experiences in the trip to Hamburg is the ride around the harbor on a small steamer.

Overlooking the harbor is a dominating statue of Prince Otto von Bismarck. The Iron Chancellor is buried within a few miles of Hamburg and his memory is revered by the citizens of the Hansa town which he made part of the empire.

There are two lakes in the center of Hamburg, the outer and the inner Alsters. Boats from the rowing club, sail boats, canoes and little row boats give the city a holiday appearance during the summer months. Around the outer Alster are the beautiful villas of some of Hamburg's great families. A trip along the shore of this lake by car or bus is an introduction to the great independent middle class of this city.

The business section of Hamburg has been developed along fine and spacious lines. The administration office of the Hamburg-America Line is the type of building which represents this city. It is large and dignified, with a very decided restraint in its architecture.

STATUE OF ROLAND IN BREMEN
One of the most famous statues of the legendary hero.

NEW BREMEN'S OLD MOAT

Whereas Hamburg is said to be slightly influenced by Denmark, Bremen differs from the larger port in that it is more a Dutch city. This difference, however, is not great. The extremely neat appearance of the residential section of Bremen and the well scrubbed aspect of its business section are most impressive. There is much in Bremen which suggests its remote past. The famous Gothic statue of Roland is there. The name is supposed to be derived from the fact that in early times the town meetings were held at a place called "Rotes Land." Few buildings in the Old World have the atmosphere of the Gothic Rathaus or City Hall in Bremen. It was erected in 1405 and later a beautiful façade was added. The great hall of this building embellished with frescoes of sculptured wood and ship models makes it an authentic reminder of Germany's romantic past. In the great Rathskeller below, men of the council and the people of the city gather as they have done for more than five hundred years. Finally it may be said that Bremen has one of the finest sea ports in the world. It is strange to see some of the largest and most modern ships standing by a city which is surrounded by an ancient moat.

LÜBECK— S. P. Q. L.

Hamburg and Bremen because of their continued commercial activity have become large cities. The quiet atmosphere of an old fashioned port is no longer there. To find this one must go to Lübeck, one of the most charming cities in northern Germany. Because Lübeck is located twelve miles from Lübeck Bay, an arm of the Baltic Sea, the great avenues of trade have passed by that city. Ocean liners would find it impossible to come up the little Trave River. The only ships which visit this port are the small coastwise vessels, the fishing fleet, and a few small boats which carry on a trade between Lübeck, Copenhagen, and parts of Sweden and Norway. The very fact that Lübeck has not developed renders it more interesting as a city to visit. The ancient warehouses still stand as they did many years ago, and the gate which was closed against the invading Danes is one of the rare sights in northern Germany. Over the gate are the letters S. P. Q. L. which indicate that Lübeck was a republic which fostered the tradition of its ancient Roman predecessor. Great Gothic churches stand in Lübeck. Although alterations during the centuries have rendered their interiors less pleasant than those of pure Gothic style, the structures are very impressive. The simple lines and the use of brick suggest the sober restraint of these Baltic Romans.

Perhaps one of the most interesting places in all of Germany in which to eat is the Schiffer-Gesellschaft. This ancient restaurant was formerly the eating place of hardened mariners who plied their way across the stormy Baltic.

The country around Lübeck has a distinctive beauty. The inland lakes and the famous beach of Travemünde on the Baltic draw thousands of visitors every summer.

DRESDEN CHINA

One of the former capitals in Germany is Dresden. Here the kings lived who ruled over Saxony. Through years of war they managed to build one of the most charming cities to be found anywhere in the world. One cannot speak of Dresden without remembering one of its greatest rulers, Augustus the Strong. It was he, more than anyone else, who made Dresden the great Rococo city of Germany. The story is told that at one time he traded his own soldiers for a group of Chinese vases which the king of Prussia had. The area including the palace, the court church, the opera house and the Zwinger is world-renowned for its ornate beauty and great delicacy. The Zwinger itself, which surrounds a large square, has been considered the finest single piece of Rococo architecture to be found anywhere in the world. There are few places that suggest the gayety, the color, and the pleasantness of eighteenth-century court society as much as does this remarkable group of buildings. A mass of statues and statuettes, wreaths and flowers, it is truly a garden in stone.

In the palace itself is one of the finest displays of royal jewelry to be seen anywhere in the world. Although not equaling in value the collection in the Tower of London, many of these jewels are unique in their form and construction. The swords and scabbards, buckles and spurs of former royalty are displayed in such a way as to give the visitor the full benefit of their glamour and richness.

Courtesy The Art Institute of Chicago

WALL-PAVILION OF THE ZWINGER, DRESDEN

One should not visit Dresden without seeing Dresden china. There is a collection of porcelain in the city, including the Meissen manufacture and many others, which is hard to match. Of course many are not satisfied with simply seeing the porcelain which has been made, but want to see the manufacturing establishment itself. This is in Meissen and can be reached by a short trip by train, car, or boat.

Raphael's Sistine Madonna, the most expensive picture in the world, hangs in Dresden. Also in the city are works of Correggio, Titian, Rubens and Rembrandt.

The country surrounding Dresden is particularly romantic. The charming Pillnitz and Moritzburg castles are well worth visiting as they suggest perhaps even more intimately the ease and life of royalty in Saxony. Perhaps one of the loveliest bits of Germany is to be found in Saxon Switzerland. This hilly country on the side of the Elbe River not far from Dresden is surprising in its beauty. A number of exceptionally fine restaurants and cafés make Saxon Switzerland a very enjoyable place when hiking or motoring.

LEIPZIG FAIR

Leipzig, the largest city in Saxony, is famous for its music, books, trade fairs and railway terminal. The railway terminal, the first place that a visitor sees, is built to handle the enormous amount of traffic which goes through this great commercial city in the center of Europe. Leipzig is the greatest exporting city in Germany. German industry depends upon Leipzig to sell goods throughout the countries of the Danube basin and as far as Asia Minor. For centuries this has been the city's work, and the trade fairs have been used to attract buyers and sellers from all over the world. Goethe, as a student in Leipzig, saw the Russian traders come to the fair with their pelts, dressed in strange oriental costumes which bespoke the lack of continental civilization in the country from which they came. Today, although some of the business formerly handled by Leipzig has shifted to London, it is still intensely interesting. Machinery, cloth, Christmas decorations, china, toys, tools and furniture, indeed almost anything that man buys and sells in the line of finished products is shown in Leipzig twice a year. The visitor who takes the precaution of reserving a room well in advance can study the most up-to-date ideas in practically every line of production by simply wandering through the halls of this great fair. Doubtless the most dramatic sight at the fair is the machinery exhibition. To visit it is to see dozens of different types of production all under one roof. Some of the machines are set up so that they operate as the buyers stand and watch them. Nowhere else in the world is there a trade fair to compare with the long established fairs of Leipzig.

BOOK AND MUSIC CENTER

In addition to being a commercial city, Leipzig has one great industry—the manufacture of books. The Germans are noted for the number of books they make and sell. Leipzig is the very center of that industry. The finest productions in the art of book making are kept on display and it is possible to view some of the great collections. Any lover of books will be thrilled to see the type of work done in Leipzig and to study how it is done.

Since the days of Johann Sebastian Bach, Leipzig has been one of the great music centers of the world. Students from all corners of the globe flock there to study in the purest traditions the works of the great German composers. The performances in

Courtesy German Railroads Information Office, N. Y.

LEIPZIG, GERMANY, AT FAIR TIME
Oldest and greatest trade fair is the one held in Leipzig twice a year. The old inner
city consists largely of exhibition buildings.

the Gewandhaus and the motets of St. Thomas' church choir make it possible for the casual visitor to come closer to this, the most brilliant side of the city's life.

Here in Leipzig, according to tradition, the Devil, or Mephistopheles, performed the miraculous feat of riding a hogshead of wine up the stairs of Auerbach's Keller as though it were a horse. This famous old wine cellar is now one of the city's finest restaurants.

Interesting from the point of view of German history is the monument of the Battle of Nations. Here Napoleon met defeat at the hands of the Germans and here he started on the road to his ultimate downfall. The monument is a shrine to the spirit which threw off the oppressor in 1813 and which paved the way for German grandeur during the balance of the nineteenth century.

PROVINCIAL WEIMAR

Not far from Leipzig is the town of Weimar. It was here that Goethe lived during the period of his greatest production.

In addition to being a shrine for Germany's leading poet and philosopher, Weimar is a charming introduction to a small provincial city. The tiny Residenz of the former Duke, the little State Theater, the park, and even the hotels suggest the easy-going life which more than a hundred years ago made possible Goethe's great contribution to the world. This was the life of Germans in the days of poets and dreamers. It has little to do with the magnificence of Berlin or the bustle of Leipzig. Yet it reminds one that some of man's noblest achievements have been in the realm of thought.

MUNICH

No section of Germany is so beloved by all the world as Bavaria. Bavaria is essentially an agricultural country, with its lands divided between high mountainous country, a high and invigorating plateau and the pleasant valleys of rivers. Here life has gone on apparently undisturbed by the rest of the world. The people have lived close to the soil, and their virtues are those of a simple, natural race. The capital of Bavaria is Munich, the ideal entrance to a vacation land. It has been remarked that in view of the size of the city, there is no way of explaining how the citizens are able to support themselves. There are, of course, the famous breweries; and a certain amount of china and some machinery is produced here, yet one has the impression that some sort of manna descends upon this city to keep it going.

The life of Munich with its round of holidays and celebrations forms a perfect background for the student, and every German student plans to take at least one semester of his university work there. In addition to the University, there is the famous academy of art and technical school. Munich holds a high position in the field of creative art. A large colony of artists living the Bohemian life of Paris, tempered by trips to the mountains and contact with the fresh and pleasant countryside around Munich, has been able to produce throughout the years some of the outstanding modern works in painting and sculpture.

The artistic phase of Munich life was started by Ludwig I. In 1825 Ludwig said, "I shall make Munich such an honor to Germany that no one who has not seen Munich can pretend to know Germany." As good as his word, he set about systematically to develop his city as the center for art and music. He ambitiously rebuilt the main street and inaugurated the movement which has resulted in having different streets in Munich built according to various type of architecture. Ludwig Strasse is of fine Renaissance design, and Maximilian Strasse is Gothic. Perhaps the finest modern Gothic in Munich is the new City Hall which according to some may be compared with Milan Cathedral in its perfect symphony of sculptured stone. In other parts of the city the pure Greek style of architecture has been reproduced with great effect.

CITY OF MUSEUMS

Munich is a city of museums, some of them containing collections of the masters, some of a historical nature. But doubtless, the most interesting is the German Museum. Here one can see the progress of science and industry through the ages as it is presented with marvelous German thoroughness. The exhibits are set up in such a way that by pressing a button, one sets many of them into motion so that in a few minutes a completed process of industrial production can be studied. The idea of advance and progress has been used as a guide in developing the museum.

Courtesy German Railroads Information Office, N. Y.

HOUSE OF GERMAN ART, MUNICH
This structure replaces one destroyed by fire.

Courtesy German Railroads Information Office, N. Y.
MARKET SQUARE IN MUNICH
City Hall with Frauenkirche in the background.

The king's former residence is interesting because it presents, as do so many others, room after room of period furniture. In some of the rooms the inlaid floors and the decorations of the walls are really glorious. Opposite the residence is the Royal Theater. This little house, a gem of Rococo architecture, is the most suitable place in the world to hold the famous Mozart festival. The conductor sits before a small orchestra in a chair, directing part of the time and playing a harpsichord part of the time, exactly as it was done a century and a half ago. The performances are as authentic as they can possibly be. Thus the

Courtesy German Railroads Information Office, N. Y.
GERMAN PEASANTS ENJOYING A SUNDAY MORNING CHAT
A street scene in Garmisch-Partenkirchen, showing German types and native costumes.

real genius of Mozart is most perfectly displayed. The City Opera House ranks among the greatest in Germany and carries on the tradition which it achieved in the days when Wagner was at the court of Ludwig II.

One should not leave Munich without first inspecting the impressive war memorial. Under the massive cubical stone covering, in helmet and full uniform, is a sculptured figure of a soldier of heroic size. Engraved on the flags of marble on one side are the words "To Our Dead" and on the other side "They Will Return."

THE BAVARIAN ALPS

To many, Munich is the entrance to the Bavarian Alps. Not as high as those in the Austrian Tyrol, in Switzerland, or in France, these mountains challenge the others from the point of beauty. There are a number of beautiful lakes in this region lending it a particular charm. The most famous mountain resort is Garmisch-Partenkirchen. The brightly painted walls of the

houses and the magnificent Zugspitze make Garmisch a favorite
with most travelers. Yet one should not stop here, for in the
smaller mountain towns less affected by the world travel, the
tourist comes in more intimate touch with the mountain population. These mountaineers with their leather pants and quaint
costumes, their religious shrines and love of native dances, are a
people who have won the hearts of tourists from all over the
world. Few people ever leave this region without having made a
promise to return to it some time, preferably as soon as possible.

WAGNER UNDER THE STARS

Ludwig II, the patron of Richard Wagner, made himself immortal in another field of the arts. He constructed in one of the
loveliest spots in the mountains a romantic castle which he called
Neuschwanstein. Here, according to legend, Ludwig would sit
under the stars as Wagner played music which he had recently
composed.

OBERAMMERGAU

In this wonderland of mountains, woods and lakes, there are
a number of very interesting towns. Füssen, Berchtesgaden and
Oberammergau are the most famous. The first two have local

Courtesy German Railroads Information Office, N. Y.
SCENE FROM THE PASSION PLAY OF OBERAMMERGAU
This scene from the great religious drama shows the washing of the feet.

traditions in commerce and art which make them well worth visiting. The last, with its famous Passion Play, has become a town of world renown. In 1634 a plague which followed in the wake of the Thirty Years War struck the little town of Oberammergau. The people of the town, who are deeply religious, swore that if they were delivered from the plague they would present a spectacle of the passion week and crucifixion of Christ every ten years. This they have loyally done, and the play itself, because of its great sincerity and the true artistry of its production, holds a place of honor in the world among religious productions. One hardly feels that the people of Oberammergau are really actors as we think of actors. The play has become such a natural part of their town life that they look upon it, not as an opportunity of displaying exceptional personal talents, but as a chance for the townspeople to join in a celebration of a great religious ritual.

In northern Bavaria, the greatest city is Nürnberg. Nürnberg, the city of the Meister-Singer, the city of toys, of Albrecht Dürer, has now become the city of a great National Socialist Party celebration. Everything seems to differentiate Nürnberg from Munich. The wurst and beer have another taste, and the churches with their Protestant tradition present a different aspect. The city is more strictly Gothic than Munich. The old wall still stands and part of the old fortress which was built by Frederick Barbarossa.

DINKELSBÜHL AND ROTHENBURG

Two quaint little cities in northern Bavaria have rightfully become the mecca of those who seek the ancient past. Dinkelsbühl and Rothenburg are touched with a Gothic atmosphere and are free of the intrusion of modern life. The last five hundred years have brought no change to them.

In Rothenburg, the population regularly celebrates the town's main historical event. During the Thirty Years War the famous commander Tilly brought his forces against the town. Although the inhabitants fought bravely, the city was captured. The demand went up in the forces of Tilly that the town be dismantled, but since the women and children pleaded so ardently, this plan was set aside. However, the mayor and the counselors were condemned to death. Before the order was carried out, the Emperor's huge goblet was brought forth to regale the victorious

Courtesy German Railroads Information Office. N. Y.

BRIDGE IN MEDIEVAL NÜERNBERG

Life flows in much the same placid fashion as it did hundreds of years ago in this city of
Hans Sachs, the Meistersingers, Albrecht Düerer and Veit Stoss.

generals. Under its influence, Tilly's good nature got the best
of him and he challenged any one of the senators to drink a full
goblet of wine of his best vintage in one swallow. This accomplished, Tilly would free the council and the town. Nusch,
the mayor, undaunted by its three and a half quarts, stepped
forward to make the attempt. By some great personal ability,
he managed with one great swallow, and the wine went down.
The town was saved! This event has been called the "Meister-
trunk" of Rothenburg.

RHINE JOURNEY

No survey of the interesting and beautiful spots of Germany
would be complete without mention of the glorious Rhine valley.
Men have called the Rhine the most beautiful river in the world.
Surely it is one of the most scenic trips that can be taken. On
its banks are lovely hamlets and great cities. The famous rock
of the Lorelei and the castles of Falkenburg, Heinburg and
Schönburg, along with others, make the trip a veritable show
window of medieval Germany. The passenger steamers which
cover the whole distance between Cologne and Coblenz are large

and comfortable. The towns of Rüdesheim, Bingen and Ober-wesel are distinctive for their gayety and picturesque settings. The Rhine valley is a world-famous wine country, and it is possible to attend the various celebrations which are held at the harvest's end and after the wine has been pressed in practically any of the towns along the river's banks. The great city of this region is Frankfurt. Famous for centuries as the city in which the emperors of the Holy Roman Empire were crowned, Frankfurt has, in modern times, become a great center for trade and finance. Some of the most important private banks of Europe were established here and the Frankfurt Börse has long been a rival of Berlin.

HEIDELBERG

Near Frankfurt is the justly famous town of Heidelberg. Here one of the oldest universities in Europe is situated and here in a romantic setting in the Neckar valley, German student life has reached its highest point. A fortunate visitor is sometimes permitted to see the intimate details of this student world. The dueling, famous for centuries, is a sport which requires great courage and presents one of the most dramatic spectacles to be seen anywhere in university life. The castle in Heidelberg is con-sidered the most valuable and artistic of the ruins of Germany.

Courtesy German Railroads Information Office, N. Y.

COURTYARD OF HEIDELBERG CASTLE

Courtesy German Railroads Information Office. N. Y.

SOUTH SIDE OF COLOGNE CATHEDRAL

COLOGNE'S CATHEDRAL

Cologne, the largest and most important city in the Rhineland, is an ancient ruling city. Here the Archbishops held sway over a large section of the Rhineland in days gone by. Today the glory of Cologne is its magnificent Cathedral. The foundation stone was laid in 1248, but the building was not completed until 1880. The towers are 520 feet high and the total length of the building is 468 feet. One of the greatest monuments of the Gothic period, the old Cathedral dominates the city and can be seen for miles around.

DÜSSELDORF'S NATURAL BEAUTY

By crossing one of the beautiful bridges over the River Rhine, one can reach Düsseldorf, a city of gardens, placed in the center of Germany's great iron, steel and chemical area. Here are the main office buildings for some of the outstanding industries of

Courtesy German Railroads Information Office, N. Y.

GERMAN STUDENTS ATOP STAHLECK CASTLE

Many of Germany's old castles have been made into young hikers' inns, where students
are taught the romantic history of their country.

Germany. Here, too, living artists create work which equals that
of many a better known art center. That this combination should
exist in the Ruhr district is explained perhaps by the fact that
the Ruhr, although an area of mines and factories, is also an area
of great natural beauty. Some of the loveliest scenes in Europe
are to be found within commuting distance of some of the greatest factories.

Thus the Rhine begins its course in the fairy tale land of
the Black Forest and leaves Germany in the area of modern industry and production. It is not only a great scenic river—it
introduces the traveler to the most varying aspects of German
life.

Black Star photo   By E. W. Lewis
CANAL NEAR MONNIKENDAM, HOLLAND

HOLLAND: A COUNTRY WRESTED FROM THE SEA

ON THE NORTHERN COAST of the European Continent, on the shores of the North Sea, lies unbelievably little Holland, as diminutive as it is pretty. The country at its utmost length is only one hundred and ninety miles, and at its extreme width merely one hundred and twenty miles. By flying over the Netherlands, meaning Low Countries, in an airplane, one can obtain a bird's-eye view of nearly the entire country. The total size of Holland is less than one-twentieth the area of Texas, though Holland has twice as many inhabitants as that state. Its present population exceeds the eight million mark.

Battered by the treacherous waves of the North Sea, scoured by heavy winter storms, washed by endless rains, saturated with water like a sponge, this patch of earth, clay, and peat resembles a living organism with a greatly overdeveloped vascular system. Its arteries are the rivers, streams, and brooks; its veins, the multitude of canals, draining ditches, and trenches. In this vast network, whose threads continually intercross and intermingle, circulates the water, the life blood of Holland, at the same time the cause of its life, and the menace of its existence. For the water, which is Holland's greatest friend, is also its greatest enemy.

[195]

Three great rivers, fed by innumerable tributaries, bring to Holland the waters and commerce of Central Europe, and at the same time enlarge and enrich this country by a mass of alluvium deposits. The Scheldt and Meuse, rising in France, flow through Belgium, enter Holland at its southern frontier, and splitting into several branches, with innumerable islands and deltas, fall into the North Sea. The great river Rhine comes from Germany's industrial regions and in Holland forms several arms, some of which flow into the North Sea, while the Yssel branches off into the Zuiderzee.

The lands surrounding the rivers and canals are so low, that high dikes are built alongside every stream to protect the country from inundation. In many regions the water stands much higher than the rest of the landscape, and sails and boats may be seen on the same level as the top floors of the homes on the other side of the dike, providing a most picturesque view.

In the sixteenth century when the Dutch fought their eighty-year war of independence against the Spanish, the inhabitants cut their dikes, and a Dutch fleet sailed over the inundated lands to the rescue of Leyden, so long besieged by the enemy. Again, in the seventeenth century Louis XIV sent a huge army to conquer the Dutch. William of Orange, Prince of the Netherlands, calmly ordered the flooding of a large area, and once more the water saved the indomitable Dutch from threatening conquest.

Not always have the Dutch waters been friendly. In the Rhine delta, in 1421, a terrible catastrophe, unequaled in history, hit the Low Countries. A furious tempest broke the dikes protecting part of South Holland. The country was submerged, one hundred thousand people lost their lives, and sixty-four villages were swallowed by the furious waves. Even today only half of this territory has been reconquered from the sea.

THE CONQUEST OF THE ZUIDERZEE

In recent times the Dutch conceived the plan of adding more than ten per cent to their agricultural area. The reclamation of the Zuiderzee was the object of their ambition. The Zuiderzee, a branch of the North Sea, extends into the heart of Holland; it is separated from the North Sea by a chain of islands. The draining of this sea was one of the most fantastic engineering feats of history.

Black Star photo   By Ilse Bing
ONE OF HOLLAND'S FAMOUS
WINDMILLS

Black Star photo   By Hilmar Pabel
DUTCH FISHERMEN DISCUSSING
THE CATCH

Under immense difficulties a heavy dike was laid where the sea
was the narrowest, thus separating the Zuiderzee once for all from
the North Sea. The dike is twenty-six miles long, and contains
many huge locks. It connects two parts of the Netherlands, the
provinces of North Holland and Friesland. Already a beautiful
concrete road has been built on the top of the dike, providing for
fast automobile traffic, and a railroad is soon to follow.

Because of the many rivers that flow into it, the Zuiderzee
has become a sweet-water lake. Part of it will be retained as a
fresh-water reservoir and as an outlet for the rivers, and is to be
known as the Yssel Meer. The remainder will be surrounded by
dikes and will soon be drained, adding 550,000 acres of fertile
soil to overpopulated Holland. Part of this work has been accomplished and the traveler today may see waving grain fields and
prosperous villages where the waves of the sea held sway a few
years ago. The entire project will be completed by 1950.

Though Holland is a small country, it is divided into different
parts, each with its own tradition, history, dialect, and customs.
Today the country is divided officially into eleven provinces,
which follow their ancient boundaries. One of these, called Friesland, the inhabitants of which are called Frisians, regards itself as a
distinct, separate unit. The Frisian language is the oldest language

in Europe, excepting the Icelandic, and cannot be understood by the other people of the Netherlands. The two most thickly populated provinces are North and South Holland, which have given their name to the entire country. In the following pages the eleven provinces will be discussed under separate headings.

South Holland is one of the most important provinces of the Netherlands. It is a land of meadows, canals, bridges, and cows and cheese. But it is also a land of big cities, both ancient and modern.

THE HAGUE

Of its many cities The Hague is the most aristocratic, the most beautiful, the most modern. Here the Parliament and government of the Netherlands have their headquarters, and Queen Wilhelmina and Princess Juliana have beautiful homes. The city, however, is not formally titled the capital of the Netherlands, an honor which is reserved for Amsterdam.

Here in 1250 Count William II built a castle at the foot of the dunes, and soon a village grew up near the castle walls. Early, the town became the seat of the Stadtholders of Holland and since that time has retained its aristocratic character. For The Hague is not a commercial or industrial city, but a residential one. It is

Paul's Photos, Chicago

STATUE OF WILLIAM II, PRINCE OF ORANGE, IN THE HAGUE

Paul's Photos, Chicago

SCHEVENINGEN ON THE NORTH SEA
Holland's largest and most popular beach resort, eight miles from The Hague.

a delightful city of beautiful homes, broad boulevards, fine parks, and charming surroundings, only a few miles distant from sea, dunes, and forests. Near The Hague lies Scheveningen, Holland's most famous sea side resort.

The forest of The Hague is a beautiful wood of beech and oak trees, and forms part of the ancient forest once bordering the dunes. In The Hague itself the visitor should not neglect to visit the Peace Palace, built by funds donated by Andrew Carnegie.

LEYDEN—STATELY UNIVERSITY TOWN

The ancient city of Leyden, situated on the river Rhine, preserves a truly Dutch atmosphere. The town dates back to an old fortress, still in existence, which was built by the Scandinavian Vikings, who in the ninth century made their inroads into Holland. The town is intersected by numerous canals, quietly flowing through the streets, and spanned by quaint, arch bridges. The old corn market is built on a wide bridge over a canal.

Leyden possesses many old buildings and edifices. The *Rapenburg* lined by well-built, old, patrician mansions; the *Burcht*, an old fortress wall inclosing over twenty acres, built on an artificial

CATHEDRAL
IN LEYDEN,
HOLLAND

hill; and the Community House with its three picturesque façades, are all well worth visiting. The Town Hall, built in the fifteenth century, is grand and quaint. A flight of steps leads up to the main entrance, while the façade is decorated with a balustrade and statues standing in niches. The tower has a fine carillon, and the sweet tones of its chimes often can be heard over the quiet city.

But the University is Leyden's pride. After its siege by the Spaniards, the Prince of Orange wished to reward the brave citizens of Leyden and offered them the choice of an exemption of import duties or a university. They chose the latter, and this choice proved to be a happy one, for to it Leyden owes much of its reputation and fame. Some of the world's greatest men have occupied chairs at Leyden's University. Its library is truly famous, as are its Botanical Gardens and various museums.

South of Leyden the countryside is most charming and alluring. Far and wide one sees green meadows, separated by canals and streams, on which the white sails of an occasional ship glimmer in the sunlight. The landscape is dotted with farmhouses, hidden behind a circle of high elms, and occasional churches which indicate the presence of small villages. Every foot of land is cultivated, nothing goes to waste; there are no weeds. A tidiness and orderliness which amaze the visitor reign and make him remember Holland as the garden spot of the world.

COUDA

The city of Gouda, a great commercial city in the fourteenth century, has since become a tranquil little town, famous for its cheeses and pipes. The splendor of its past is revealed in its monuments. The Town Hall, built in the middle of the market place in 1450, possesses a unique square tower rising out of the center of the building. The façade is flanked by two octagonal spires, which are quaintly projected from the two corners. It is a beautiful though small building.

The great monument of Gouda is the Grand Church of St. John, whose stained-glass windows are of world-renown. These date back to the sixteenth century and are the creation of the brothers Crabeth. Their richness and artistic design are unequaled anywhere.

DELFT

The city of Delft is called by some the most charming town of South Holland, since it has retained entirely its ancient appearance. Its canals have not been filled, but are lined with fragrant lime trees, and are full of clear water. Some of its buildings, for instance the House of the Commune, display beautiful façades. Today Delft is known the world over for its beautiful earthenware.

On the old canal near the Grand Church one can see the *Prinsenhof*, formerly an old monastery. Here William the Silent, beloved leader of Holland during its struggle with Spain for independence, was killed by an assassin in 1584. In the wall one can still see the hole where the bullet struck. In the *Nieuwe Kerk*, dating from 1381, the tomb of William the Silent has been covered by a grand mausoleum, remarkable for its sculpture and skilful workmanship. The tomb is flanked by four figures, represent-

ON A CANAL IN
OLD ROTTER-
DAM, HOLLAND

Paul's Photos, Chicago

ing Liberty, Justice, Prudence, and Religion. In the same church also are the tombs of Grotius, father of international law, and of De Leeuwenhoek, inventor of the microscope.

The Old Church of Delft, parts of it dating back to 1250, contains the tomb of Piet Hein, famous Dutch Admiral who in 1628 captured the Spanish silver fleet on its way home from America, loaded with treasure valued at twelve million florins.

ROTTERDAM—MIGHTY CITY OF COMMERCE

Rotterdam is the second town of the Netherlands in population, and one of the largest commercial ports of Europe. Its position between France, England, and Germany is commercially most strategic. The city lies on the river Meuse and has water connections with the river Rhine. Since the building of a canal for ocean-going vessels, connecting Rotterdam with the North Sea, its trade and commerce have increased by leaps and bounds.

Rotterdam represents a typical picture of the modern commercial city. Unlike other cities of Holland, its streets, to be truthful, are often ugly and dirty; but they are filled with the hustle and bustle of a metropolis. Here the Dutch instinct and genius for trade and commerce find their true expression.

Rotterdam is also an industrial city. Its distilleries, breweries, metallurgical works, and furniture, carpet, and tobacco factories becloud the sky with their smoke. Coffee, sugar, spices, cotton, tobacco, tea, oil, and rubber from the Dutch East Indies are brought to Rotterdam, making it the storehouse of Western Europe. From one of the many towers it is possible to look down on this unceasing, restless activity which, together with the sight of hundreds of shipmasts along docks and quays, provides a thrilling view.

THE PROVINCE OF NORTH HOLLAND

No region in the world has undergone such geographical changes as the northwest part of the Netherlands. Formerly consisting mostly of marshes and lakes, these have nearly all been drained, providing thousands of acres of fertile soil. The largest lake thus drained was the Haarlemmermeer, today a flourishing polder of over fifty thousand acres. As a result, most of the province of North Holland lies considerably below sea-level. A multitude of windmills and steam engines continually pump the water from the polders over the dikes into the canals and streams connecting with the sea.

HAARLEM

Haarlem, the capital of North Holland, gives the impression of a quiet and prosperous city. There is nothing here of the nervous tension and hurry of the great cities of Amsterdam and Rotterdam. Its streets, most of which converge on the central market place, are usually quite empty and peaceful.

The Meat Market, a fine example of the Renaissance style, was built in 1601. On the other side of the market place the ancient Palace of the Courts of Holland may be admired. Part of the building served also as a Dominican cloister for a time. Today the building is used as the town hall and as a museum, containing many art treasures. Formerly, the paintings of Frans Hals, who was a citizen of Haarlem, were housed here. These paintings, however, have been removed to an old orphanage. They are truly

Black Star photo   By ABC Press Service
WHERE HYACINTHS CARPET HOLLAND'S FIELDS

masterpieces, and many travelers come to Haarlem solely to admire these paintings, noted for their brightness and richness of color.

TULIPS, HYACINTHS, AND DAFFODILS

In the spring the environs of Haarlem are clothed in a most festive garb. As far as one can see the fields reveal a grand variety of colors. From Haarlem to Leyden, whites, blues, reds, yellows, and pinks change off in a most colorful panorama. The air of this beautiful spot, resembling a huge oriental garden, is laden with the sweetest of scents. Special trains and busses carry the people of Holland and tourists from the entire world to this garden spot of Europe to feast their eyes and noses.

One cannot think of a prettier walk than from Haarlem to Heemstede. A carpet of tulips and hyacinths in all shades of colors stretches out to the left and right of the road as far as one can see. Hillegom is most famous for its tulips, while the town of Overveen is best known for its hyacinths. The town of Bloemendaal derives in some years an income of a million dollars from its flowers alone.

This territory, so ideally suited for horticulture, because the soil is a mixture of peat and sand, stretches out along the dunes of North and South Holland for a distance of over forty miles. The flowers themselves, of course, are not the primary product; rather the bulbs are most desired and are exported to America, England, and other countries in huge quantities.

The region is covered with villas, gardens, and woods, and gives the impression of an immense park. No wonder that Tsar Alexander I of Russia, on a visit to King William I of Holland, exclaimed, while riding through these flower fields: "Your country is a veritable garden."

AMSTERDAM, A CITY BUILT ON PILES

Amsterdam, a fascinating, flourishing city of eight hundred thousand inhabitants, is the capital of lovely Holland. The name means literally, "Dam in the river Amstel," for in the thirteenth century the beginnings of modern Amsterdam were laid on this dam. Today the Dam is still the center of this large modern city, since all the important streets and car lines converge here.

The city is laid out in a regular, though unique fashion. At an early date a canal, or *gracht,* was built around the city in the form of a half moon, both ends of which flowed into Het Y, a bay of the Zuiderzee. As the city expanded, canals were laid parallel to the first canal, thus surrounding the town. At all times one could journey around the entire city in a boat. The most famous of these canals are the Heerengracht and Keizersgracht, which today are lined by five rows of trees and are faced by long lines of aristocratic mansions. Innumerable secondary canals intersect the principal ones. As a result the city boasts of having over three hundred bridges and fully merits its name of "Venice of the North."

Since the fourteenth century Amsterdam has been one of the largest commercial cities of the world. By hundreds of canals, streams, and railroad lines, it is connected with every town in Holland and Central Europe. A wide canal, having the largest locks in the world, not excluding those of Panama, connects it with the North Sea, thus admitting ocean vessels to its harbors. The city is a great financial center and famous the world over for its diamond-polishing industry.

On the Dam the traveler may see today the *Beurspoort,* or gate of the old Bourse, built in 1600. Another old building reminiscent of old glory is the *Waag* or Public Weights Building. Occupying an entire side of the square is the Royal Palace, which in olden days served as the town hall of Amsterdam. Its façade and sculptured frontispiece are truly beautiful and impressive. A unique feature of this building is the fact that it is built on 13,659 piles, driven into the marshy ground for its support. Nearly all buildings in

Paul's Photos, Chicago

SUNSET IN AMSTERDAM

The famous old Tower of Amsterdam is limned against sun-illumined clouds.

COLONIAL MUSEUM IN AMSTERDAM, HOLLAND

Amsterdam are given a similar foundation. A group of statues on the Dam are by the Dutch sculptor Quellyn. The *Nieuwe Kerk* (New Church) which also stands on the Dam, is noted for the tombs of famous Dutchmen. Here lies buried Admiral de Ruyter, who in the seventeenth century, in one of the innumerable sea wars between Holland and England, sailed up the Thames and destroyed the English fleet.

The *Kalverstraat* is the most interesting street of Amsterdam. It is a narrow street, lined with fine stores, cafés, and luxury shops. Here the stranger, seated behind a café table, may watch Dutch life go by. Not so far away are the old canals of Amsterdam, with their majestic trees. It is as though one were suddenly transferred into another world. The surging life of the Dam is replaced here by the quietness and solitude of the old patrician homes, beautiful but melancholy, recalling to the visitor's mind Holland's Golden Age, when she ruled the seven seas.

The visitor to Amsterdam ought not to neglect to see the Ryks Museum, which contains one of the finest collections of art treasures in the world. The house itself is worthy of the masters whose works it contains. One feels as if one enters a temple, which it actually is; a temple of art. The Dutch school of art is nowhere more completely represented. Most famous of all is the "Night

Watch" by Rembrandt, a painting as beautiful as it is immense, since it occupies the entire side of the hall in which it is located. There are other masterpieces by Frans Hals and Jan Steen. At the Rembrandt House, where Rembrandt lived for twenty years, one may inspect some drawings and etchings by Holland's greatest painter.

This region surrounds the river Zaan and is known for its many windmills and shipbuilding yards. In the town of Zaandam the tourist is shown the cottage of Tsar Peter the Great, who lived here in 1697. The emperor of Russia, noted for his zeal to modernize his country, came to Holland to learn shipbuilding and other trades, Holland being at that time the foremost commercial country of Europe. Today, the borders of the Zaan are as busy as ever, with over 250 important factories built along its shore.

Edam, typical old Dutch village, is situated on the Zuiderzee. It is famous for its tasty Edammer cheese. The church of Edam dates back to the fourteenth century and merits a visit.

Volendam, also on the Zuiderzee, is a fishing village. Like the island of Marken, this town is widely advertised for its quaint style of dress and unusual customs. The constant flow of visitors, however, has somewhat spoiled the natural charm of these otherwise so simple people.

Enkhuizen deserves the name of being a dead city. In the sixteenth century its population was over forty thousand, while now there are no more than seven thousand inhabitants. Formerly it was an important port on the Zuiderzee and counted over five hundred ships. Its old edifices and fortifications are full of historical interest.

ALKMAAR, CITY OF CHEESES

An interesting boat trip may be taken from Amsterdam to Alkmaar, which takes the visitor through the entire length of the province of North Holland, through typical Dutch canals and lakes. The boat lands in the heart of the city, near the old Weigh House, a delightful and extraordinarily beautiful old building. It dates from 1582; its delicate tower contains a belfry of thirty-five bells. At the hour, when the clock strikes, little horsemen may be seen doing their round in an opening of the belfry, and somewhat higher a little warrior blows his trumpet.

The Weigh House overlooks the market place, where on Fridays there is an immense stir. Early in the morning one can see large heaps of cheeses piled up high during the night, coming from near and far, from cheese factories and farms. The cheeses shine resplendently in the early morning air, since they are polished with linseed oil. They are carried by members of one of the several cheese bearers' guilds, dressed in white, with ribbons of different colors decorating their hats, denoting the guilds to which they belong. The cheeses are taken to and from the Weigh House, where they are weighed, on large *briers* or litters, which are painted in the colors distinguishing their carriers. The weight of these cheeses must be great, for the bearers perspire freely. The cheeses are piled together in lots of twenty to four hundred, and the buyers pass by, sinking their "cheese-tasting knives" into one of the cheeses. If taste and smell are suitable, a bargain may be struck, and the lot is covered by a canvas, signifying it has been sold.

THE PROVINCE OF ZEELAND

This province well deserves its name of "land of the sea," since most of its area is made up of six large islands surrounded by rivers, creeks, gulfs, and bays of the North Sea. In the past, these islands were somewhat isolated from the rest of Holland, and as a result the people have retained much of their unique customs and dress. Because of the many tourists, however, there have been

Paul's Photos, Chicago

Homer Smith photo, Chicago

IN THE LAND OF THE ZUIDERZEE
Mother and son at the door of their ancestral home in Vollendam, Holland.

GOTHIC TOWN HALL, MIDDELBURG,
HOLLAND

many modern adaptations of late. Much of the province consists of polders wrested from the sea, and in this fashion a quarter of a million fertile acres have been added to it in the course of the centuries.

The island of Walcheren is the most important. The city of Flushing is the main port of this island and of the entire province as well. It is an ancient town with a great past, but is even more of a busy port today. Express trains arrive here from Germany and Central Europe, connecting with the daily boat service to England. The river Scheldt is extremely wide near Flushing, and large ocean vessels may be seen passing by on their way to and from Antwerp. The harbor presents a colorful sight because of the presence of many fishing boats and trawlers.

MIDDELBURG AND ITS BUTTER MART

The city of Middelburg is the capital of Zeeland. During the Middle Ages it was a town of great renown because of its cloth-weaving and commerce. The town is quite beautiful and contains fine mansions and other relics from the past. No rebuilding or modernization has taken place, so that barely a house can be found built later than the eighteenth century, while many homes are much older than that. Most of the streets are rough and narrow, paved with old-fashioned cobble stones.

The Town Hall on the great market is certain to attract the attention of the tourist first. The construction of it was begun in 1507. The façade is most beautiful and decorated with statues of counts and countesses of Holland and Zeeland. The roof is adorned with several pinnacles. The tower, one hundred and eighty feet high, watches over the market place in dignified manner.

The most beautiful building in Middelburg is the abbey, situated in the heart of the city. Its antique courtyard, old gates adorned with sculpture, and ancient cellars and vaults dating from the thirteenth century, are delightful to behold. Its halls witnessed many great historical events. The Counts of Holland used to make their home here. A meeting of the Knights of the Golden Fleece was once held within its walls. Today the building provides a meeting place for the Provincial Council and is the residence of the Governor of Zeeland.

A tall tower, called "Long John" by the inhabitants, was somehow attached to this medley of buildings. The tower stands over 280 feet high. Its belfry contains a fine carillon, with forty-one chimes, the melodious sounds of which may often be heard floating over this land of rain and mist.

A colorful and unforgettable spectacle, the Butter Market, takes place every Thursday on the great market of Middelburg. The odd costumes of the farmers have been given great publicity, so that many tourists may be seen intermingled with this unusual crowd. The peasants wear a vest of a dull, black color, their trousers are held together by a belt with silver buckles, costing as much as fifteen florins, and their heads are covered by plain, round hats, looking much like a black cap without a frontpiece. The dress of the women is much more unique and ornate. Their arms are always bare, winter or summer. Their bodices are laced tight, while their hips carry many heavy skirts, a combination which no doubt would be uncomfortable for any woman not accustomed to it from childhood. They wear large aprons and stiff, tight, white caps, which are adorned with gold or silver ornaments. The heavy, garnet necklaces are quite pretty and are held together by gold clasps. The women are extremely fond of jewelry, and

Black Star photo   By Ilse Bing

FISHING BOATS AT ZEELAND DOCKS

the towns of Zeeland possess an unusual number of jewelry shops, in front of the windows of which the picturesque women may be seen standing, casting longing eyes upon the desired jewels within. The colored handkerchiefs worn by many women are of interest because these reveal the religious affiliation of the wearers. When the dominant color is blue and violet, the girl or woman professes the Calvinistic belief; should it be red and yellow, the wearer is Catholic.

The countryside of Zeeland and the fertile fields show that this land is quite prosperous. The homes of the farmers are of interest because they are quite old and because of their unique interiors. The ceilings of colored tile usually have the date of building inscribed in them. As generations came and went, they left all sorts of treasures, such as earthenware, cabinets, furniture, and jewelry for their descendants, who carefully preserved them. Hence every farmhouse presents, as it were, the picture of a museum of antiques. Every farmhouse has its flower garden, where exotic flowers in the spring enliven the flat, green landscape.

THE PROVINCE OF UTRECHT

Unlike many other parts of Holland, this province lies well above sea-level, and is known for its sandy hills, woods and shrubbery, villas, and beautiful scenery. What attracts the tourist here most of all is the city of Utrecht, the capital of the province.

The city of Utrecht dates back to the time of the Romans, who had a fortress on this site. Later the Frisians and the Franks occupied the city, and it became the capital of the Frisian kings. Most prominently in its history figures the saintly Willibrod, English missionary, who converted these warlike Teuton tribes to Christianity and became the first bishop of Utrecht in the seventh century. Later the archbishopric of Utrecht became of great importance in European affairs, because the archbishop also wielded temporal power, and often was able to muster large armies in the field, and subjugate surrounding territory as far as Germany.

Of interest in Utrecht is the presence of the "Old Roman Catholics," also called Jansenists, who refuse to recognize the pope as their master. They possess three large churches here and have an archbishop of their own.

The Cathedral of Utrecht, called The Dom, is its greatest attraction. The idea for building the church was conceived by St. Willibrod, since the chapel of St. Thomas built by him had been pillaged and destroyed by the Frisians, then still pagan. A stone on the marketplace indicates the site of the old chapel. The building of the cathedral was delayed, however, and not till the year 947 was the first mass celebrated in the edifice. In 1017 the church was renovated and officially dedicated in the presence of Emperor Henry II of Germany and his entire court.

Unfortunately the church has been severely damaged. The church and large tower, once connected by a high nave, now stand separately since the nave collapsed in 1670. A road and

Paul's Photos, Chicago

DAUGHTERS OF HOLLAND
Showing two types of farm costumes.

streetcar line now passes between the two. The church itself has retained much of its ancient grandeur, especially its interior, which is truly imposing. It contains a few beautiful monuments, and in the crypt are kept the hearts of two German emperors who died in Utrecht.

Many places, too numerous to mention, remind the visitor of Utrecht's early greatness. In its modern aspect the city is no less pleasing. Its scenic environs of canals, woods, and boulevards, and well-kept modern homes are delightful to visit, especially by automobile.

THE PROVINCE OF FRIESLAND

The Frisians are a race apart from the rest of Holland, and speak a language of their own. On the farms and in the villages the people have preserved their old customs and garb, though the cities, except for their historical relics, are quite modern in appearance and spirit. Most of the land of Friesland during the course of the centuries has been wrested from the sea, and the country is surrounded by huge dikes. As an additional precaution, some villages and farmhouses are built on so-called *terpen*, which are man-made hills of clay. The countryside is interspersed with canals, lakes, and rivers, thus making Friesland famous for the opportunities it affords for yachting.

The capital of Friesland, Leeuwarden, originally a port on the North Sea, now lies in the center of the province, clearly indicating how the sea has been forced to retreat. One of the most charming buildings of the city is the ancient Weigh House, built in the style of the Dutch Renaissance, for centuries the center of the butter mart. The interior of the House of the Provincial Government is well worth seeing, because of its beautiful frescoes, depicting scenes from Frisian history, and its exquisite stained-glass windows showing the emblems of Friesland's thirty-two districts and eleven cities.

The Museum of Frisian Antiques is remarkable for its collection of historical objects pertaining to the province. Especially a great variety of medieval art pieces, taken from various monasteries and convents, deserves mention, as well as the silver and gold work for which the Frisian goldsmiths of the sixteenth century were famous. The Court of Chancery was constructed by King Philip II of Spain in 1566 and served the province for 250

A TYPICAL BIT OF HOLLAND
A picturesque landscape in Friesland.

years as the court of justice. The southern wing is not completed, but this palace is nevertheless one of the most beautiful Gothic structures of the Netherlands. Today the building is used as a provincial library and holds the archives of the province.

Not so far from Leeuwarden lies the *Popta Slot*, an old castle, which may be reached by means of a lovely boat trip. In 1722 when the last member of the Popta family died, he left the proceeds of the castle grounds to some nearby almshouses, built by him. The will contained the stipulation that not the slightest thing within the castle might ever be changed. Hence today the interior of the building is exactly as it was two hundred years ago, with ancient kitchen utensils, furniture, beds, and everything else within untouched and in its old place. The building is kept clean, however, and once a year the trustees of the almshouses have a sumptuous dinner within the castle.

The town of Dokkum is the most ancient town of Friesland, its beginnings dating back to the year 248. Today, more than any other town in Friesland, it has preserved its medieval charm.

The six old fortresses, formerly used for defense, are still intact. The old walls, surrounded by moats, still encircle the entire city as in the Middle Ages.

Near the city of Dokkum is the Well of St. Boniface, which allegedly sprang forth upon the saint's prayer. Boniface was an English missionary, who came to Friesland in order to convert the rough warriors to Christianity. But he was murdered by the then pagan Frisians about 680, and the scene of this crime, the Murder Wood, is still visited by hosts of pilgrims.

QUAINT HINDELOOPEN

The small town of Hindeloopen and environments are known for their quaint customs and costumes. The farmers in their homes have a continual display of one or two *pronk-bedden*, that is, show-beds, which are never used. They are covered with the finest linen and laces, and have beautifully embroidered pillows. These beds are built high into the wall, and have curtains that are never closed.

When someone dies, the body is placed on a bier in the church, awaiting burial. Different kinds of biers are used, according to the profession or trade practiced by the deceased person. The costumes worn by the women are very unusual. An infinitely long black band is wound around the waist so often that it forms a thick girdle. A long silver chain dangles from this waist band, to which a pair of scissors, needle case, and silver pin cushion are attached. The bodices are laced tightly, and a black skirt is covered by a white apron. The women also often wear a black necktie. When out of doors, a sort of mantle is thrown loosely around the shoulders. The latter may be of different light colors, and is covered with designs of red flowers and green leaves.

The costumes of farm women vary all over Friesland, but there are certain similarities. Laces, muslin dresses, silks, and jewelry are freely displayed by the women on Sundays and feast days. This is true of other regions of Holland as well. In Friesland and also in the provinces of Drenthe, Overyssel, and Gelderland, the caps of heavy gold worn by the women are quite famous. The caps are usually covered by lace, but shine brightly in the sunlight. In order to wear them, the women have to cut off all their hair. The custom dates back to the early Middle Ages, and the cap may represent the savings of a lifetime. Modern influences have already made heavy inroads on all of these quaint customs, and may eventually lead to their complete disappearance.

THE PROVINCE OF GRONINGEN

The province of Groningen is one of the richest agricultural sections of Holland, but offers little of interest to the tourist. Its main attraction is the city of Groningen, which is the capital. This city is fairly large and has a modern air about it, though actually it is quite old; records show it joined the Hanseatic League in 1282. The province, too, has a modern atmosphere. The farms are larger than anywhere else in the Netherlands, and the lands are worked by modern machinery, and produce large crops of wheat, rye, sugar beets, and potatoes. As in Friesland, the barns are connected with the farmhouses and the two are often built under one roof. But, unlike Friesland where the barns serve to house cattle, in Groningen these are used solely for the storing of agricultural products, because there is little dairying. The people of Groningen are noted for their extremely enterprising spirit.

In the city of Groningen the St. Anthony's Almshouse, built in 1664, should be visited by the tourist. These charming houses are built around a quaint courtyard. The gate whereby one enters has an unusual architectural beauty and is of rococo design. The cathedral of Groningen dates back to the thirteenth century. Its magnificent tower, 432 feet high, contains a set of fine chimes. The organ inside was built by Rudolphus Agricola, who lived in the fifteenth century, and is thus one of the oldest church organs in existence in the world.

THE PROVINCE OF DRENTHE

The province of Drenthe presents a surprising contrast to the other parts of Holland. Here the traveler is confronted with wild scenery, large, lovely spaces, with few inhabitants. Most of the country is covered with heath, which in the blooming season affords a most picturesque landscape. Here and there a single shepherd and his dog may be seen watching sheep. An occasional cottage made of heath sod, breaks the monotonous view. The two chief towns of Drenthe are Meppel and Assen, a couple of pleasant small towns.

The *Hunnebedden* of Drenthe are the subject of much speculation. These are large graves, built of huge rocks, standing on the lonely heath. It is supposed these were built by some giant, prehistoric race, of which nothing is known, except the primitive remains left by them in the graves. It is not understood how and from where the heavy rocks were taken to the heath, since no such huge stones are available in that part of the country.

THE PROVINCE OF OVERYSSEL

The province of Overyssel resembles more the rest of Holland, with its usual canals, streams, and ships. The country is quite charming, however, and can be seen to best advantage by motorboat or yacht. In the north the country is marshy and has many lakes.

For the tourist the little village of Giethoorn is most unique and picturesque. The hamlet lies between a series of lakes and it has no streets. The houses are separated by little canals and each home has its own punt, a small boat propelled by poles, and its own little bridge, which is built up high to permit the passage of sail boats. The baker and butcher, pushing their boats swiftly through the water, call at every home. All traveling is done on the canals. In the winter time young and old put on their skates, and often long trips to neighboring cities are made, since as much as a hundred miles a day may be covered by a good skater.

The capital of Overyssel is Zwolle, a place which has all the appearances of the typical, calm Dutch town of the nineteenth century. Most famous here is the old Sassenpoort, a large Gothic gateway of the old city walls. More ancient in its appearance is the town of Kampen on the Zuiderzee, a flourishing town during the Middle Ages. Today everything here is calm and quiet, except for the occasional rattling of a bicycle or wagon on the rough cobblestones of its narrow streets. The pride of Kampen is its beautiful and ancient Townhall, one of the most exquisite old buildings in Holland, dating from the year 1345. Its sculptured façade, its carvings, and woodwork stand fair comparison with that of any Renaissance architectural product in Europe.

THE PROVINCE OF GELDERLAND

Much of the province of Gelderland is sandy and hilly, and most of its northern part is wild and covered with heath. This is a country of ancient castles and châteaux. Near the town of Apeldoorn, the Queen of Holland lives in a beautiful summer-

ON AN ICE-
SHEATHED HOL-
LAND CANAL
Skating is probably
the greatest winter
sport in the home-
land of the Dutch.

Paul's Photos, Chicago

house, called Het Loo. The surrounding estates are used chiefly
for hunting and contain some beautifully laid out gardens. Near
Zutphen is the old thirteenth-century Castle of Nyembeeh, where
Sir Philip Sidney, gallant Englishman, lost his life, while aiding
the Dutch in their struggle for independence.

Arnhem, a town of prosperous appearance, is the capital of
Gelderland. Nearby is the Beturve, a low-lying territory between
large rivers, famous for its orchards and fertile farm lands. In
blossom time the people come from all over the Netherlands to
see the apple, pear, and cherry trees in all their beauty. The surrounding woods of Arnhem are extremely lovely and offer an
ideal resting place. Near the town of Rozendaal, meaning "Valley of the Roses," is a large castle, the huge tower of which dates
from the thirteenth century.

The oldest city of Gelderland is Nymegen, where Emperor
Charlemagne had his home. The position of the town, overlooking
the river Waal, is superb. In the pleasure gardens of Valkanhof,
the tourist may still see the ruins of the palace of Charlemagne,
who lived here about the year 770. Near the old church of
Nymegen, the Grammar School, a grim-looking building of 1544,
gives the visitor an interesting glimpse into those times.

THE PROVINCES OF NORTH-BRABANT AND LIMBURG

The two southern provinces of Holland border on Belgium
and lack the features of the typical Dutch landscape, such as

windmills and canals. The people here are Roman Catholic in their belief and the farmers dress differently and not as picturesquely as their northern countrymen. Like the latter, however, they do wear wooden shoes.

The capital of this province is named Hertogenbosch, meaning "Woods of the Dukes," since in the early Middle Ages the Dukes of Brabant made this site their favorite hunting ground. The beautiful and huge cathedral, dating from the eleventh century, is the main attraction. In the vicinity of the city is the old and beautiful castle of Heeswyk, whose walls rise directly from the moat surrounding it; it has a fine bridge connecting it with the outside world. The prettiest town of North Brabant is Breda, famous for its carillon and many statues.

This province extends deeply into Belgian territory, where it approaches the Belgian city of Liége. Maastricht is the main city of Limburg and means "Ford in the River Meuse," since here the Roman legions used to cross the river on a bridge built by them. The town is of modern as well as historical importance. Its history is marked by innumerable sieges, as it is the gateway to Holland, and stood in the way of many would-be conquerors. Here the visitor can see the oldest church in the Netherlands, the Church of St. Servatius, the east crypt of which dates back to the year 560. A room within the building, called the Emperor's Hall, allegedly was once occupied by Emperor Charlemagne. The church is full of treasures and tombs of Frankish kings, only recently discovered. It is built in the Romanesque style, which is unusual for northern Europe; most other churches are Gothic.

The environs of Maastricht are unusually charming. There are old mines of limestone, formerly worked by the Romans, to which all sorts of legends are attached. Houses, built like caverns in the side of these limestone hills, are still clean in their appearance. The tourist may also visit the lovely ruins of several castles in the neighborhood.

Paul's Photos, Chicago

ANTWERP AND THE SCHELDT RIVER

BELGIUM is a small, but thickly populated country, sand-wiched between France, Luxembourg, Germany, Holland, and the North Sea. The number of its people exceeds the eight million mark. This little kingdom is inhabited by two distinct linguistic groups: the Walloons in the south and the Flemings in the north. The former speak French, the latter use the Flemish tongue, a variant of the Dutch language. Both languages are official. A traveler by train sees to his surprise that each station exhibits two names, both indicating the same town. Both French and Dutch newspapers are read in Brussels, the capital of Belgium, the population of which is partly Flemish and partly Walloon. A common faith, the Catholic religion, and a common political tradition, dating back for over five hundred years, keep these two peoples together as one nation.

A GLORIOUS PAST

Belgium, at the beginning of its history, was settled by a mixture of Frankish and Teutonic tribes. This area in the eighth century belonged to Charlemagne's empire. The powerful Flemish cities, such as Bruges, Ghent, Liége, and Ypres, rose during the

Middle Ages. Their wealth came from the manufacture of woolen cloth, the wool for which was imported from England. These cities could muster large armies and successfully defy attempts of German and French kings to subjugate them. Thus the spirit of liberty and tolerance was developed. After the Napoleonic wars the Congress of Vienna joined Belgium and Holland under the rule of the Dutch king. But the Dutch were somewhat domineering, and the Belgians complained that they lacked a proper share in the government. The Belgians, with the aid of French troops, revolted, and in 1832 Belgium became an independent nation under King Leopold I. Since then, under succeeding kings and democratic government, Belgium has developed into a strong, prosperous country.

BELGIUM, COUNTRY OF ART TREASURES

Unlike France, the architectural glory of Belgium is not found in its cathedrals. They are modeled after Rhenish and French religious structures. The interests of the well-to-do commercial class of the Flemish cities in the late Middle Ages were not primarily religious; rather, trade and commerce were glorified. Originality and creativeness were expressed in the construction of great civic buildings.

The outstanding structure is the Cloth Hall at Ypres, which was built in the beginning of the thirteenth century. It was destroyed during the World War, but afterward rebuilt along its original design. Of the same architectural type are the *Halles* at Bruges. The belfries at Ypres, Bruges, and Ghent contain famous carillons. In the fourteenth and fifteenth centuries a number of civic buildings were erected in a more ornate style. Of these the townhalls of Bruges, Brussels, Louvain, and Ghent are splendid examples.

During the late Middle Ages it had seemed that only Italy could produce great sculptors and painters. But in the fifteenth century a group of native painters of Flanders, styled the "Flemish School," soon inspired artistic endeavor all over western Europe. Their activity was centered mainly in Bruges, but studios sprang up also in Brussels, Antwerp, and Tournai. Somewhat earlier the abbeys already had inspired mystical and religious plastic productions. The leading masters of the Flemish School were the two brothers, Jan and Hubert van Eyck. By realistically observing life about them and by introducing new and beautiful

MARKET DAY IN YPRES, BELGIUM
Much of the city was destroyed in the World War, but it has been rebuilt, and
old landmarks have been restored.

color schemes, they transformed canvases into living panoramas.
Other great painters of that day were Van der Weyden and Mem-
ling. Outstanding works of the latter are found at St. John's
Hospital in Bruges.

After a transitional period, during which Flemish painting
was greatly influenced by Italian art, a new school, centered at
Antwerp, rose to still greater heights of artistic achievement.
Rubens was its chief representative. A noted pupil of Rubens
was the well-known Anthony van Dyck. After him a definite decline set in until an artistic revival occurred in the nineteenth
century. One can find paintings of modern and contemporary
artists in the various Belgian museums.

Those interested in gold and silversmith craft can feast their
eyes in Tournai, where original works of the Hugo brothers of
Oignes (thirteenth century) are on exhibition. The art of tap-

estry weaving reached its height in Belgium during the sixteenth century. Belgium weavers were and still are the chief source of supply for the aristocratic salons of Europe. Belgium is famous also for the manufacture of lace products. This industry received its impetus when Emperor Charles V ordered every school in the low countries to teach this craft. Thus Flanders and Brabant became known the world over for the manufacture of fine lace.

BELGIUM'S RIVERS AND VALLEYS

The River Meuse, which runs from France through Belgium and into Holland, divides Belgium into two distinct geographical parts. North of the river the landscape is flat, and uninteresting, and only an occasional canal or muddy river breaks the monotonous view. Here, however, the famous Belgian cities, so well known for their historical and artistic attractions, more than make up for the deficiencies of the landscape. The forty-mile seashore, too, with its fine, sandy beach and rolling dunes, its modern hotels and mild bathing season, provides a beautiful environment. South of the river Meuse one observes an entirely different scene. Here Nature has been less sparing with her charms. Woody hills and mountains, valleys and rocks, rivers and rivulets make up the pictorial landscape.

FLEMISH CITIES

Gone is the greatness that once was Bruges. Gone from its harbor and canals are the ships that once plied the Seven Seas. In the latter part of the fifteenth century the Golden Age of Bruges came to an end when its outlet to the North Sea, the River Zwyn, gradually filled with sand. Today Bruges is one of the dead cities of Flanders. Its population is only one-fifth of what it was in its prime. But Bruges has preserved the relics testifying to its ancient grandeur better than any city in Belgium.

One can imagine himself standing in the midst of the *Groote Markt* or Grand Market, still the center of town life. Nearby are the life-size statues of two Flemish heroes, Pieter de Conick and Jan Breidel, by the sculptor Dévigne. These two men were masters of the once powerful guilds and in 1302 led the burghers of Bruges to shake off the yoke of the French king. The high tower or belfry is the most imposing structure in the Grand Mar-

ket. It symbolizes the freedom
and independence of Bruges.
The erection of such towers,
whose bells served to call the
burghers to arms, was the first
privilege extended growing cities by their feudal lord. The
tower of Bruges was destroyed
three times, and the present one,
begun in 1291, required a full
century to build. Concerts on
the carillon of the belfry are
still given on holidays and on
special occasions. The belfry
slightly inclines to the southeast. This has been true ever
since its erection. Formerly, a
spire graced the top of the belfry, but this was destroyed several times by lightning and has
not been rebuilt since 1741.

Paul's Photos, Chicago
BRUGES, BELGIUM, CITY OF CANALS
Small canals and waterways link many parts
of the city with the ship canal from Heyst,
on the North Sea coast twelve miles away.

Any traveler in Bruges ought to visit the top of the belfry,
notwithstanding its 402 steps. From here one has a beautiful
view of the entire city, with its many canals, and ancient walls.
The Flanders countryside, interspersed with bridges, green fields,
and villages, can be seen for miles. In early days the belfry
played an important rôle in the defense of the city. The watch-
man stationed in the belfry could easily sight any hostile group
which approached the city from afar. The beautiful *Halles*
stand on either side of the belfry. They were built in the early
thirteenth century, and the left wing formerly served as the
cloth-hall and cloth-trading center of Bruges.

As one walks through Bruges one is reminded constantly of
its ancient grandeur. Glimpses of ancient house-fronts and architecture, carvings, stonework, and carved doors meet one on every
hand. The *Hôtel de Ville* is a perfect specimen of Middle Gothic
architecture. The Count of Flanders began the building of it in
1376. The structure is quite ornate, with much painted and
gilded statuary work. Its wooden roof is notable for the high

quality of its carvings, dating back to the year 1400. The building contains some fine paintings and murals depicting the commercial, ecclesiastical and civic history of Bruges.

The interesting Béguinage, more than anything else in Bruges,
furnishes opportunity to the tired tourist to indulge in the poetry
of the past. During the Middle Ages the knights setting out for
the Holy Land did not always return. Hence a certain Lambert
Le Bègue conceived the idea of providing a place of shelter and
comfort for their mourning widows. First, he was ridiculed, but
in time such homes sprang up in many Belgian cities. Today
these are still inhabited by widows and women desiring a sheltered
life. These miniature towns are rich in art treasures.

The *Chapelle du Saint Sang,* the lower floor of which dates
back to 1128, contains the Holy Blood, brought back during the
crusades from the Holy Land by Theodoric, Count of Flanders.
This blood of Christ is alleged to have been preserved by Joseph
of Arimathea, and Theodoric obtained it at great cost and
sacrifice.

The *Hôpital de St. Jean* should not be neglected on a visit of
Bruges. Since 1188 it has served as a hospital, and the sick are
still attended there by the charitable nuns of St. Augustine. It has
a small gallery of paintings, which contains the masterpieces of
Hans Memling. The famous shrine of the Holy Arm of St.
Ursula was painted by him. Modern life has done little to change
the outward appearance of Bruges. Its women are still busy
making the fine lace for which Bruges once was famous. In its
many lace shops, this exquisite hand work may still be bought
today.

GHENT

Ghent is a city that combines the ancient and modern. It has
a glorious past but is a flourishing city today. It is the second largest port of Belgium, and connected with the River Scheldt by a
ship canal. The population of Ghent exceeds 173,000. One may
expect that the process of modernization has affected Ghent more
than Bruges; but the presence of more recent buildings has not
detracted from the beauty of the old structures. The fine Belfry
attracts everyone's attention. It was designed as early as 1183 in
Early Gothic style. A huge, gilded dragon stands on the tapering
turret. It is alleged that during the crusades this dragon was

taken from the Mosque of St. Sophia in Constantinople by Baldwin of Flanders and brought to Ghent. From the top of the tower one can see far and wide, and on a clear day can discern Antwerp along the Scheldt. The Chimes in the Belfry are famous. During the summer, every Saturday evening their melodious tones may be heard over the city.

The Cathedral of Ghent would pass by unnoticed but for the famous altar paintings by Jan and Hubert van Eyck, called "The Adoration of the Lamb," a theme taken from the Book of Revelation. The figures are delightful to behold, yet a realistic, Flemish atmosphere pervades the scene. The new Jerusalem looks much like a Flemish city. The Lamb of God is pictured standing on an altar. He is clothed in white linen, the blood running from his veins. The Holy Ghost descends upon him in the form of a dove, while the Father looks down from Heaven. Other pictures show the figures of John the Baptist, the Holy Virgin, Adam and Eve, St. Cecilia, and a total of more than two hundred figures.

The *Château des Comtes* was constructed in 1180 by Count Philip of Alsace in order "to restrain the pride of the men of Ghent." This serves to show that at an early date the burghers of Ghent displayed a spirit of independence. The castle is an unique monument to which no other feudal fortress of that period is comparable.

In the heart of the city, along the river front of the Lys, stand three buildings reminiscent of bygone days. The Skippers' House, or Guild Hall of the ship captains, is said to be the finest in Belgium. It was built in 1531. Nearby, the House of Grain Measures has a somewhat simpler style. The Staple House, dating back to the thirteenth century, is one of the oldest remaining structures of Ghent.

The Crossbow Guild of Ghent, founded about 1300, is still flourishing today. Competitive meetings are held regularly, and at the yearly tournament the winner is crowned "King" of Ghent's crossbowmen. His name is engraved on parchment, which since the year 1500 has contained the names of these "Kings." Similar tournaments take place in other cities in Flanders.

The Béguinages, founded in the thirteenth century, constitute one of the most interesting peculiarities of Ghent. They are veritable little cities, enclosed by walls; their only way of communication with the outside world is by a gate. Unlike nuns, the

Béguines do not take vows, but are subjected to religious customs and other rules. The ladies elect a *Groot Juffer* or Grand Lady as their superior. They devote their lives to the performance of good works.

THE CHARM OF BRUSSELS

Brussels is the capital of Belgium. Its streets are clean, its avenues and boulevards broad and lined with trees. Its market place is large and imposing, surrounded by impressive, ornate buildings of a mixed Gothic and Renaissance style. The older part of Brussels is surrounded by a host of towns, making up larger or cosmopolitan Brussels. Fast and efficient transportation connects these suburbs with the business center. Distinguished residential districts, beautiful parks and forests, imposing civic buildings, and botanical gardens furnish an ever varying scenery.

The broad market place of Brussels has been the center of public life for centuries. Here the great markets or *kermisses* were held, feasts were celebrated, and the knights held their tournaments. Often, too, the *Grande Place* has been the scene of bloodshed. Here in 1568 the Duke of Alva had twenty-five Flemish nobles executed, and in the same year the heads of the Counts of Egmont and Hoorn, distinguished Flemish patriots, rolled on the block, in full view of Brussels' citizenry. The *Hôtel de Ville* (Town Hall) is the most imposing structure on the market place, and, as such, it draws immediate attention. Its beautiful façade is in the Gothic Style, but strongly influenced by Renaissance ideas of ornamentation. The eastern wing was completed as early as 1402, while the western half was not begun till 1444 upon the order of Charles the Bold, Duke of Burgundy, at that time Lord of Flanders. The designer of the beautiful tower and spire was the well-known architect, Jan van Ruysbroek. Prominent among other historical buildings on the market place are some former Guild Houses dating back to the late Middle Ages. Opposite the Town Hall stands the Bread House, now used as a museum. The "Hall of the Sea Captains" is unique in that its gable is constructed in the form of a ship. Some distance from here the tower of the Palace of Justice reaches skyward. This building is one of the most imposing in Europe and contains more than 245 rooms, most of them used by the Belgian Department of Justice.

Black Star photo
By Tucker

The visitor need not limit his interest to the historical in Brussels. Immediately outside of the city, nature offers boundless attractions. To the north one can find relaxation in the beautiful park of Laeken. A castle in this park is used by the Belgian royal family as a summer home. A ride of fifteen minutes by motor car brings the tourist to the battlefield of Waterloo. In addition, though Brussels has little night life, its theaters and sidewalk cafés offer unlimited opportunity for entertainment and amusement.

LOUVAIN

Louvain is only twenty miles from Brussels, on the road to Liége. The town has an excellent university that enjoyed especial fame in Europe during the fifteenth and sixteenth centuries. Louvain suffered greatly during the World War. After the war

Paul's Photos, Chicago
THE FAMOUS TOWER OF THE HOTEL
DE VILLE, BRUSSELS

Paul's Photos, Chicago
TOWN HALL AT LOUVAIN,
BELGIUM

it was rebuilt with the help of American finances. The Town Hall, dating from the fifteenth century, is small, but exceptionally beautiful. Its ornamentation is rich. More than 280 niches were provided for statues, and these have all been filled in the course of the centuries. Artists have pronounced the Louvain Town Hall the most beautiful example of the ogive, or pointed-arch style of architecture, in Belgium.

ANTWERP'S BUSY PORT

With the decline of Bruges, Antwerp became the chief commercial city of Belgium and today ranks among the great ports of Europe. In contrast to Brussels, Antwerp has more of a cosmopolitan air about it. Present-day Antwerp is one of the great diamond-cutting centers of the world. A trip to Antwerp's busy docks proves highly fascinating. Antwerp is stretched out for miles along the River Schelde, whose two banks are connected by two long tunnels, one for pedestrians and one for automobiles. Huge electric cranes may be seen loading and unloading steamers from the four corners of the earth. The best view is obtained by renting a small motorboat. Such a trip enables the traveler to visit the giant Kruisschans Locks, five miles from the city, through which the huge ocean liners pass on their way to and from the port. Antwerp is a Flemish city. Seldom does one hear anyone employ the French language. The upper classes know French, but use it only when necessary in their business dealings. Antwerp, like so many Belgian cities, combines the old and the new. The modern city with its boulevards, parks, homes, and civic buildings resembles any large, prosperous European town. The old city with its guild houses, cathedrals, and art treasures arouses feelings and thoughts reminiscent of the greatness of Antwerp during the sixteenth century. The Cathedral of Notre Dame in Antwerp is the largest church in Belgium. The church is built in the shape of a cross. The main entrance portal is especially beautiful and has been carefully restored. The beautiful dome towers high above, resting imperceptibly on high Gothic pillars. Wherever one turns the eye, a forest of columns greets it. The altar is adorned with one of Rubens' masterpieces, "The Assumption." Many call this painting the greatest existing representative of religious art. Another painting by Rubens, "The Descent from the Cross" hangs in the south transept. The renown of the cathedral of Antwerp is thus mainly due to the presence of so many art treasures in its interior. The famous "Elevation of the Cross" by Rubens is found in the north transept.

No visitor should pass by the church of St. Jacques. This church is sometimes called the Westminster Abbey of Antwerp, since for centuries it has been the burying place of the aristocratic families, whose vaults and slabs of stone can be seen throughout the church. Rubens was also buried here, the city paying the greatest respects to him.

MALINES OR MECHELEN

The city of Malines or in Flemish, Mechelen, lies half way on the road between Antwerp and Brussels. It has a population of approximately 60,000. The cathedral built in honor of St. Rombaut furnishes the greatest attraction for the visitor of Malines. St. Rombaut was one of the early bishops of Belgium, who was

Black Star photo.   By Mondiale

CATHEDRAL AT ANTWERP

martyred on the site of the cathedral in 775. In his day he was accredited with supernatural powers—he healed the sick, and cured the blind and cripples. The cathedral has a large, massive tower, built in the fifteenth century in Late Gothic architectural style. In the interior the altarpiece is decorated by van Dyck's painting, the "Crucifixion." The chimes in the belfry of St. Rombaut consist of forty-two bells. Concerts are regularly given and the carillon programs alternate the classical music of Germany, France, Holland, Italy, and other countries.

The church of St. Jean at Malines is noted chiefly for its beautiful altarpiece, painted by Rubens. Such paintings as "The Adoration of the Magi," "The Beheading of John the Baptist," "St. John the Evangelist in the Cauldron of Boiling Oil" are famous over the entire world. They are regarded by many as Rubens' best works. When visiting Malines, one should not forget the old Guild houses. The House of Solomon, a fine edifice built in the rich Renaissance style, is the home of the Fishdealers' Guild. The Guild house of the Crossbowmen dates from the sixteenth century.

YPRES

It seems hardly possible to believe that Ypres in the twelfth century was a large manufacturing town with a population of two hundred thousand souls, and with four thousand looms humming day and night supplying all of Europe with woolen goods. But even earlier than other Flemish cities, Ypres fell upon evil days. In 1383 the envious burghers of Ghent sent an army and burnt a large part of the city. Later the Black Plague, which swept Europe in 1347, wars, and sieges did their share, so that by the end of the fifteenth century its population had shrunk to a mere fifteen thousand. Now the population is approximately seventeen thousand.

Before 1914, however, the Town Hall and the Cloth Hall, built under one roof, constantly reminded Ypres of its former greatness. The beautiful belfry standing between the two buildings was the oldest in construction. Begun in 1201, it took more than a century to complete this famous tower.

The World War brought bombardment, death, and destruction to Ypres and most of its beautiful buildings were destroyed. But nothing could destroy the brave spirit of the Belgians. Out of its ashes a new Ypres arose. A new belfry was built, entirely along its original design and structure. The fate of the Halls still hangs in the balance. Their ruins are surrounded by scaffolds and it seems nigh impossible to restore them to their former glory. In the cemetery of Poelcappelle over three thousand bodies were picked up from shell holes. Nearly all visitors pay their respects at the beautiful Menin gate erected in honor of the fallen British. Here a trumpeter sounds "The Last Post" at every sunset.

THE CITIES OF WEAVERS

The traveler from Ypres to Courtrai comes through a fertile region of waving grain fields. Down the Lys River he sees the massive Broeltorens, Twin Towers, standing near the river front. The ancient bridge between the towers connects the city with the west bank of the river. Here, near the city gates, was fought the Battle of the Golden Spurs in 1302. The weavers of Ypres and Bruges, under the leadership of the Guilds, waged a death struggle with the invading French armies, to maintain their liberties and independence. After the struggle the Flemish burghers gathered eight hundred golden spurs from the battlefield and these were hung in a nearby church as evidences of triumph. There is an atmosphere of prosperity and business-like activity about Courtrai. The population which was once about one hundred thousand is now approximately thirty-seven thousand. The city is famous for its linen industry.

The Church of Notre Dame contains "The Elevation of the Cross," painted by van Dyck.

As much as any city in Belgium, Oudenarde retains its ancient appeal. In olden days the city was famous for its tapestry weaving. In recent years, its main attraction is the beautiful *Hôtel de Ville*, an impressive building which is rather decorative and gives the impression of a richness of style. The environs of Oudenarde are well worth exploring. Villages and fertile patches of land provide a truly rustic atmosphere. The River Scheldt, a mighty water at Antwerp, is here but a small stream.

TOURNAI

The antecedents of Tournai go back as far as the time of the Romans who built a fort on this site on the River Scheldt. Today, with a population of about thirty-six thousand, the town gives a

fine appearance, with trees lining nearly every street. Most of
the walls have been leveled down, boulevards and promenades replacing them. The river is filled with barges going downstream,
bringing coal and ore from southern Belgium and northern France
to the large Belgian cities. The city is still famous for "Brussels
Carpets," which are made not in factories, but in the homes of the
weavers.

The Cathedral of Notre Dame at Tournai was built in the
twelfth century, and unlike most Belgian churches, which are
Gothic in style, the Cathedral of Notre Dame is chiefly Romanesque. Much of its grandeur is derived from the large tower in
the middle of the building, but, in addition, each transept is
flanked by a steeple, adding greatly to the total effect. The beautiful stained glass of the high choir windows leaves the inside of
the church subdued, even on the brightest summer day. The
cathedral contains several art treasures. A painting by Rubens,
"The Rescue of Souls from Purgatory," is noteworthy, but has
been retouched quite carelessly. A beautiful image of the Virgin,
painted and gilded by Nicolas de Verdun, dates back to the thirteenth century. There is an unusual collection of embroidered
robes, one of which was donated to the church by a visiting bishop
in 1165. A mantle worn by Emperor Charles V when presiding
at the meeting of the Knights of the Golden Fleece, beautifully
embroidered with scenes of the Passion and the Last Supper, also
belongs to the collection.

THE FLEMISH COUNTRYSIDE

Though Belgium is a land of many cities, its countryside is
well populated. In Flanders, particularly, there are many small
farms. All the work is done by hand, and Flanders really presents
the picture of one large truck garden with only shallow ditches
separating the different patches of land. Flanders is also a region
of rivers and canals. Through its flat countryside many rivers
wind slowly to the sea. Canals either connect the rivers with each
other or are dug direct from city to city. The waterways are
filled with barges, motorboats, and sailing ships, adding much to
the scenic effect. A towpath is constructed along each canal,
and often one may see a horse, hitched to a long rope, pull one
of the many barges through the water.

Most of the towns are connected by hard roads, not all of
which, however, are designed for fast automobile travel. Bicycles

are a favorite mode of human locomotion and so are the famous Belgian dogcarts. Dogs are used in pulling milk carts, vegetable carts, and other vehicles. During the World War the Belgian dog with untiring effort pulled machine guns, supply carts, and Red Cross supplies along the front. In Belgium one fully realizes the meaning of the expression, "to work like a dog." The big, beautiful Belgian horses are no less famous. They are so expensive that not every farmer can afford to have one. These animals are too large and heavy to run fast, but are used to pull heavy loads of farm products.

Old villages dot the Flemish landscape. Most of them have a small inn, perhaps centuries old, where the weary traveler can rest or obtain a meal. The old church, the town hall, and a handful of small stores and houses comprise the rest of the village. On Sunday the village is the liveliest, for on that day nearly all the farmers from the surrounding rural districts attend the church. During the week the peasants work hard in their fields. With the first gleam of dawn they may be seen on the country roads, dressed in short trousers, cap, and wooden sabots, in order to reach the fields as soon as there is sufficient light to see. Yet these people are not unhappy. They feel they are part of the soil, for the Belgian peasant owns his own strip of land, however small it may be.

THE BELGIAN COAST

Between France and Holland, for forty miles, the Belgian coast stretches out along the North Sea. The beautiful sandy beach and mild summer climate attract thousands of visitors from the entire world to the numerous bathing towns along the shore. There are spots where the summer may be spent suitable to every purse and every inclination. The Belgian beach has a layer of fine sand and ranges in width between sixteen hundred and six hundred feet. The North Sea is always interesting and beautiful. There is never a completely calm sea; the salty swell perpetually breaks on the shore. Most famous along the Belgian coast are the dunes, hills of sand thrown up by the wind and covered with wild grassy plants. They may reach a considerable height and at certain places are over a half mile in width. Along certain parts of the beach the sea has thrown up a natural dike, which from Ostend to Westend reaches a length of ten miles. At high tide the

SAND DUNES OF BELGIUM

waves come up to the dike, then with thundering noise run back into the sea. Beautiful promenades are built on the dike.

Golf courses are found all along the shore and dunes. Airdromes and landing fields are established at several towns, while Ostend boasts of a flying school. Planes often are seen circling over the dunes and beach. Regular air communications are provided with the chief capitals of Europe, making this European playground readily accessible. A beautiful, paved highway, called the Royal Route, runs along the entire shore into France and Holland. An electric train, with fast and frequent service, follows the same route.

Ostend is one of the most fashionable watering places of Europe. Its normal population is fifty thousand, but during the bathing season from May to September it boasts of two hundred thousand inhabitants. No city in the world offers such a variety of attractions. Most famous is the *Kursaal*. Built along the promenade, its beautiful frontage faces the sea. Its well-patronized roulette wheel and baccarat table make it the Monte Carlo of northern Europe. Within the building the strictest formality is maintained, only persons having passes being permitted to enter.

Inside are splendid theaters, and a beautiful concert hall where an orchestra of a hundred players regularly offers the world's finest music. Horse races are held regularly at the large racecourse or hippodrome where much betting takes place. Various dance halls offer entertainment and relaxation. Fashion shows are held where beautiful models display the latest Paris fashions to the socially élite. Luxurious hotels may be seen at every hand, but there are also hotels for tourists of more moderate means. During the season, limousines from every country in the world arrive daily. On the beaches one hears an intermingling of many tongues, but there is a strong undercurrent of English and American. Nearby are the ancient Flemish cities which can be visited on side trips, and thus the appreciation and admiration of art treasures can be varied with modern entertainment and healthful exercise.

Besides bathing, Ostend offers unlimited opportunities for golf, tennis, auto and speed-boat racing, and various other sports. The fashionable shops on the Rue de la Chapelle and Rue de Flandres are visited by everyone. The town bubbles over with gaiety, and no one ever seems bored.

But there is also another Ostend, indifferent to the host of fun-making visitors, yet interesting to them. Originally, Ostend was a fishing town. It has a fishing fleet of over two hundred and fifty boats. In the fishing season, the sturdy Flemish fishermen may be seen leaving their homes on the backstreets to set sail for the fishing banks of the North Sea. At other times, they may be seen on the quays, drying their nets and fixing their sails. Carts loaded with shiny brass milk cans, pulled by huge dogs, deliver their burden daily into the city.

OTHER TOWNS ALONG THE SEACOAST

Of the several bathing places along the shore, La Paune is the closest to France. It is a quiet beach resort where one may spend a restful summer in real comfort. The dunes here, too, present an unusual sight, since they are covered with green grass. A favorite sport on the smooth beach is sand yachting, for which a wooden frame on four rubber wheels and with a huge sail is employed. The country and villages in the interior behind the dunes are beautiful, and numerous sight-seeing trips, by either bus or private car, are the order of the day. During the World War the king and queen of the Belgians made La Paune their home.

NIGHT VIEW OF THE CHURCH OF ST. PETER AND ST. PAUL, OSTEND

Blankenberghe has grown into one of the largest and most important bathing places along the Belgian Coast. It is a charming town of six thousand inhabitants. Its wide beach is covered with a thin layer of fine sand. The pier, uncommon in Belgium, extends far into the sea and offers a fine parade for sea lovers, ending as it does in an elegant pavilion. The promenade extends for two miles along the shore. On one side it is lined with hotels and fine shops, on the other side the beach is crowded with bathers. There are nine hundred cabins built here, and these, in addition to a large number of tents, add a color and charm to this beach. At Blankenberghe tournaments in various sports are organized for international competition.

When motoring along the Royal Route, one passes more than twenty resort towns. Of these, besides those already mentioned, the town of Zeebrugge is of great interest. It has a fine harbor, and a sea canal connects it with Bruges. During the war it was used as a base for German submarines, until the English sunk ships filled with concrete blocks in the canal entrance. A museum, showing the unique contents of a German bombproof shelter used by the submarine crews, may be visited.

THE VALLEY OF THE MEUSE

From France the Meuse winds into Belgium, crosses the border just south of Dinant, then goes north and west, entering Holland north of Liége. The mountains of the Ardennes, to the east and south, stretch out, and, as in a painting of wild, rugged scenery, the stream surrounds them like a silver frame. The course run by the Meuse is varied and unpredictable. At times it rolls forth majestically in a wide valley flanked by woody hills. Then again it may narrow to seethe wildly between ravines and high rocks, on the top of which are seen the ruins of old castles.

Shortly after the Meuse enters Belgium, it passes by the pretty town of Dinant. Part of the town is built down below, near the river, while another part is situated on the steep cliff that rises out of the valley. On one of the high rocks, stands the tower of *Mont-Fort,* from the top of which a beautiful panorama greets the visitor. Nearby is a prehistoric cave. The grottoes of Dinant, named The Marvel, are famous for their mysterious atmosphere. An impressive-looking fortress or citadel, built on the surrounding rocks in 1530, overlooks the city as if it still tries to protect

the citizens from foreign foes. The Belgians love Dinant and
have made it into one of their favorite resort towns. The attractive surroundings, the pleasure boats plying up and down the
river to Namur, the unlimited opportunities for fishing and
swimming, its ready accessibility by boat, motor car, and train—
all contribute to this result. In addition, because of its favorable
geographical location, Dinant serves as a center from which to
make further explorations and trips into the Ardennes.

The most pleasant way to reach Namur from Dinant is by
river steamer. On the way one meets many barges, pulled by
heavy horses, plodding along the towpath. Native Walloon
washerwomen are doing their wash in the river. Cottages, hidden
in the foliage of the valley, temporarily house vacationers.
Anglers from Namur, old and young, male and female, using
tackle of every description, stand on the banks, trying to ensnare
the guileless fish. At other places the boat glides between steep
cliffs and rocks and at Profondeulle passes by the famous marble
quarries. At Yvon the Meuse is joined by two swiftly running
tributaries, the Bock and the Molignée, whose cool waters are full
of trout. At Godinne one steams past the beautiful Gardens of the
Château d'Annevoie. Still farther downstream the pretty villages
of Dave and Wepion lie half-hidden in the valley. Unforgettable
are the sights afforded by this river trip.

Namur lies at the junction where the Sambre River joins
the Meuse. The city is built in tiers, with rows of houses and
streets placed above each other, overlooking the two rivers. As
one ascends and finally reaches the heights, one faces the remains
of an ancient fortress and the citadel which, in olden days, protected the city and its beautiful valley. The dungeons in the
citadel date back to the year eleven hundred, and were carved
out of the rock by the once powerful Earls of Namur. A scenic
road, called the "Wonder Road," leads from the city to the fort.
The fortress was rebuilt in the latter half of the seventeenth century by the famous Dutch engineer, Coehoorn, and served as an
outpost against the invading armies of the French "Sun King,"
Louis XIV.

Of interest in Namur is the ancient Boucherie, in modern
times converted into an archeological museum. In it one can see
skulls of prehistoric men taken from the caverns of the province,
pottery, and a host of other antiquities taken from tombs dating
back to the fifth century.

THE PULPIT OF THE CATHEDRAL IN ANTWERP

As one proceeds downstream on the Meuse, the village of Marche-les-Dames attracts one's attention. Here, in 1934, King Albert I, beloved king of the Belgians, came to a tragic death, while climbing the steep pinnacle of *Coneille*, one of the huge rocks near the river. Picturesque Huy, situated where the river Hoyoux joins the Meuse, is called the gateway of the Ardennes. The town is built along the river slope, and is guarded by its imposing citadel. The valley of the Hoyoux, the ruins of Beaufort Castle, the famous grottoes of Throu-Manto, Hay-Belle-Maison, and various other attractions are of interest.

BELGIAN INDUSTRIAL REGION

Continuing downstream, the river Meuse now enters upon a broad valley. Gradually the hilly slopes of southern Belgium, covered with rich vineyards, are left behind. Quite suddenly the picture changes from one of ancient grandeur and memories to the living symbols of the machine age. Between Huy and Liége a forest of smoke stacks borders the river. Coal mines, steel mills, iron foundries, factories, and machine shops are intermingled into one great industrial jungle. The atmosphere is thick with smoke and dust, while the shrill noise of factory whistles and the thundering roar of machines and trains fill the air.

In the midst of these developments stands Liége, ancient Walloon city of nearly two hundred thousand inhabitants presenting the picture of modern large-scale manufacturing in the midst of old surroundings; it recalls a past, different in character, but as great as its present-day glories. Hence, Liége does not possess the ugliness and gloominess of most industrial centers. Its position on the river Meuse is most picturesque. From the heights surrounding, Liége appears as if snugly tucked away in a hollow. For a thousand years Liége was ruled by its powerful prince-bishops, who combined ecclesiastical and worldly powers. The magnificent Palace of these Lordly Bishops is still the pride of the city, and today is used as a court of law. For centuries Liége has been a military stronghold, and a girdle of fortresses surrounds the city in a thirty-mile circle.

As the Meuse proceeds northward it gradually widens and becomes navigable for larger ships. Humming industrial towns flank its banks. At Herstal, automobiles, motorcyles, and bicycles are manufactured. Jupille is a quaint old town; its ancient walls still intact, it is noted for the beautiful Fayembois estate. Châteaux, centuries old, may be seen at Argentean and Dalhem. At Visé, close to the Dutch border, gourmets may feast on the famous "goose á la Visé," and more energetic visitors may row or paddle to Robinson Island, where the rivers Seer and Voer join the Meuse. The Albert Canal between Visé and Lanaeken is of interest because of its engineering feats and the unusual Lanklaer locks.

THE BELGIAN ARDENNES

In order to appreciate the Ardennes one must have seen the rugged rocks, the rivulets and waterfalls, the immense pine forests, the sun quietly setting behind the woody hills, and the ruins of ancient châteaux overlooking the valleys of wildly running streams. The Ardennes comprise the country south of Liége and extend as far as the borders of France and the Grand Duchy of Luxembourg. To the west and north the Meuse River winds around them, while to the east there is Germany. The rugged beauty of these hills is greatly enhanced by a series of rapidly flowing rivers, most of which run northwest, and all are tributaries of the Meuse. The most scenic of these are the Vesdre, the Warche, the Amblève, the Ourthe, the Lesse, and the Semois rivers. Whether one prefers to fish for trout in the stormy brooks, or likes to walk on the woody hill slopes, or quietly wishes to spend the days on the invigorating plateaus, or swim in the rivers, the Ardennes afford all these and many other opportunities. The Ardennes are old. The peasants are friendly and hospitable.

To the north of the Ardennes lies fashionable Spa, famous for its mineral baths. Some come here for their health, others for pleasure, or for both. The town lies 820 feet above sea-level, and is situated at the foot of a woody hill. The visitor soon discovers that Spa lives up to its name of "Pearl of the Ardennes." The waters of Spa, containing carbonic acid gas, carbonate of iron, and other minerals, are known the world over for their healing powers. Though the springs are used chiefly for bathing, the waters are also imbibed freely by visitors, with invigorating effects. The baths are gorgeous buildings, built above the springs, providing every kind of comfort and luxury. Other springs are found in the forests of Spa. They are sixteen in number and lie

THE MONUMENT
OF LAECKEN
It represents the
nine provinces of
Belgium.

in a circle around the city. All sorts of entertainment and sports
may freely be indulged in. There is a racecourse, a shooting
ground, an air field, a fine golf course and the gorgeous lake of
Warrffox. Excursions can conveniently be arranged to the ruins
of Château Franchimont and the grotto of Remouchamps.

THE VALLEY OF THE VESDRE

The beautiful river Vesdre runs along the northern edge of
the Ardennes. To enjoy its scenic grandeur one should take the
road leading from Liége to Verviers, which at times runs alongside
the winding river, at times ascends the surrounding heights overlooking the woody valley. Not far from Liége the river breaks
through the Chevremont hills, on the top of which an old Car-
melite convent commands a view of the valley.

Following the river upstream, one first touches on the town
of Chaudfontaine, famous for its mineral waters, sought by visitors from all over the world, while the fine *Kursaal* offers a variety
of entertainment. At Pepinster, where roads from Spa, Liége, and

Verviers intersect, the Château des Mazures and the Vieux Bon
Dieu de Taneremont are the main attractions. The latter is a
holy shrine visited yearly by devout pilgrims. In contrast, the
city of Verviers is a large manufacturing center, noted for its
textile cloth. Its broad boulevards and mansions of the rich give
the town an air of prosperity. The city of Eupen, in ancient
days famous for its weaving, lies farther east, close to the German
border. Because of its high altitude it is a favorite health resort,
with various sanitariums in the neighborhood. The river Vesdre
here is joined by several mountain streams, which wildly flow
down the hills, forming charming waterfalls along the way.

THE VALLEY OF THE WARCHE

The rivulet of the Warche has its origin in Germany, flows
through a plateau having an altitude of over two thousand feet,
the highest in Belgium, then enters upon a territory of gorgeous
scenery. At Robertsville the stream flows into a lake. A few good
hotels are situated near the lake. From here a hike along the
river bank to the ruins of Renarstene may be undertaken. At
Malmedy the Warche flows into the Amblève River. Malmedy is
an ancient town, to which its antique houses still testify. Its
mineral baths are as good as those of Spa, but less expensive. Situated as it is in a valley, near the fork of two rivers, surrounded
by trees, the town affords an ideal place of rest.

The Amblève River is most typical of the Ardennes. This
swift stream is a tributary of the Ourthe, which in turn runs
into the Meuse. Impetuously does the Amblève move forward till
it passes the town of Stavelot. This town possesses many relics of
a bygone age. In this Walloon city there are families, whose
ancestors, having the same names, were natives of Stavelot during
the Middle Ages. Some of its citizens even possess Roman sur-
names, such as Marius and Massius, dating back to Roman times.
Near the town the Amblève plunges downward, forming the
famous Cascade de Coo. At Remouchamps the river disappears
into the rocks. By renting a boat one may follow the stream
into one of the largest subterranean vaults of the world.

THE VALLEY OF THE OURTHE

The Ourthe is the largest river of the Ardennes, its beginnings
reaching back into Germany. At first there are two branches,
an eastern and western stream, which have worn out a deep bed

in the slate rock till they unite at the famous Héron rock, where they provide a most unusual sight. The Ourthe then runs northward and joins the Meuse at Liége. Before the western stream joins its eastern sister, it is surrounded by the thick forest of St. Hubert. Here, near the village of Amberloop, the ferocious Huns under their King Attila, once waged battle. Towards the west, on a high plateau, rises the city of St. Hubert. The town is famous for its Abbey Church, built in the eleventh century. By the ninth century the journey to this holy spot had become a famous pilgrimage, and today, during the week in which falls the saint's birthday, thousands of pilgrims stream to St. Hubert to be cured of ills and diseases.

La Roche en Ardenne, a town on the banks of the Ourthe, is noted for its ancient church and castle ruins, dating back to the eleventh century. Barvaux-sur-Ourthe is famous as a bathing and boating resort. At Sy the Ourthe widens considerably and more calmly pursues its way. The geological stratifications of the surrounding rocks are of great interest to student and tourist alike. At Comblain-au-Pont magnificent grottoes have been discovered of late and soon will be opened to the public. Around Esneux many castles and châteaux are found. The environs of Tilff reveal the more modern mansions and country homes of the wealthy from Liége and Brussels.

THE VALLEY OF THE LESSE; THE GROTTOES OF HAN

From humble beginnings at the highest elevation of Belgium, the Lesse, flowing westward, soon develops into the most mysterious stream of the Ardennes. In the caverns of its rocky valley prehistoric tribes, wild beasts, and invaders used to take shelter from storms, leaving rich archaeological treasures. The Lesse flows into the Meuse at Anseremme. Here, by means of flatboats, piloted by skilful boatmen, one may for fifteen miles ascend the former stream in the midst of unusual scenery. On the River L'homme, a tributary, the traveler may visit two ancient cemeteries and a fortress, all dating from the fifth and seventh centuries. At Rochefort the River L'homme mysteriously disappears temporarily from view and all attempts to locate the underground river channel have failed. During the searches a large grotto was discovered in a hill. The grotto is separated into three distinct halls, whose weird rock formations and grill shadows give the tourist a foretaste of a still more unusual experience at Han.

Han is a Walloon word meaning "hole in the ground." Here the River Lesse suddenly and quite obscurely vanishes into the bowels of a nearby mountain. Despite a long series of scientific searches the river bed cannot be found, till the stream unexpectedly, and just as enigmatically, reappears in the midst of the grotesque grotto of Han. This cave embraces more than twenty lofty halls and is connected with the outside by a narrow passage, through which visitors must enter in single file. Inside, the cone-shaped rock formations, or stalactites, take on fantastic proportions. The largest room is the Hall of the Dome, over 165 feet long, 150 feet broad, and 160 feet high. It has been estimated that the river Lesse runs 230 feet below the floor of this hall.

THE VALLEY OF THE SEMOIS

The River Semois has its origin near Luxembourg, runs westward through the southern Ardennes, and joins the River Meuse at Monthermé, in France. This capricious stream follows a most sinuous course, since the distance covered is only fifty miles as the crow flies, as contrasted with the hundred and fifty miles of river windings. Laboriously, the stream twists itself around a rocky projection, on which lies the ancient town of Bouillon. Overlooking the town stands the original castle of Godfrey de Bouillon, youthful leader of the First Crusade in the eleventh century. The Semois is a paradise for lovers of trout fishing. The valley is indescribably beautiful. Near Lacuisine where the country is most wild and savage, the Ardennes appear in their full glory. Thick forests cover the river banks and ancient castle ruins forlornly stand on crumbling rocks. The Semois valley is most typical of the Ardennes.

BELGIAN MAR-
KET WOMEN OF
THE ARDENNES

PARIS FROM THE BATTLEMENTS OF NOTRE DAME
The majestic Eiffel Tower may be seen in the right background.

FRANCE might well be called "The Land of the Heart's Desire," for there is little one could ask which cannot be found in this wonderful country. Do you like winter sports? France offers her mountains where you may ski, skate, or toboggan. Are you a gourmet or a connoisseur of fine wines? No country is readier to satisfy your desires. France is a nation of gaiety. Paris, its heart and soul, is rightfully known as the gayest capital in all Europe and fairly teems with foreigners in search of the joy which only the French know how to engender.

Yet underneath all the sparkle is a mellow beauty, which is a part of the French tradition. Brittany, with its peasants in their delicate, starched *coifs*, its graceful cathedrals, Renaissance châteaux, keeps the past alive.

France is easily crossed in any direction in a day. Rising in the morning under the shadow of Notre Dame in Paris, one can easily reach Marseilles in time to go to bed at as reasonable an hour as the fascinating Mediterranean port will allow. Such a rapid glance as this, however, does not permit a satisfying view of all the glories through which one must pass. So he who would know France well must make many such flying trips or else leisurely excursions in various directions.

[249]

Arriving in France by whatever approach possible, every itinerary leads the traveler sooner or later to Paris. The capital city, which is the center of commerce, finance, and industry, is one of the richest cities in the world in culture and intellectual life. Political and commercial affairs are carried on in the Hôtel de Ville and The Bourse. The first Hôtel de Ville, built in the ninth century in the market place, The Grève, was demolished in 1532 by Francis I and rebuilt. The Bourse, established in 1734, is a splendid Graeco-Roman building, whose cornerstone was laid by Napoleon. The Hôtel des Invalides, founded by Louis XIV as a home for disabled soldiers, contains a museum of arms and armor. Here, in the Church of the Invalides, immediately beneath the dome, is the tomb of Napoleon in a circular crypt with walls of highly polished granite, decorated with marble reliefs. From the mosaic floor rises the sarcophagus containing the remains of the great leader. By day a golden glow of sunlight filters through the stained-glass windows, while at night a weirdly impressive blue light renders the tomb one of the most awesome of all Parisian spectacles. In the same building are the ashes of Rouget de Lisle, who composed the song to which the Bastille was stormed in the French Revolution, the world-famous "La Marseillaise"; and also two chapels which contain the sarcophagi of Jérome and Joseph Bonaparte. The effect of dignified isolation is maintained by the Esplanade, with its rich, fine trees, in front of the Invalides.

A short walk brings the sight-seer to the famed Champs-Élysées, the most popular promenade in all Paris. This avenue with its beautiful gardens extends from the Place de l'Etoile to the Place de la Concorde. Pleasure-seekers come here from all parts of the world to stroll along the avenue and to sit in

Paul's Photos, Chicago

WHERE NAPOLEON SLEEPS

The Hôtel des Invalides, under the dome of which is the tomb of Napoleon.

THE ARC DE TRIOMPHE, PARIS, BUILT TO HONOR NAPOLEON'S VICTORY

the sidewalk cafés. The avenue, laid out in the seventeenth century, is the center of the modern life of the city. Smart dress designers and famous perfumers have their establishments along the avenue.

At one end of the Champs-Élysées stands the Arc de Triomphe, the grandest and most colossal triumphal arch of modern construction. Place de l'Etoile (meaning "of the star") was named from its position as the center from which radiate twelve splendid avenues. The huge arch is decorated with statuary and high relief representing the various battles in which the French were victorious. The climb of two hundred seventy-three steps to the top of the arch affords a glorious view over the city. Beneath the center of the Arc de Triomphe is the French tomb of the Unknown Soldier, at which each year many thousands of

Paul's Photos, Chicago

LANDMARKS OF PARIS
The Obelisk of Luxor, brought to Paris from Egypt, is in the foreground, while
the Eiffel Tower looms at the left.

men and women from all parts of France pay tribute to the memory of those gallant nameless ones who lost their lives in the World War. And as a symbol of the undying memory in which their sacrifice is held, a light atop the arch is kept constantly burning.

PLACE DE LA CONCORDE

At the opposite end of the Champs-Élysées is the Place de la Concorde, which in spite of its peaceful name has witnessed many tragedies. Here was erected the guillotine, by which Louis XVI and Marie Antoinette, along with more than two thousand others, were beheaded. Here were encamped three foreign armies. And here many civil struggles took place. Adorning the Place de la Concorde today is the giant Obelisk of Luxor, a solid piece of stone weighing 240 tons. On either side of it is a huge fountain. There are also eight splendid statues, representing the most important cities of France. At night elaborate and skilful lighting enhances the beauty of the Place.

The Eiffel Tower, built originally for the Exposition in Paris in 1889, is still the highest structure in the city; and again at

Paul's Photos, Chicago

CHURCH OF THE SACRED HEART, PARIS
This beautiful Byzantine structure, standing on a lofty height in Montmartre, can be seen for many miles.

the Exposition in 1937 it towered in supremacy of height over the modern exhibition buildings. From the top of the tower Paris is seen in clear outline, and the Seine can be followed by the eye for miles beyond the city limits.

Parisian nightly gaiety thrives along the Left Bank of the Seine. Here the night clubs and cafés present their brilliant entertainment to sophisticated patrons. The Left Bank is also famous as the artists' quarter. Everywhere are throngs of students, all partaking of the gay, careless attitude which has characterized Parisian studio-life since the days of François Villon.

Crowning the hill is the famous church of Sacré-Coeur, home of the largest bell in France. The bell, which weighs over nineteen tons, was unfortunately cracked the first time it was used. However, it can be heard for miles around and requires sixteen men to toll it. The church is built in elaborate Byzantine style and has a magnificent dome.

The Pantheon, originally erected to honor Saint Geneviève, is now dedicated to the commemoration of illustrious men of France. Symbolizing this purpose is the high relief over the front entrance, depicting France distributing wreaths to her great men. The building itself is in the form of a Greek cross surmounted by a large dome. The portico is a free imitation of that of the Pantheon in Rome. Among the great men immortalized in this hall of fame are Voltaire, Napoleon, Mirabeau, Rousseau, Lafayette, Victor Hugo, and Zola. The famous statue of Rodin's, "The Thinker," has a prominent place in front of the portico, while on the dome are several fine frescoes.

Covering nearly three acres in the heart of the city, the Opera House in Paris was built on the site of nearly five hundred houses which were demolished to give room for it. Its magnificent façade impresses the visitor as he approaches by the Avenue de l'Opéra. The interior, with its grand staircase leading from the foyer, is by no means less impressive.

Not far from the Opera House is the Church of La Madeleine. The cornerstone of this superb classic structure was laid by Louis XV. Unfinished when the Revolution broke out, the work was resumed by Napoleon who intended it as a temple to Victory. Again interrupted in 1814, it was finally finished under Louis Philippe in 1842. Its dignified elegance is embellished by a carved representation of the "Last Judgment" over the front entrance and by splendid bronze doors depicting the Ten Commandments.

Paul's Photos, Chicago

CHURCH OF LA MADELEINE, PARIS

The home of one of the world's largest collections of books and manuscripts, as well as of old coins and engravings, is the Bibliothèque Nationale. Although not particularly remarkable for its architecture, there are few places in Paris which have such a thoroughly delightful atmosphere; and no reader of books can enter there without feeling the urge to spend many a day among its treasured volumes.

CHURCHES OF PARIS

Ranking high among the churches of Paris is the comparatively new St. Vincent de Paul, which was built in the basilica style at the beginning of the last century. Several handsome frescoes depicting scenes from the life of St. Vincent, a bronze crucifix, a Virgin and Child group, and remarkable stained-glass windows vie with the façade, which consists of twelve fluted Ionic columns topped by a relief again representing St. Vincent.

One of the oldest and most interesting churches in all Paris is the St. Laurent. First built in 593, additions and renovations have been made from time to time. Fortunately the original type has not been seriously altered. Highly valued features are the painting by Greuze, "Martyrdom of St. Laurent," and the Gothic façade which was built in the middle of the last century.

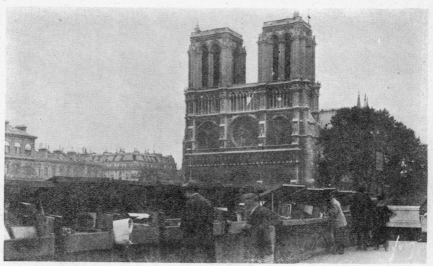

Paul's Photos, Chicago

BOOKSTALLS OF THE SEINE
These stalls line the Seine for many blocks, and here the collector may occasionally pick up a rare volume, print or engraving.

ARCHITECTURAL GEM OF PARIS
SAINTE CHAPELLE

was built by King Louis IX in 1245 and is said by art critics to be the most perfect specimen of pure Gothic architecture. This ethereal structure has been a source of inspiration to students of art for centuries as well as to multitudes who have admiringly gazed at it. The esteem in which Sainte Chapelle is held is evidenced by the reproductions of it that have been made in several foreign countries.

Paul's Photos, Chicago

In many respects the cathedral of Notre Dame is superior to many other Gothic buildings of Europe. It was begun in 1163 as the cathedral of the Archbishop of Paris, but most of the building was done in the thirteenth century, when Gothic architecture was at its best. One can hardly decide which is the best time to see it first, but it is truly magnificent at night when electric floodlights play on it and the white towers rise from the trees with all their purity, strength and grace unimpaired by the surrounding buildings which detract from its loveliness by daylight. And probably the best spot from which to view the cathedral is the Seine, for from the river one sees the whole with much better perspective than can be found elsewhere. Near the edge of the Ile de la Cité one sees first the graceful flying buttresses which support the edifice and help to carry its weight. Beyond them rises the body of the church surmounted by its sky-piercing spire, and beyond that the two noble towers. In the south tower hangs the great bell of Notre Dame, which weighs thirteen tons, and whose clapper alone weighs more than a thousand pounds. It was this bell of which Victor Hugo wrote in his famous novel, *"The Hunchback of Notre Dame."*

The west front of Notre Dame was once profusely ornamented with carvings in the best Gothic tradition, but much of this carving was destroyed in the French Revolution; in fact, the destruction of the whole cathedral was once decreed, but the order was rescinded in time to save most of the beautiful old building. There still remains a very fine relief representing the "Burial of the Virgin," and another of "The Last Judgment" on the west front. The Galerie des Rois, a series of niches holding statues of twenty-eight of the kings of Judah and Israel, which was destroyed during the revolution, has been restored. The large and magnificent rose windows of stained glass over the north and south entrances are of the thirteenth century.

Leaving the cathedral one passes along the Quai du Marché Neuf and the Quai des Orfèvres toward that block which contains the Palais de Justice, the Conciergerie, and Sainte-Chapelle. The quais are among the most interesting sights in Paris. All along the water front are old men with portable bookcases, *bouquinistes,* as they are called, who sell any sort of book in the world, provided it is not new.

THE PALAIS DE JUSTICE

Across the street is the Palais de Justice, in the center of the old Cité of Paris. The original Palais was erected by Charles VII in 1431, and given to Parlement, the high court of justice. The building was successively damaged by fires and revolution, so that only a few old parts are left; but it has been entirely restored and is still used by the various courts of justice. Among the interesting sections which had to be replaced is the old *Salle des Pas-Perdus,* or Hall of Those Not Lost, which is 80 yards long by 30 wide, and one of the largest in the world.

A few steps from the home of justice is Sainte Chapelle, which, though very small, is one of the finest of all Gothic churches. It was built by St. Louis for the reception of some holy relics, and he saw to it that it was a fitting home for the most sacred objects he could procure. A part of its beauty is due to the fact that it was completed in a relatively short space of time, when Gothic architecture was at its peak. The building consists of two chapels, of which the upper is perfect in proportion and detail. Nearly the whole wall space has been filled by windows of extremely lovely old stained glass illustrating the Old Testament and the lives of the saints, except the large rose window which is a representation of scenes from the Revelation of St. John the Divine. The elegance of the stone tracery sets the windows off to perfection. The pillars and surface inside the church are done in delicately harmonizing polychrome, and against the pillars are statues of the Twelve Apostles. For some reason, the relics, for which this architectural gem was constructed, have been moved to Notre Dame, where they may still be seen.

In the same block with the Palais de Justice and Sainte Chapelle is the Conciergerie where Marie Antoinette and other famous victims of the Revolution spent their last hours. If one can get in, for the building is now used as a prison for those awaiting trial, one can see the cell which was occupied by that unfortunate queen, and the cell in which Robespierre spent a short time before he followed her to the guillotine. One may also see the *Salles des Girondins,* a small museum in which are kept relics of the revolution. There is an armchair in which the queen sat, several paintings, and a black wood crucifix with an ivory Christ, which she is said to have kissed before entering the fatal tumbril.

Recrossing the bridge from the Conciergerie, one is soon on the *Place du Chatelet* where the notorious prison once stood. That, however, has been replaced by the *Fontaine de la Victoire,* which was designed by the artist Bosio to commemorate Napoleon's first victories. At the base are the figures of Fidelity, Power, Justice, and Vigilance, from which rise columns inscribed with the names of the battles the monument commemorates. Crowning all this is a statue of Victory which is distributing laurels.

THE PALAIS ROYAL

Perhaps no building in Paris reflects the history of the city so well as does the Palais Royal. It was originally built by the great Cardinal Richelieu, who named it the Palais Cardinal, and who planned the policy of France for nearly fifteen years within its walls. He willed it to the master whom he had served so faithfully, and by whom it was renamed the Palais Royal. It was then occupied by the Queen, Anne of Austria, and her two sons, the future Louis XIV and his brother Philip. After Louis ascended the throne, the wild debauches of Philip and his descendants brought the palace a bad reputation, which was made even worse when the grandson of Philip was forced by his riotous extravagance to retrench and build arcades around the edifice already let to shop-keepers. *Cafés* were installed there which became the favorite haunts of revolutionists, and it was in one of them that Camille Desmoulins organized the capture and demolition of the Bastille. In keeping with changing politics, the palace was successively called *Égalité* and *Palais du Tribunat.* With the Restoration the palace went again to the Orléans family, who occupied it till the Revolution of 1848, when the mob broke in and wrecked the apartments of the king and ruined the art treasures which were there. And again the name changed, this time to Palais National; but with the rise of Napoleon III it regained the name Palais Royal which it has held ever since. It was burned in 1871, and the palace which replaced it is now used by the Council of State.

THE LOUVRE

Housing some of the most valuable collections in the world is the Louvre, which generally heads the list of interesting places to be seen by travelers. The strange name is supposed to have been

THE LOUVRE, PARIS, FRANCE'S MOST FAMOUS ART GALLERY
This section is called "The Gallery of Apollo."

derived from the word *louverie,* or wolf resort, because it is on the
site of a hunting château built early in the thirteenth century by
Philippe Auguste. Toward the end of the fourteenth century the
royal castle of Charles V was built here, with all the proper
strongholds and keeps of the time. But that edifice, too, was torn
down, and not a trace of it remains today. In its stead there stands
the magnificent structure built by Francis I and his successors.
The parts designed by his architect, Lescot, are considered the
most perfect and richest examples of early Renaissance architecture to be found in France. Each king of France up to Louis XIV
contributed to the building, but after the death of Louis XIV it
was neglected until Napoleon caused it to be restored and renovated. In the civil war of 1871 much of the part leading to the
Tuileries was damaged by fire, but before the main structure was
ruined the Versailles troops arrived and put an end to the ravages.

Since 1793 the Louvre has been used as a museum. It contains
one of the finest collections of art treasures the world possesses.
Among its famous pieces that all the world knows is the "Venus

de Milo," which was found by a peasant at Milo and sold to the
French government for a mere 6,000 francs! No price could buy
it now. One of the most impressive treasures of the Louvre is
the "Victory of Samothrace," which, placed at the top of a flight
of marble stairs, has a setting so perfect that one is breathless at
first glance. Many of the masterpieces of the world's greatest
painters and sculptors are to be seen in the galleries of the Louvre.

Near the Louvre is the famous Place du Carrousel, so called
because in 1662 Louis XIV held there a great tournament, or
equestrian ball, to which all the honored guests came in elaborate
and expensive riding habits. There is now a magnificent arch,
which was erected by Napoleon, to the glory of the French army.
It was on this arch that Napoleon placed the four horses which
he carried away from St. Marks in Venice, and which were returned to their Italian home in 1815 by the Emperor Frances of
Austria after the battle of Waterloo. Later, Louis XVIII had
other horses designed by Bosio, which are to be seen there today.
Here also is an equestrian statue of Lafayette.

Immediately facing the Place du Carrousel are the famous
Gardens of the Tuileries. There are many fine marble statues and
groups in this garden, which was largely planned by Le Nôtre

THE MAGNIFICENT VENDÔME COLUMN
Reaching a height of 142 feet, this column rises from the center of the Place Vendôme
in Paris. It was erected by Napoleon I.

who laid out Versailles. The palace around which the gardens were originally planned was burned and the remains torn down.

Constructed by Napoleon to commemorate his victories over the Austrians and Russians, the column of Vendôme was made from the metal in 1,200 guns taken from the defeated forces. Surmounting the column, which is decorated with reliefs depicting scenes from the campaign of 1805, is a statue of Napoleon, a copy of the original that was melted down to be recast into the equestrian statue of Henry IV which is now to be seen on the Pont Neuf. During the civil war of 1871 the column was torn down, but it was later rebuilt.

THE BOIS DE BOULOGNE

One of the finest avenues starting from the Arc de Triomphe is the Bois de Boulogne. It leads to the famous Bois, a public park, which was once a royal game preserve and is now a popular equestrian center. The avenue itself is thronged with gay horsemen and horsewomen; and the wood itself is full of delights. There are many fine bridle paths, two lovely artificial lakes, an impressive waterfall, many beautiful well-shaded spots for one to enjoy. Chief attractions are the smart cafés, the racetrack of Longchamp, and the ruins of the old Abbey of Longchamp. The racetrack is on the site of a famous convent erected by St. Louis's sister Isabel in 1256; the convent was destroyed during the Revolution and never re-erected. Near the Longchamp track is the

LAKE IN THE BOIS DE BOU- LOGNE, PARIS

Courtesy French Government Tourist Bureau, N. Y.

equally famous, though not so large, Champ de Courses d'Auteuil, used for hurdle races and steeplechases.

The official residence of the President of the French Republic is the Palais de l'Élysée. Built by the Comte d'Evreux in 1718, it was occupied by Madame de Pompadour during the reign of Louis XV. It was next the residence of the Duchesse de Bourbon until the Revolution, when it became the government printing office, and in turn a public ball and gaming room. Rising again, it became the residence of Murat, then Napoleon, Louis Bonaparte, Queen Hortense, the Emperor Alexander I, and the Duc de Berri. Still later, it was the place in which Napoleon III planned his coup d'état which made him Emperor in 1851. And twenty years later it was again the symbol of another French loss of liberty and prestige, when the German Kaiser occupied it for three days.

VERSAILLES

Originally a mere hunting lodge, Versailles played a part in Louis XIV's campaign to impress the world and became the envy of every monarch of the seventeenth and eighteenth centuries. In imitation of its magnificence many palaces sprung up all over Europe. In 1661 Louis XIV began to transform the tiny château into the immense palatial system which dazzled the world.

From the courtyard one views the façade over a quarter of a mile long, made up of various types of architecture. In the center is the hunting lodge of Louis XIII, to which Louis XIV added wings. The older brick and stone hunting château still presents a pleasing appearance, even when compared with the awe-inspiring additions of "The Grand Monarch." From the garden one gets an entirely different impression. Rising from the edge of the strictly formal park is the Château de Versailles. Classical in style, the many-windowed marble walls stare down upon one with majesty. Viewed too closely the perspective is lost, the true dignity of the palace cannot be appreciated. The best view is from across the canal. Looking down the tree-lined, grassy stretch, with its great fountains, to the palace, one can appreciate the true majesty of the edifice and its gardens and easily believe that kings have lived here.

The gardens themselves are laid out with geometric precision. Grass lawns are evenly marked off by marble promenades, groves of trees stand at attention, statuary of classical restraint is profusely but precisely placed.

The interior of the palace with its elegant furnishings pre-

ONE OF THE WONDERS OF VERSAILLES
The palace grounds are famous for their shaded avenues, fountains, parks and
groups of statuary.

sents the same superior appearance. Much of the furniture which
Louis installed is now gone, but there is still an air of formality,
giving the impression of life governed completely by rule. The
Hall of Mirrors, 240 feet in length, is entirely lined with gold-
framed mirrors! What self-conscious perfection of appearance
they must have demanded!

Yet this palace witnessed human emotions. The Grand Monarch died here after ruling for 72 years. Then in 1757 Damiens
here attempted to assassinate Louis XV. The revolution crashed
violently upon the palace. Its magnificent walls witnessed the
fierce fighting waged here and the terrified flight of Marie Antoinette.

Great political events have occurred here. The Independence
of the United States was recognized by Great Britain at Versailles.
The revolutionary States-General began its sittings in the tennis
court of the palace, where they swore on oath to remain in session
until the deplorable condition of French politics and administration had been altered. Queen Victoria was a guest of Napoleon
III in the residence of the haughty Bourbons. And from Versailles
William of Prussia was proclaimed Emperor of Germany.

Because the formality of the palace proper did not please the

young and beautiful Marie Antoinette, who had come from the
more homelike court of Vienna, she turned the Petit Trianon into
an imitation rural home and enjoyed its delightful simplicity. The
Petit Trianon is a delightful spot, with its low roofs, ivy-covered
brick walls, in contrast to the palace. The Grand Trianon, a
villa apart from the rest of the buildings, though handsome, lacks
both the magnificence of the grand palace and the intimate charm
of the Petit Trianon.

FONTAINEBLEAU

The palace of Fontainebleau might well be called the palace
of undoings. Here in the reign of Henry IV the illustrious career
of the Marshal Biron was ended by his arrest for treason. Here
Louis XIV undid the efforts of his predecessors by revoking the
Edict of Nantes and ended religious tolerance in France. And
it was here at Fontainebleau that Napoleon had his divorce from
Josephine pronounced.

The exterior of the château is less impressive than of others
which Francis I built; but the interior has all the elegance and

PALAIS DE FONTAINEBLEAU

gracious luxury which the Italian and French artists of the Renaissance could devise.

The buildings are planned around five courts. The oldest is the Court of the Dungeon, which is slightly more reminiscent of the Middle Ages than of the Renaissance. In the Court of the White Horse—so called because of a statue which was once there —Napoleon bade farewell to the Old Guard after his abdication, and shortly afterwards, upon his return from the isle of Elba, reviewed them before going to Paris.

The chapel of the Trinity has a fine ceiling painted after the manner of Michelangelo by the French artist, Fréminet. But perhaps the greatest art treasures of the palace are the exquisite Gobelin and Flanders tapestries which adorn the Salons de Réception, in one of which Louis XIII was born. The palace is rich in memories of august men and women of the past: Marie Antoinette, Anne of Austria, the two Medici queens, Pope Pius VII, and the various kings who lived there in less dignity and more comfort than was possible at Versailles. Fontainebleau is a peculiarly gracious and pleasing château, without the record of horror and violence which is attached to so many of the famous buildings of France. The lake on which it is built and the truly magnificent forests of the grounds carry an air of peacefulness.

WHERE THE WORLD PLAYS

Many people think first of Monte Carlo and the Riviera when France is mentioned. And justly, too; for they are the playgrounds of the world of wealth and sophistication. Burke's Peerage Social registers vie with one another nightly at the gaming tables of Monte Carlo and daily on the fashionable beaches of Cannes, Juan-les-Pins, and Nice. The Mediterranean resorts, with their enchanting coves and red rocks, welcome guests at any season; for they offer the most delightful climate the year round.

Nice has justly been called the pleasure resort *par excellence*, for it is the center of the social whirl of the Riviera. The inhabitants make an especial effort to entertain extravagantly all distinguished visitors, which gives the city a definite place among the social centers of the world. Situated in the center of a veritable amphitheater of hills which are sprinkled with the villas of the wealthy pleasure-seekers and the vineyards and gardens of the industrious natives, Nice admirably lives up to its pleasant surroundings. As a background rises a sharp rock, crowned with

Paul's Photos, Chicago

ON THE PROMENADE AT NICE, ONE OF THE WORLD'S
GREATEST PLAYGROUNDS

the ruins of a picturesque medieval castle. Almost within the shadow of the past flourishes the ultra-modern city with its parks, with its handsome palms, its bustling Place Massena, and its sophisticated Promenade des Anglais with the urbane villas for which Nice is famous. The arrangement of the hills which shelter the town from the north is an added encouragement to visitors who relish the warm climate. And if that were not enough in itself, the clubs, theaters, receptions and horse-racing, which are conducted with every consideration for chic and excellence, render the place irresistible.

A pleasurable twelve miles beyond Nice is Monte Carlo, the most beautiful spot on the Riviera, as far as natural scenery is concerned. So lovely is it, in fact, that many who never go inside the famous and alluring Casino spend much time there merely for the sake of the surroundings. The Casino itself is a showy building enhanced by many statues, whose grounds offer every known variety of palm. Surprisingly enough, aside from the temptation of the gaming tables, the place is famous for its excellent music.

Equally as famous and as smart as the Riviera is the Silver Coast, as Biarritz is called. On the west coast of France very

Paul's Photos, Chicago

ON THE BEACH AT BIARRITZ, FRANCE

near to Spain, it enjoys an entirely different local atmosphere, that of the Basque rather than the almost Italian background which is so noticeable on the Southeastern coast. With gracefully curving coast line, magnificent resort hotels and villas, smart cafés and the most sophisticated nightclubs to enhance the delights of the smooth, wide beach and the temperate climate, it is no wonder that the world flocks to Biarritz on the Basque coast, and that even those who possess villas at Nice are frequently to be found here.

Similar in character and local conditions are the three most famous resorts on the north coast of France, le Touquet, Dieppe, and Deauville. These channel beaches, cool and refreshing after the heat of a Parisian or London summer, are popular especially among those who are in the midst of a social or business routine and want a few days of rest. But there is no lack in smartness at these beaches. Le Touquet, for instance, with its impressive promenade and drive along the shore edge, with its wide beach and chic cafés, attracts the same set as the other resorts, but at a busier season.

"MONT BLANC YET GLEAMS ON HIGH"

In spite of the thousands of tourists and pleasure-seekers who throng to the French Alps both summer and winter, one still finds the power and tranquillity, the majestic calm of which Shelley and Byron wrote over a century ago. The towering, implacable beauty of Mont Blanc, the placid smoothness of Lac Leman, the shimmering glory of the sea of ice, all these can lift one's soul above daily worries, above the distracting turmoil of modern life. A few moments of silent reverence before such splendors, and the discordant phases of life disappear.

Small wonder then, that the French Alps are so popular, and that there are so many fine resort hotels and amusements. Skiing, skating, and general holiday atmosphere are found at the hotels. In the heart of the gaiety and excitement which make up the resort portions of the Alps is Chamonix. Boasting not only a nine-acre skating rink, bobsleigh and toboggan runs, but an eighteen-hole golf course, and a School of *Alpinisme,* where one may learn to climb mountains with a minimum risk, Chamonix is well supplied with attractions which draw every class of vacationers. Every type of hotel, from the magnificent type one sees in the movies to the small family hotel is to be found; and at all of them are courteous attendants, who are only too glad to show the beauties of the place and to point out the innumerable excursions and climbs which radiate from this resort of resorts.

WHERE ITALIAN KINGS ONCE RULED

Back in the days when the ancestors of the present King of Italy were only dukes, but powerful and important to the rest of Europe, their capital was Chambéry, a delightful town in a pleasant valley. Although not in the winter sport section, the place is popular; for it is an alluring little town, with many interesting buildings. Perhaps the most attractive is the old Château of the dukes of Savoy, set in towering old trees. But almost equally important is the Cathedral of St. Francis of Sales, a very lovely old church, and one rich in memories with which to delight the visitor. The surrounding landscape is also charming, and the lakes, du Bourget and d'Aiguebelette, can hardly be surpassed.

Leaving the Alps, let us go to Rheims. There, in days gone by, generation after generation of French kings was crowned and anointed with holy oil. The cathedral of Rheims, where the awe-inspiring coronation took place, is one of the finest examples of Gothic architecture. The tall, lacy building, reaching slender, graceful arms to heaven, is a lovely Medieval hymn in stone. Its triple-arched doorway, with the rose window above which is the glory of the cathedral, is surmounted, as are the flanking doors, with tier after tier of sculpture. On each side and above it are niches and arches with various statues. For the people of the Middle Ages the cathedral was the Bible. It was their source of church knowledge, and into the cathedral the master builders poured the lore of miracles and of holiness. No other architecture so well expresses the spirit of its age, as does the Gothic, and few other cathedrals so symbolize the spirit of the Gothic as does Rheims.

The cathedrals of Mont Saint-Michel and of Chartres have long been considered the essence of medievalism and art as a part of the French spirit. The cathedral at Chartres, one of the greatest marvels of Gothic art known to man, is grace itself caught and forever expressed in stone. The two spires hardly seem real, so slender and fragile do they appear. Nearly two thousand sculptured figures, from heroes and saints to monstrous dragons writhing in the agony to which evil was condemned, decorate the exterior. Within, bathed in the multi-colored light which strains through the jewel-like glass windows, the like of which can be found nowhere else, are two of the most ancient and illustrious shrines to the Virgin in France. There is also a miraculous relic, the gown of the Annunciation, which Charlemagne is supposed to have received from the Emperor of Constantinople. The whole building is a paradise on earth, a home of angels and saints quaintly carved, but as alive today as any modern art.

In contrast with the charming peace of Chartres which is dedicated to the loving and pitying Virgin, is Mont Saint-Michel, which, dedicated to Michael, is the epitome of the militant strength of the Medieval Church. Reflecting the spirit of the Norman barons, from the very neighborhood of the monastery, who went with William to take England, reflecting the spirit of the Crusades, and of the Church as a temporal power which sent forth armies to conquer disobedient kings, Mont Saint-Michel is

Courtesy The Art Institute of Chicago

CHÂTEAU OF CHARTRES, FRANCE

strong, granite-built, and thoroughly masculine, except for a few later additions. Built on the summit of a sugar-loaf of a rock which rose from the perilous sea, the church followed the shape of the rock, with its largest portion, the central tower, as the focal point around which the rest of the edifice hung perilously—and much of it did fall later. About the whole of the oldest part, which dates from the eleventh century, clings an air of simple, quiet strength. The newer additions are of the more ornate and graceful tradition of the later Gothic style; but there is no discord or lack of harmony. One gets rather the impression of a strong, quietly handsome man married very happily to a young and beautiful woman.

A STATE WITHIN A STATE

Even before the Hundred Years War La Rochelle was a strong and virtually independent city ruled, with a slight bow to the king, by her mayor and aldermen. By throwing in her lot with France instead of England during the great struggle between those two nations she won for herself even greater concessions from the French king. Considered practically impregnable because of her strong position on the sea, she dared oppose every wish of the central government which did not meet with her approval. When the Reformation turned France into one large battlefield she became the stronghold of the Huguenot party, and no matter how bad things got in other centers, La Rochelle was always safe and always managed to withstand sieges laid against her. But that was only until Richelieu decided that the Huguenot political party had to be broken. He ruled that since La Rochelle was the heart of that political organization, La Rochelle must fall. Going about the matter scientifically, he blockaded the town so well from the sea that three great navies from England were incapable of breaking through with food. After a siege of months the Rochellais finally had to capitulate, not to arms, but to hunger. Today there are many relics of that courageous but tragic resistance. There is the table into which the Mayor Guiton stuck his dagger, with the demand that it be thrust into the heart of the first man who mentioned capitulation. This table is in the old Town Hall, by all odds the most interesting building in the city, both historically and artistically.

Not far from La Rochelle to the north is the famous Loire wine district, whence come such choice wines as Vouvray and Saumur. And about an equal distance to the south is the Bordeaux region, which boasts of five *"premiers grands crûs,"* 119 *"crûs classés,"* and a large selection of excellent local wines. And nearby is produced the famous Armagnac Brandy, not to mention Cognac and Sauternes. But these impressive names merely scratch the surface of the French wine list. There are the wines of the Midi, of the Rhone, of Alsace, of Burgundy, and the Champagne wines.

Centering around Rheims, Epernay and Châlons, with the famous river Marne as the most important valley, are the slopes on which grow the grapes that become the bubbling amber known the world over. The history of this region as a wine-producing center goes back to the third century, when the Romans introduced the vines from which Champagne was made. From the fourteenth century on Champagne was the favorite of the kings of France who were always presented with the best in the district whenever they went to Rheims to be crowned. Perhaps that fact accounts for the medieval custom of frequent coronations in France. It was not until the seventeenth century that a Benedictine monk discovered the method of bottling the wine so that it retained its sparkle and limpid pallor. Since that time Champagne has held the title of the wine de luxe.

But this section is not dedicated to gaiety only, for on the same gentle slopes where grow the grapes of joy, not long ago great nations were locked in deadly battle. The Marne, which drains those vine-covered hills, was the scene of two of the most decisive battles of the Great War. But slightly to the east is the Meuse-Argonne region, with Verdun and Château-Thierry near by.

The lovely old city of Strasbourg has a mixture of French and German culture. Because of the many times the city has changed hands, it is one of the most interesting spots in the country. Not least among its many charms is its magnificent late Gothic cathedral, which is so ornate with statuary and filigree work that it seems to be made of starched lace rather than strong stone.

MARSEILLES, THE FRENCH ORIENT

Hurrying south, one reaches Marseilles, which presents other combinations of cultures. But the varied types of Marseilles are not due to military conquest, but to economic adventure. Since the earliest times men of all nations have flocked to and from Marseilles, bearing with them all sorts of exotic and useful objects of trade. Many races meet and blend in this most fascinating Mediterranean port. As exotic as Port Said, as French as Paris, Marseilles is always exciting.

Not far from Marseilles is Arles, the blistering wind-swept city where Van Gogh painted his best works. The molten sunlight which makes everything quiver and dance gave him the inspiration and the colors for which he had been searching all his life. And in the center of the town, surrounded by modern buildings, are a remarkably well preserved Roman amphitheater and arena, adding ancient tradition to the town.

THE RAMPARTS OF CARCASSONNE

The best preserved of all the fortified towns of the Middle Ages is Carcassonne. In the heart of the old Provence, the land of culture and chivalry, it is quite fitting that we should find

Paul's Photos, Chicago

MARSEILLES, GATEWAY TO THE NEAR EAST
This ancient port has many beauty spots.

this monument to the cities of that time. Evoking marvels of
the past, reminiscent not only of the Crusades, but of the delightful Medieval romances, the home of stories like those of Arthur
and his knights, Carcassonne stands today almost exactly as it
stood in the days before the cruel and unjust Albigensian Crusade,
which put an end not only to the harmless Albigensian heresy but
to the graceful culture, the cult of the lovely lady, which flourished around this region.

The city against which the Albigensian Crusade was leveled—
for most of the knights who fought in the Crusade were after new

FAMOUS OLD FIREPLACE IN THE MUSÉE DE CLUNY, FRANCE

Paul's Photos, Chicago

GATES OF CARCASSONNE
This castle in southern France is said to be one of the most perfectly preserved
relics of the Middle Ages.

lands and wealth—was Toulouse, the capital of the powerful
Count Raymond of Toulouse. For centuries this county had been
one of the most powerful in all France, and had paid slight attention to the nominal king of the country. When the Pope asked for
a Crusade against the heresy to which the Count and almost all of
the graceful people of Provence ascribed, the king, Philippe
Auguste, would have nothing to do with it except allow his
knights to join if they wished. And with an opportunity to win
new possessions in the name of religion they were only too eager to
do so. In great swarms they attacked the country and seized most
of it for themselves. The heresy was wiped out, as was the charming culture of the section, but the northern knights were not able
to hold their acquisitions, and the only one who gained in the end
was the king who managed to establish a more secure control
over the section.

Toulouse has never been the same since the Crusade which killed off her best people and broke her spirit, but there is still an element of the old charm which impresses itself upon every visitor. Rich in relics both of artistic and historical interest, possessed of one of the many fine churches of France, it is one of the most delightful cities in the country. It is worth a passing comment that after the Crusade Toulouse became a stronghold of fanatical orthodoxy, and although located in the center of the Calvinistic Huguenots, remained loyal to the church through the religious wars of the sixteenth and seventeenth centuries.

BORDEAUX

Following the Garonne from Toulouse to its mouth one arrives in Bordeaux, a city which combines culture, historical interest and commerce gracefully and harmoniously. Famed as the home of the delicious Bordeaux wines, and also of the best sardines in the world, the city would seem to be mainly an economic center. But behind that modern exterior lies a tradition of other things. Since the early Middle Ages Bordeaux has been famous for its splendid university, which is still one of the sixteen leading educational centers in France. Rich in memories of the Hundred Years War, Bordeaux is also the home of several very beautiful churches which, from the times of constant feudal strife, have been places of refuge and contentment for the heavy-laden.

By going slightly to the east on the road from Bordeaux to the château region of the Loire, one may pass through Limoges, the home of the famous and exquisite Haviland china. And then a slight jog to the west again will lead to Poitiers, where one may see one of the finest of all Romanesque churches in France, Notre Dame la Grande. Low, hardly taller than it is wide, with round rather than pointed arches, with many statues, but few of the windows which mark the Gothic cathedral, of crude workmanship, Notre Dame la Grande is nevertheless an architectural treasure. It is said that in 1202 when the English were besieging Poitiers a traitor promised to give the keys of the town to the enemy. The Virgin took the keys Herself to protect the city, and it was only when the mayor turned to her to implore her aid in finding the missing keys that her intervention was discovered. Since that time the statue in whose hands the keys were found has been known as Notre-Dame-des-Clefs.

THE CHATEAU REGION OF THE LOIRE

Directly north of Poitiers is the famous château region of the Loire, where the loveliest of Renaissance French châteaux are to be found. These châteaux, built for homes of kings of the sixteenth century, were meant as buildings in which the gracious and cultured life of the Renaissance could be lived to its fullest. Consequently there is none of the awe-inspiring fortification, none of the crampedness of the medieval castle which was more a fortress than a home.

Most famous perhaps of all the châteaux of the Loire is Chenonceaux, which was built by Francis I and given by him to the fascinating Diane de Poitiers. The gracious château built over a little stream on slender arches is rich in memorials of the Valois kings and of the lovely Diane, and also of Catherine de' Medici. That queen, when her husband died, made no reprisals against her rival for his affections, but merely insisted that she give up the château and take another less beautiful in exchange.

Almost as famous and certainly more magnificent, if not so pleasantly artistic, is Chambord, another royal residence in the same locality. Surrounded by a low wall and a wide lawn, the château raises its dignified beauty above the countryside like a highest jewel. Chambord has an imposing façade, with towers at either end and a whole group of them in the center, which render the balance and symmetry perfect and graceful. Within are spacious rooms, designed to set off to advantage the best art treasures which an intelligent royal patronage could procure, impressive winding staircases, and many relics of the days when these châteaux were homes of kings rather than show places of a nation. Other châteaux of similar beauty and architecture which are of the same period and locality are Blois, Cheverny, Chaumont, Amboise, and Pierrefonds, which is east of Paris.

ORLÉANS

Also on the Loire is the famous old city of Orléans, which has long been one of the most important cities of France. In the Hundred Years War this city gave her name to the Maid who delivered her from the English. Later a cadet branch of the Bourbon family took the name as its own. In the early Middle Ages when universities were crowded with students who had just awakened to the possibilities of education, Orléans was one of the most populous

Courtesy Railways of France.   Photo by le Boyer

A NORMANDY FARMYARD
Showing the rich agricultural life of northern France.

cities of them all, for Orléans was a center for literary studies and
an advocate of the gay and interesting life rather than of any
practical but arduous course. In spite of the gay student body,
Orléans was the home of a famous cathedral and of pious *bour-
geoisie*. Today it is one of the French towns which manages a
profitable commerce without seeming anything but a fascinating
memory book.

North of Orléans, and on the Seine, is Rouen, the city of a
hundred belfries. It is another city intimately connected with the
tragic and inspired Jeanne d'Arc. It was at Rouen that she was
tried by the superstitious and vengeful English court, headed by
the Bishop of Beauvais. In spite of her naïve but forceful defense
of her innocence, she was burned at Rouen, May 30, 1431, as an
apostate, a relapsed heretic, and an idolatress. Another of the
attractions of Rouen is its famous cathedral with three tall spires,
of which the center one is the tallest and slenderest of all. Rouen
has a profusion of churches, many of them of the Gothic or
Romanesque type; and all are beautiful.

EMBATTLED TOWERS IN THE MISTS

One might leave France from Le Havre, which is at the mouth
of the Seine; but a more typically French memory is held if one

sails from Cherbourg. Cherbourg is a bustling seaport town, with all the excitement and fascinating ugliness which are a part of thriving ports. As the ship steams out of the harbor, the traveler looks back to see what a few minutes before had been mean dock fixtures suddenly transformed into embattled towers. Cherbourg is generally misty, and that mist, like the mist of time, transforms everything and surrounds it with a halo of romance and beauty.

France is a bustling, industrious nation, which keeps an eye on the future and on the developments of modern economic civilization, yet never forgets her past. She loves that past and is proud of it. Apparently laughing at mundane pursuits, she nevertheless realizes that they enable her to carry on her tradition of culture and of gaiety, her tradition of beauty and of charm. From Monte Carlo to the tip of Brittany, and from Biarritz to Belgium, France is a union of culture and industry.

Courtesy French Government Tourist Bureau, N. Y.

A STREET IN MONTMARTRE, PARIS

Courtesy Czechoslovak State Railways, N. Y.

"MARKTBRUNNEN" IN KARLOVY VARY (CARLSBAD)

SO SITUATED as to be a cultural bridge between the Germanic tradition on the west and the colorful Russian civilization on the east, Czechoslovakia is vastly interesting to the visitor. In addition, it is a country admirably suited to tourist travel. Smiling river-valleys alternate with picturesquely craggy mountains, and the far stretching fertile plains of the Danube find their counterpart in the deep mountain lakes of the High Tatras. Among the unique sights in Czechoslovakia are its sandstone rock-towns and the ice caves in the Karst regions.

The whole country is stamped with its distinctive civilization, which stretches far back into the past, with numerous traces of bygone ages surviving to the present day. Ascetically simple Romanesque chapels and fantastic Gothic houses on crooked medieval lanes, imposing palaces of the Renaissance aristocracy and souvenirs of curved baroque architecture are Czechoslovakia's

Black Star photo By Dr. Croy

FAMOUS ICE CAVE AT DOBSCHAU, CZECHOSLOVAKIA

offerings to the visitor. Ample opportunity exists for admiration of the seemingly inexhaustible treasures of the country's artistic heritage.

Although the Czechoslovakian republic is one of the newer European states erected in 1918 on the ruins of the Austro-Hungarian monarchy, it has a tradition as vivid as that of any of its contemporaries. Its capital, Prague, is believed to have been founded in 722. It was famous in the fourteenth and fifteenth centuries through the activities of the religionists, Jerome and Huss. Almost destroyed in 1424 by the Hussites, who advocated scriptural authority over papal primacy, the city was rebuilt nine years later. A decisive battle of the Seven Years War was fought there in 1757, which resulted in the defeat of the Austrians by Frederick the Great of Prussia.

THE CZECHS AND SLOVAKS

The country, as the name indicates, is a political union of two national groups. The Czechs originated in Bohemia, Silesia, and northern Hungary; the Slovaks in Moravia and Slovakia. Both are a Slavic people, and a slight difference in dialect marks their only important dissimilarity. Their combined population makes up two-thirds of a total of fifteen million; German population constitutes 23 per cent. Doubtless their mutual feeling of intense nationalism and their simultaneous revolt against Austrian rule contributed to the Czecho-Slovak union. After long years in which it lay smouldering, nationalist agitation for independence burst suddenly into flame during the World War. After a national Czecho-Slovak council in Paris in 1918, under the presidency of the late Professor Thomas Masaryk of the University of Prague, the independent existence of Czechoslovakia was declared official. Masaryk was inaugurated first president of the new republic, but his memorable career in public office was terminated by his death in his third term of office. Edvard Benes was elected president to succeed him.

SILVER AND SHOES

Czechoslovakia is by no means backward as an agricultural and industrial country. During the monarchy, Kutna Hora, a small Bohemian town, enjoyed royal favor as a rich silver-mining center. Serious emphasis is laid by the government on the manufacture of high-class goods at prices that compete with those anywhere. The main products are cereals and potatoes; coal, iron, and salt; and textiles, glass, machinery and chemicals. Shoes have made Czechoslovakia a ranking competitor in the world's footwear market. An efficient system of communication and the full backing of the state have contributed much to aid the growth of commerce.

Courtesy Czechoslovaki-
an Chamber of Commerce

SPAS

Because of its position in a region of former volcanic activity,
Czechoslovakia is a country of spas, a great number of which
enjoy world-wide reputation for their curative springs. The most
notable of these is Carlsbad, a resort founded in the fourteenth
century by Emperor Charles IV, for whom it was named. Carlsbad is not only a famous watering place with a large transient population, but also a thriving old town of more than twenty-four
thousand natives. There is the *Marktplatz,* or market place,
against a background of houses and trees perched on the steep
mountainside, stately and impressive. Many famous European
merchandising houses are represented among the attractive shops
in its main streets. Carlsbad's social life is characterized by the
prosperous-looking crowds in its magnificent parks, cafés, and
hotels. From these terraces visitors can enjoy the panorama of
the health resort surrounded by its forested hills.

Among the seventeen Carlsbad medicinal springs, ranging in
temperature from 107° to 164° Fahrenheit, the most famous is

the *Sprudel,* which yields about 400 gallons of hot mineral water (163°F) per minute. In addition it annually provides 600 tons of the famous "Sprudel Salt" and a daily two tons of carbonic acid gas. A part of this is used for the baths, of which 7,000 a day are given in the season—steam and Turkish baths as well as mud and intestinal baths.

The healing springs of Franzensbad are also renowned. This Bohemian resort is situated on the surface of a volcanic region once particularly active. In the neighborhood there is an extinct volcano called the *Kammerbühl,* which was explored by Goethe. Owing to the efficacy of the iron springs, the waters of the Franzensbad have been found to be especially beneficial to metabolic disorders.

Together with the spas, the sanatoriums in the High Tatra mountains—the highest range of mountains in Czechoslovakia— have been increasingly frequented by the ailing in recent years. The purity and comparative dryness of the air, the low barometric pressure, and the rich ultra-violet rays of the mountain sunshine give a healthful atmosphere to the region. Combined with the mild climate, they produce a toning effect on an organ-

Courtesy Czechoslovakian Chamber of Commerce

FOUNTAIN AT FRANZENSBAD
One of Czechoslovakia's many spas.

Courtesy Czechoslovak State Railways, N. Y.

COLORFUL SCENE OF A MORAVIAN PILGRIMAGE

ism exhausted by the fierce rush of modern life. The curative influence of the High Tatras is particularly marked in respiratory disorders, and it is therefore not surprising that here in the mountains there should have sprung up, within a short period of time, a large number of nursing-homes and sanatoriums.

THE MORAVIAN BRETHREN

Although Roman Catholicism is the prevailing religion in Czechoslovakia and therefore in Moravia, there exists in the republic a sect which first appeared in the time of Huss in the fourteenth century. These people are the so-called Moravian Brethren. In 1740 a group of Moravian immigrants came to America and settled in Pennsylvania, founding a permanent colony named Bethlehem. This became the Moravian center in North America. There are about 150 Moravian churches in the United States, accommodating almost twenty-five thousand communicants, and the world membership of Moravianism is 230,905. The Brethren are active in missionary work, and simple and earnest in their manner of living. Their fundamental doctrines do not differ appreciably from those of other Protestant churches. Despite the original concept of pure Christian teaching, their rituals tend to be colorful and pompous, marked by much use of relics, banners, and other paraphernalia.

The high regard for color and display ascribed to the Moravians is held by all Czechoslovakians and is evidenced in their manner of dress. Bright-hued peasant blouses are always among the prized souvenirs taken home from Czechoslovakia by the woman visitor. So richly and elaborately worked is the embroidery on these blouses that they are admired almost as much for the skilled labor which produces them as for their gay color and design.

It is not difficult for these simple, laughter-loving people to find excuses to don their finery and partake in merry-making and celebration. The feast days and holidays are many and are enjoyed to the utmost. Any man or woman is fond of putting his or her best foot forward when it is shod in beautifully worked red-leather boots. Much of a girl's attractiveness is gauged by the fullness of her skirts, the efficiency with which she has adorned the front and back of her blouse with needle-work, the delicacy with which she has crocheted the lace on her sleeves, or the ingenuity with which she has fluted her head-cloth. Often, the fullness of her skirts and sleeves has been so enhanced by minute pleating that a girl almost seems about to ascend into the air lifted by the lightness of her own swirling skirts.

Courtesy Czechoslovak State Railways, N. Y.

FAMOUS TYNKIRCHE, PRAGUE

PRAGUE, THE SPLIT CITY

Prague, the largest city of the Czechoslovakian republic, is situated in Bohemia, which was formerly a kingdom in the Austro-Hungarian Empire. The city is located almost one-third of the way from Dresden to Vienna. Like Budapest, it is built on both banks of a river —instead of the Danube, the stream is the Moldau—which is crossed by a number of fine bridges. One of these, the Charles Bridge, built in the fourteenth century, is adorned with statues of the saints and is one of Europe's surviving medieval spans. The city is situated upon low hills which rise

CASTLE OF EM-
PEROR CHARLES
IV AT PRAGUE

Courtesy The Art Insti-
tute of Chicago

gradually from the river; it comprises seven districts, of which the *Altstadt* is the most interesting and the most important commercially. Here, clustered about the *Grosser Ring,* or the Great Square, are the Gothic *Tynkirche,* the old Hussite church; the *Kreuzherrenkirche,* constructed after the plan of St. Peter's at Rome; and the palace of the former Bohemian kings. Nearby are the old buildings of the University of Prague, the oldest of all Germanic universities, some of which date from the Middle Ages. Bent on preserving the historic beauties of Czechoslovakia's capital, Prague maintains a society without whose permission no picturesque old building may be torn down. Prague was the third largest industrial city of the Austro-Hungarian monarchy, exceeded only by Vienna and Budapest. Its population in 1930 was 848,081.

THE DREADED GOLEM

Of interest is one of Prague's most persistent legends, that of the Golem. It is related that at some time in the Middle Ages the Jewish people, being cruelly persecuted, were led, by divine revelation, to mold a monstrous effigy in clay. After certain rites had been performed, the monster came to life and, following the will of its makers, avenged the Jews' wrongs. Across the forehead of this creature, which was called the Golem, was written the word *Aemaeth,* or Truth. When the downtrodden Jews felt that the Golem was becoming too strong and might turn on its makers, they reduced the creature to its original state of clayey inanimation by erasing the first letters so that nothing remained but *Maeth* (he is dead). This procedure could be repeated as often as necessary, and many still believe that when the Jews need its protection, the Golem can again rise to their rescue.

Prominent among other leading cities and towns of Czechoslovakia is Pilsen, long noted for the excellence of its beer. This town boasted a printing press of movable type in 1468, only a few years after Gutenberg's invention of the first press. Among other towns are: Bratislava on the Danube, the chief Czechoslovakian port; Brünn, a famous hill-top town; and Kosice.

WORSHIPERS
AT A ROADSIDE
SHRINE IN
CZECHOSLO-
VAKIA

Paul's Photos, Chicago

X—19

Paul's Photos, Chicago

STREET SCENE IN OLD VIENNA

A CORNER IN THE VOLKSGARTEN, ONE OF VIENNA'S MANY PARKS

USTRIA, A STATE OF GERMANY since March, 1938, combines the modern with the old and historic. It is a place of infinite variety where striking contrasts in scenery, climate, custom, and costume afford the visitor many different and delightful experiences. Here we may find medieval towns still retaining all the romance and mystery of the Middle Ages. Here also we may find progressive cities where science, industry, and culture have reached a high stage of development. It is a land abounding in scenic splendors, quaint traditions, noteworthy buildings, and impressive historical monuments.

IN THE HEART OF EUROPE

Although no longer at the head of the great Austro-Hungarian Empire, Austria still occupies a key position in troubled Central Europe. With her borders forming the boundaries between Germany on the one hand and Italy, Yugoslavia, Czechoslovakia, and Hungary on the other, Austria's position is a vital one in the uncertain affairs of Europe.

2

A large portion of the state lies on the eastern slopes of the Alps. From the rugged heights of Tirol in the west, however, the mountains gradually descend, falling away in northeastern Austria to the fertile valley of the famous "blue Danube." Here, in one of the most populous and productive sections of the state, is romantic old Vienna, for centuries the chief cultural center of Europe.

Austria contains a predominantly German population of slightly over six and a half million and is divided into a number of federal provinces or "Bundesländer." The present state comprises Upper Austria, Lower Austria, Burgenland, Styria, Carinthia, Salzburg, Tirol and Vorarlberg. It forms only a part of the huge empire which suffered such a severe dismemberment at the end of the World War. The Austrian people, however, are rapidly overcoming the problems of readjustment and retain much of their traditional gaiety and hospitable charm.

For nearly a thousand years Austria's rulers, aristocrats, and scholars have supported the arts and encouraged cultural development. The results of this patronage are seen on every hand. From the beautiful frescoes and delicate woodcarvings in the tiniest churches in obscure valleys to the magnificent art collections of the Hapsburgs in Vienna, the esthetic tradition is apparent. Nor has music been neglected. The land that mothered Mozart, Haydn, and Strauss, and was beloved of every great composer from Beethoven to Lehar, remains to this day a music-lover's paradise.

Nature, which has deprived the Austrian farmer of much agricultural land, has been kind to the tourist. Four-fifths of the

SCHÖNBÜHEL, ONE OF THE MANY CASTLES OF THE DANUBE VALLEY

Paul's Photos, Chicago

entire land is typically Alpine. Gleaming hills of snow and
sparkling mountain lakes help to make skiing, tobogganing, and
ice-skating major Austrian sports. Thickly wooded slopes and
rocky crags encourage hunting and mountain climbing. Health
resorts and spas are numerous throughout the land, for the mineral
springs of Austria gush with the most radio-active waters in the
world. From the snow-covered peaks of the Gross-Glockner to
the sheltered valleys of the Danube, Austria is a vast natural playground. It is filled with a great variety of attractions, not least
among which is the friendliness of its charming people.

DOWN THE BLUE DANUBE

The Danube flows southeastward out of Bavaria into Upper
Austria. At Passau, a quaint old town on the Bavarian border, we
start our journey downstream toward Vienna. Our boat carries

2

us past wooded glens and mountain gorges of surpassing beauty. History and legend march with us along the shores of the river which, although not blue at this point, is certainly one of the most imposing waters of all Europe. The Huns and the Avars, as well as the heroes and heroines of the *Nibelungenlied,* passed this way before us. Monasteries and castles of another age stand guard over a countryside whose natural loveliness never fades.

Linz, the capital of Upper Austria, appears before us on both sides of the river. We break our journey here to inspect the thriving provincial city which was once an important Danubian fort under the Romans. The winding, narrow streets of the old town contrast strangely with the wide thoroughfares of the modern city. Rising almost four hundred and fifty feet into the air, and dominating the skyline is the spire of the magnificent Gothic cathedral, built here between 1862 and 1924. Nearby are to be found the Hall of Diet, with its fine Renaissance detail, and the Museum of Upper Austria, housing collections designed to show the development of the state from prehistoric times to the accession of the Hapsburgs.

An hour's journey from Linz takes us to the interesting Abbey of St. Florian. It offers the tourist a splendid example of that Baroque architecture which, with its high ornamentation and its wealth of imaginative detail, is to be encountered throughout much of Austria. The abbey is further distinguished as the burial place of Bruckner, the great composer. In his commemoration important music festivals are held each year at Linz and Steyr.

In "Bruckner's country," as this part of Austria is called, we may be fortunate enough to see the quaint and traditional costumes which some of the inhabitants wear on holiday occasions. The well-known "Dirndl" costume of the women, with its puffed sleeves, full skirt, and dark silk apron, is especially typical of the district. The charming simplicity of this dress, however, gives way to a more elaborate attire worn at weddings and similarly important functions. Upon these occasions, the women may be seen in their beautiful, long, silk dresses, their exquisitely worked collars, and their curious, helmet-shaped hats which gleam with gold embroidery. The men are equally attractive in short, leather trousers, wide belts, colorful jackets, and broad-brimmed bonnets.

Bidding farewell to Linz, we board the boat and continue our journey down the lazy Danube. After drifting past the ancient town of Grein, we come to the narrows of Strudengau where the

THE ABBEY OF
MELK IN AUS-
· TRIA

It is almost 1000
years old, was re-
built in baroque
style, and its library
contains many rare
books and manu-
scripts.

Paul's Photos, Chicago

river suddenly awakens. We are carried swiftly along past castled
rocks and steep cliffs. The imposing towers of the great Benedictine Abbey at Melk soon come into view, marking the entrance to
the celebrated Wachau valley.

HISTORY IN STONE

The Wachau, situated between Melk and Krems in Lower
Austria, is considered the most beautiful section of the Danube.
Our boat winds through it past rocky promontories, wooded
slopes, and sunny vineyards. Here and there old castles and ruins
stand silhouetted against the sky, mute and stony reminders of historical events. Each curve in the river brings us a different landscape and a new experience.

We pass the crumbling old fortress of Aggstein where once lurked those robber barons who stretched their formidable chains in the path of merchant vessels. Farther along is the broken ruin of Durnstein. Here, legend tells us, Richard the Lionhearted was imprisoned in 1193. Here, in his loathsome dungeon, he joyously raised his weary head as the song of Blondel came drifting to his ears. We pass the crimson roof of Artstetten, symbol of tragedy. To this place, on a night of thunder in 1914, was brought from Sarajevo the mutilated body of Francis Ferdinand.

Throughout our journey to the capital of Austria there is hardly a cliff or a hill that does not add its colorful story of the glories of nature which surround it. Even as we drift through the verdant meadows leading to the beautiful Vienna forests, we are reminded of the immortal melodies inspired by these scenes.

ROMANTIC VIENNA

Vienna, the lovely old city of countless romantic memories, lies on a level plain amid the beautiful Carpathian foothills and the celebrated *Wiener Wald* or Vienna Woods. A frontier stronghold under the Romans, the seat of the Babenbergs in the tenth century, and a prosperous trading center during the Crusades, Vienna became the capital of the dynasty which, founded by Rudolf of Hapsburg in 1278, continued to flourish until 1918. The city stood as a rampart of Christendom against the Turks in 1529 and 1683. In the eighteenth century, under the guidance of Maria Theresa, it established that tradition of social and cultural brilliance which has persisted to the present day.

The Ringstrasse, along which are situated many of the important public buildings of the city, is the most famous of many delightful avenues. It was built by Francis Joseph in 1857 on the site of the bastioned walls which, for centuries, kept the Turks out of Western Europe. It is 150 feet wide, three miles long, and encircles the inner city.

The Opera House, located on the Ring near the heart of the city, was built by Van der Nüll and Siccardsburg in 1861. The edifice is beautifully decorated in French Renaissance style and still witnesses performances of the Vienna State Opera which are considered among the finest in the world.

Farther along the Ringstrasse looms the bulk of the National Museum of Fine Arts. We find here, among other notable treasures, the collections amassed in the sixth century by Ferdinand of

Paul's Photos, Chicago

THE OPERA HOUSE OF VIENNA

the Tirol. In addition to the splendid Greek and Egyptian departments, there are thousands of paintings among which are to be found collections of Velazquez, Dürer, and the Dutch masters. The Museum of Natural History, a sister building, contains interesting exhibits of the natural sciences.

Directly off the Ring stands the Hofburg, the Imperial Palace of the Hapsburgs for seven centuries. After passing through the main gateway, which contains the tomb of Austria's Unknown Soldier, we are confronted by an impressive mass of buildings representing a number of different architectural periods. Although numerous additions have been made to the oldest section which dates from 1275, the general effect is pleasing. Within the Palace are to be seen the imposing private and state apartments with their magnificent Gobelin tapestries. The Secular Treasury contains priceless displays which include the Crown and Relics of the Holy Roman Empire, the Collar of the Order of the Golden Fleece, and the golden cradle of the little King of Rome.

Also within the gates of the Burg is the Spanish Riding School, the sole surviving exponent of the High School of Equestrian Art. Here we may watch the splendidly equipped stallions of the cele-

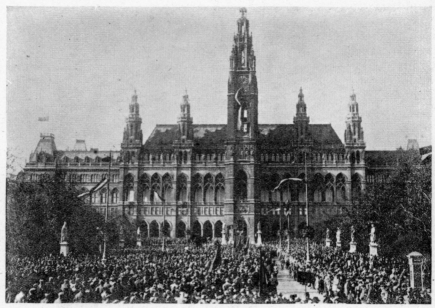

Paul's Photos, Chicago

FESTIVE CROWDS CELEBRATING THE FOUNDING OF THE AUSTRIAN
REPUBLIC GATHER IN FRONT OF THE CITY HALL OF VIENNA

brated Lipizza breed go through their intricate evolutions. For
those who are more scholastically inclined, the Este Art Collection
and the National Library are easily accessible within the Burg.

On the outer side of the Ring is the Rathaus or City Hall, a
Gothic building embellished with Renaissance detail. Nearby is
the Burg Theater, erected at the time of the American Revolution.

Within the inner city, adjacent to the Ring, we find the Academy of Fine Arts, with its splendid schools; the Liechtenstein
Palace, containing what is perhaps the most valuable private art
collection in the world; and the Belvedere Castle, built by Maria
Theresa and housing a number of excellent art galleries. The
Schubert and Haydn Museums located nearby are shrines to which
many music-lovers pay homage.

Of the numerous splendid churches of Vienna, St. Stephen's
is the most impressive. Although it was dedicated by one of the
Dukes of Babenberg in the twelfth century, it is today considered
one of the finest Gothic cathedrals in the world. Its ornate spire,
completed in 1433, rises from the heart of the city to serve as a

landmark for the surrounding countryside. The impression of solemn majesty which the interior presents is strengthened by the vast proportions of its architecture, by the all-pervading gloom of its perpetual twilight, and by the almost palpable silence of its atmosphere. The cathedral has many features which endear it to all lovers of old Vienna. Its giant bell, for instance, which weighs almost twenty tons, was cast from the cannon captured in the Turkish wars.

In the flowering suburbs on the outskirts of the city stands the summer palace of Schönbrunn, one of the most glamorous buildings in Central Europe. It is surrounded by a veritable fairyland of rose gardens, formal terraces, and fountained parks which lead gradually up a hill to a monument known as the Gloriette. The Schönbrunn Palace was copied after the palace of Versailles and was the favorite resort of Maria Theresa.

In the days of its usefulness the palace must have been well stocked with food, for it contains 139 kitchens. Of its 1,441 rooms, many are completely furnished and open to inspection. We may see, among others, the rooms occupied by Francis Joseph; those used by Napoleon, his wife, and his son; the "million-dollar-room" with its priceless Persian miniatures; and the blue and silver room which witnessed the abdication of Karl when he relinquished the crown and the capital which had belonged to the Hapsburgs for centuries. In the extensive park of Schönbrunn are the renowned botanical and zoölogical gardens, laid out in 1735, sixty years after the palace was started.

The gaiety of the Viennese is traditional. Balls and dances are frequent and lively, for the people of this city consider themselves the greatest dancers in the world and miss no opportunity of displaying their talent. A joyous spirit seems to reign here and night life is prolonged and merry. Business and pleasure are mixed in the friendly atmosphere of Vienna's innumerable cafés and bars.

In the Prater, the main park of the city, we may enjoy a variety of amusements in a beautiful natural setting. At Grinzing, situated in the suburban section, we may join the Viennese in the high festivities which inaugurate the new-wine season. Upon these occasions melodious voices, raised in the singing of old love songs, may be heard far into the starlit night.

A two-hour journey by train takes us to the Semmering. Lying across the pass between Lower Austria and Styria, at an elevation of some three thousand feet above sea-level, the Semmering

MUNICIPAL
APARTMENT
HOUSES AT
VIENNA

is surrounded by some of the most gorgeous scenery in the world. It is a winter resort of international fame, with splendid hotels, great indoor swimming pools, and facilities for every kind of sport and amusement.

Continuing our journey southwestward, we cross the Semmering. Pass, travel downward through the dense forests of Styria, and finally arrive at Graz, capital of the province. Built on both sides of the silver Mur and cupped on three sides by ascending wooded hills, Graz occupies one of the most delightful locations in the world. As Austria's second largest city, it has its full complement of theaters, museums, libraries, and schools. Kepler, the mathematician, taught here at the university in 1594.

OLD WARNING

Dominating the city is the "Schlossberg," a hill with a quaint clock tower and old cable railway. The fortifications which at one time guarded the summit were demolished in 1809 during the Napoleonic wars. In the older section of the city, we come upon the Renaissance Landhaus, built between 1556 and 1563. It still bears a sixteenth-century notice forbidding its occupants to quarrel, draw daggers, or fight with bread knives.

In the Arsenal, unaltered since the seventeenth century, we may see, if time permits, some 28,000 pieces of armor, many of which show grim evidence of having been used. Other interesting structures include the fifteenth-century Gothic cathedral, the baroque mausoleum of Ferdinand II, the imperial palace, and the house which Johann Meyer adorned with frescoes.

As we travel south and west through Styria toward the province of Carinthia, we may observe some of the native costumes typical of the district. The men may be seen wearing short leather pants or long green-striped trousers. Their quaint gray jackets are trimmed with bright green cloth. The women wear colored aprons and bodices, white skirts, and silken neckerchiefs. Add to this costume a kerchief fastened artistically around the head and the "Steirergewand" is complete.

The province of Carinthia, because of its warm lakes and its sheltered position amid the mountains, has the most moderate summer climate of the entire Alpine district. Klagenfurt, the capital, lies in the sunny valley of the Glan River. It is an old city but it has been almost completely rebuilt. It possesses, however, besides its superb mountain lake scenery, several spots of interest.

The Provincial Museum is rich in relics of Alpine folklore and of the sagas in which the region abounds. The Landhaus contains a sixteenth-century Hall of Diet, emblazoned with the heraldic symbols of the old Carinthian houses. In addition to these are the botanical gardens, with fine specimens of Alpine flora, and a sixteenth-century cathedral.

Carinthia is especially full of the folk customs which, even today, are a vital part of Austrian life. On Easter morning throughout the province may be seen the huge bonfires which are kindled at this time on the mountain tops. As we stand in the valley and watch the flames rising in a circle around us, we are reminded of the magic fire spell which Wotan cast around the unfortunate Brünnhilde.

"Tub thrusting," which takes place at Whitsuntide in the Gail valley is another fascinating old ceremony. Those who take part gallop bareback past a tub which is dangling in the air at the end

BURGENLANUD
FOLK-DANCE

of a rope. If the horsemen smash the tub with the lances which they clutch in their hands, they receive the plaudits of the assembled multitude. Girls dressed in the short skirts and the strangely folded kerchiefs of their traditional costume enthusiastically cheer their favorites.

Salzburg, capital of the province of the same name, is situated northwest of Klagenfurt in a world-famous section of the country unrivaled for its beauty. Lying on both sides of the winding, sparkling Salzach River at a point where plains and mountains meet, it rises amid lush greenery to the fortressed summit of the Hohensalzburg. The festival plays attract great crowds every year, but comparatively few people realize that Salzburg possesses many points of interest that are in themselves worth seeing.

The seventeenth-century cathedral is a remarkable building whose Romanesque architecture was derived from St. Peter's in Rome. The simplicity of its interior emphasizes its dimensions and produces a surprising effect of vastness. From any place in the immediate neighborhood we may hear the silver-voiced carillon which pours out beautiful melodies twice during the morning and once again at twilight.

The old Abbey of St. Peter contains the Peterskeller, frequented during the holiday season by visitors who appreciate the tantalizing bouquet of the wines the monks have been cherishing for decades. The cemetery of St. Peter is a curious burial place where we may see rocky walls so honeycombed with vaults as to remind us of the catacombs of the early Christians.

In Salzburg, also, are the Mozart Museum, marking the birthplace of the composer; the beautiful Mirabell Castle, with its lovely gardens; the Palace of the Archbishops; and the Kapuzinerberg, upon whose lofty heights Mozart lived and composed *The Magic Flute.*

A short distance from Salzburg is the Castle Hellbrunn where the prince-bishops were wont to frolic. One of them caused to be constructed within the grounds an elaborate system of water pipes which was so designed that at a given signal fountains would spring up in the most unexpected places. Summer-houses would become shower baths, paths would send up streams of water, and dinner guests would be thoroughly drenched while eating. Practical jokes were perpetrated in those days as they are at the present time.

SALT MINE TERRITORY

The Salzkammergut, the region east of Salzburg, is one of the most popular resort sections of Austria. Wooded hills and rocky mountains; gleaming glaciers and gigantic caves; gorgeous lakes and fascinating salt mines—all contribute in making this district attractive to the visitor. The sunny, flower-sprinkled shores of its many lakes are dotted with pleasant resorts such as St. Wolfgang, Mondsee, and Bad Ischl. Students of prehistoric lore are especially interested in the remains of the civilization of the early Celtic cave dwellers at Hallstatt. Nearby are the weird and fantastic Dachstein Caves with their giant ice-grottoes and chill, subterranean lakes.

Turning westward once more, we proceed toward the province of Tirol, the land of mountains. Majestic Alpine splendors, curious folk customs, and historic monuments give the province a many-sided appeal. Here, where the snow-capped mountains meet the fleecy clouds, where the air is crisp and clear, and where the smell of the green pine forest is like some rare incense, nature reveals her beauties in a truly wonderful fashion.

Homer Smith photo, Chicago

BATHING BEACH AT BADEN, NEAR VIENNA

The devout peasants, cut off from the rest of the world by a chain of peaks, still retain many of their traditional characteristics, superstitions, and costumes. The women of the Inn valley continue to wear their quaint native dress on Sundays and holidays. On these occasions they may be seen wearing tucked skirts, close-fitting bodices, light-colored aprons, and flat, black hats with platelike brims and gold cords.

INNSBRUCK

Innsbruck, the capital of the province, is situated on the river Inn and is almost completely encircled by high mountains. The *castrum* built here by the Romans who followed Caesar into Gaul was called "Veldidena." As a junction of the great medieval trade routes, it was a place of rest familiar to thousands of travelers. Among the innumerable important personages who have paused here are Frederick Barbarossa, Goethe, Maximilian I, and Andreas Hofer. The place they knew is still a Gothic town with slight touches of baroque and Renaissance architecture surviving from the times when the Hapsburg court flourished here.

"Old Innsbruck," the section radiating from the Maria-Theresien-Strasse and the Herzog-Friedrich-Strasse, has scarcely been touched by the incursions of modern life. Many historical monuments are to be found here. The fifteenth-century castle with its beautiful Goldene Dachl (a gilded copper roof) upon which Maximilian can still be seen laughing; the Triumphal Arch of Maria Theresa's day; the Hofkirche (Court Church), where the bronze King Arthur stands guard with the statues of the Teutonic kings over the black marble tomb of Maximilian; the Tirol Folk Museum with its gay array of peasant art and costumes; the Hofburg, where the staunch Hofer ruled his native land in direct defiance of His Napoleonic Majesty; and the Berg Isel, where he once defied the marshals and where he broods in bronze today—all these landmarks of another day remain thrilling beyond description.

VORARLBERG

Directly west of Tirol lies Vorarlberg, the province which unites every variety of landscape. In the north spread the friendly and harmonious ranges of the Bregenzer Wald. In the west and northwest are the undulating plains of the Rhine valley and the shores of Lake Constance. In the east rise the rocky mountains of the Arlberg district. In the south, the beautiful Montafon valley leads up to the wonderful glaciers of the Silvretta.

Bregenz, the capital of the province, is charmingly situated above the shores of Lake Constance. For over a thousand years, legend tells us, the capital of little Vorarlberg had overlooked the sapphire lake before the Bregenz maid headed her white steed into the waters on her way to warn her native town of the impending Swiss siege. The older portions of the town look their age, but the surrounding country is as greenly fresh, as gay with its little carnelian-colored towns, as it was before history was recorded.

Within the town are the Provincial Museum, the parish church, and Martin's Tower—all worthy of our notice. The Pfander, reached after a thrilling ride on the cable-railway, affords a splendid view and we look down upon the meeting place of three nations.

We leave Austria with a feeling of regret but with the pleasant knowledge that we shall return some day to renew our acquaintance with this hospitable land. For all who have once participated in the delightful experiences which Austria affords will surely want to revisit this beautiful, cultural, and historic "heart of Europe."

Variety is the keynote of the state. Sports such as hunting, fishing, skiing, and mountain climbing; spas and health resorts located amid the magnificent natural scenery of a country whose superb mountains, rivers, and lakes provide a veritable paradise for photographers; quaint native costumes whose originality arouses the envy and admiration of the tourist; innumerable places of historic interest; and every conceivable type of amusement combine to make our trip through Austria an unforgettable experience.

ST. STEPHEN'S CATHEDRAL IN VIENNA
Construction was started in 1147.

Black Star photo. By Illustrated Press, Budapest

SUPPER AFTER THE DANCE
Even the smallest children are dressed like grown-ups for the festive Hungarian dances.

AT MENTION OF HUNGARY first thoughts are likely to be of vast, rolling wheat fields, goulash, violin music and gipsies, and peasants garbed in fantastically colored costumes. Over all this hovers a haze of mystery. Hungary seems so far away, and somehow un-European. Although the Kingdom of Hungary, the kingdom without a king, is but three hours by rail from Vienna and six and a half days from New York by steamer and airplane, the visitor is carried as on a magic carpet to the past of a thousand years ago. This forest-clad, castle-crowned land lies deep in the heart of central Europe. Yet it is the portal to the East and, like all gateways, has a strange mixture of the East and the West.

PAWN OF EMPIRES

The land called Hungary today was known to the Roman conquerors. Then it was overrun by a succession of barbarian invaders. At length, in the ninth and tenth centuries, a wild Asiatic tribe came sweeping up the Danube into the heart of central Europe.

[307]

Black Star photo. By Illustrated Press, Budapest
BODYGUARD OF ADMIRAL HORTHY, WHO WAS MADE REGENT
OF HUNGARY IN 1920

The tribe pillaged and conquered as another Asiatic horde called
the Huns had done four hundred years before. Frightened Europe
made no fine distinctions between such tribes and cried out in terror that the Huns had come again. When they settled down along
the banks of the Danube, their country was called Hungary. But
the people called themselves Magyars. Today only a small percentage of the inhabitants represent the original, pure Magyar
stock. But Magyar customs and ideals are dominant, the Magyar language is the official one, and people whose ancestors were
German or Slavic have become completely Magyarized.

First the Turks, then the Austrians, were the oppressors of
Hungary. Restiveness under Austrian rule persisted for many
years and finally broke out in open revolt in 1848 under the guidance of Hungary's greatest patriot, Louis Kossuth. A short-lived
republic was established. This was put down; but in 1867 Austria
was compelled to grant Hungary equal partnership in the Monarchy, which from that time until 1918 was known as the Dual
Monarchy.

AN EMPTY THRONE

After Austria-Hungary's defeat in the World War a republic was set up in Hungary. It succumbed to a communistic government, which also failed. Finally in 1920 a royalist group gained control and declared that Hungary was still a kingdom. But a king was not easily to be had, for the Allies were determined that a Hapsburg should not be enthroned, and it was a Hapsburg whom the Hungarians wanted. Making the best of things, they elected a regent, choosing Admiral Nicholas Horthy, commander-in-chief of the national military forces.

The peace treaty imposed upon Hungary is known as the Treaty of Trianon, named from the palace in France where it was signed. By its terms Hungary lost two-thirds of her territory and half her population. There was some justice in this, for most of the people living in these territories were not of the Magyar race, nor did they speak the Magyar tongue. But Hungary has never accepted this arrangement and to this day is firmly determined to regain the lost areas.

DOWN THE DANUBE

By far the most interesting way to enter Hungary is down the Danube by steamer from Vienna. About thirty miles below Vienna the river suddenly enters a region of hills and cliffs. These are the Little Carpathians, southernmost portion of the great Carpathian chain, which runs through most of central Europe. This marks the boundary of Austria. In majestic sweep the Danube rolls into Hungary. The land soon becomes almost flat so that the river is free to choose its own course. It frequently divides into separate channels, creating great islands or vast marshes. As the river enters these marshy lands, the visitor realizes that at least one thing is not completely strange here; for the marshes seem to be inhabited mainly by extremely active and vicious mosquitoes. Because of its wanderings the river loses speed in its flow and progress is slow.

The first major city down the Danube is Esztergom, or Gran. Almost all places in Hungary have two names, a German one and a Magyar one. This is a country of many peoples and as many languages, although German and Magyar are the most important. Esztergom (population 18,000) was once the capital of Hungary and the site of its first church. Today it is still Hungary's reli-

Black Star photo. By Il-
lustrated Press Budapest

gious center, being the residence of the archbishop of Hungary,
who is an extremely important personage.

The town's most imposing structure is the cathedral, which
stands on one of the few hills of this region, 215 feet above the
river. It was erected (1821-1870) at great expense and magnificently decorated. It strongly resembles St. Peter's Cathedral at
Rome, and contains many precious and antique relics. Many
other church buildings, including the magnificent palace of the
archbishop, and a famous church college are found here.

HUNGARY'S MT. VERNON

Esztergom's proudest boast and its chief claim to national
importance is that St. Stephen, first king of Hungary, was born
and died within its limits. His name is frequently encountered in
journeying through Hungary, for many monuments to him are

to be found; and the very crown which Hungary's kings wore is known as the Crown of St. Stephen.

There is nothing left in Esztergom to remind one of St. Stephen save his memory, which is ever alive in the hearts of the people.

Excavations have been made in a ruined palace dating from the twelfth century. Some of its halls have been found to contain art treasures of great value. These ruins reveal the high degree of culture and the importance of Hungary in the Middle Ages.

QUEEN OF THE DANUBE

Beyond this ancient city of Esztergom the Danube suddenly turns southward for over 200 miles, cutting Hungary into eastern and western halves. The traveler on the gentle stream sees dimly in the distance a group of little hills on the flat Hungarian plain. On these hills rises the magnificent double-city of Budapest, the nation's capital.

Just before the river reaches this city, it is divided into two streams by St. Margaret's Island, on which is a beautiful park with provision for all pastimes, especially for water sports. Above all, the island contains the world-renowned Margaret's Baths, one of Budapest's many spas. Owing to its large number of thermal springs, the total daily yield of which is several million gallons, Budapest claims to be the world's greatest health resort. The waters have healing qualities, and people from all over Europe come to these spas to regain health. Beautiful hotels and sanitariums have been built around the springs.

Above and beyond Margaret Island rises the city. For over a thousand years it has been the meeting place of East and West; and here the two cultures have mixed.

THE HEART OF HUNGARY

Few capitals typify the spirit of their country as Budapest does that of Hungary. In it center the political, commercial, industrial, and intellectual life of this kingless kingdom; and its mixed population reflects the various racial elements of the nation. Its atmosphere is the quintessence of Hungary. Its very architecture is individual, containing many reminders of the exotic buildings of the East. Budapest, proud and lovely, richly deserves her title, "Queen of the Danube."

The story of Buda, on the right bank of the river, runs back to the days before the Romans, and its beginnings are lost in the

Black Star photo. By Illustrated Press, Budapest
FISHERS' BASTION, BUDAPEST, BY NIGHT
The silhouette of the famous Coronations Church, built in Gothic style and named for
King Mathias, is shown in the background.

shades of antiquity. As time passed, it assumed importance because of its geographical location. Its sharp hills made it an excellent fortification, while its central position facilitated the
gathering of the tribes. Pest, too, on the left bank of the Danube,
has ancient origins. Each was a separate city, and in 1361 Buda was
chosen as the capital, while Pest became the commercial center.

Midway between East and West, the two cities viewed the
passage of many armies and learned the horrors of battle and the
terrors of pillage. Standing in its streets today, surrounded by
modern buildings, one finds it hard to believe that gallant crusaders once passed over these roads on their way to redeem the Holy
Land, or that turbaned and fearless warriors, bearing the crescent
before them, swept westward through the Queen City to threaten

Christendom. Naturally, Buda and Pest were repeatedly captured and sacked in the centuries of warfare through which they lived. So today there is not much left from olden times, but the later, magnificent buildings more than make up for the loss.

In 1873 the two cities were united into one municipality, and called Budapest. A British engineer linked the two halves by one of the first great iron bridges in the world. Now six bridges span the river, which is over six hundred yards wide here; and the two towns are completely one in fact as well as name, with a population of one and a half million.

The government buildings, the hotels, and most of the gay life are located in Pest. The Franz Joseph Quay, famous promenade, runs along the riverbank here. No wheeled traffic is permitted upon it, so that thousands may stroll leisurely along the wide boulevard. On the riverside there are benches, where for a trifling sum one may sit for hours. On the land side of the Quay are many cafés, where centers the night-life of the city.

On the right bank, the old town of Buda climbs the slope of the hills. Exquisitely picturesque are the Rose Hill and St. Gel-

Black Star photo   By Kenessey (U. S. Pictures)

SZECHENYI FURDO, MAGNIFICENT SANITARIUM ON MARGARET ISLAND
Combines health cures with the attractions of a fine resort.

lert's Mountain. On the side of the latter is a chapel, hewn into the rocks. This shrine is a memorial to Bishop Gellert, who is said to have been the first to try to convert the pagan Magyars to Christianity.

A THOUSAND-YEAR-OLD HAND

In the middle of the old town rises Citadel Hill, upon which stands the magnificent Royal Palace. Containing 860 rooms, it was built as a symbol of Austro-Hungarian unity. It is on the site of the first royal residence that was built in Buda, in the thirteenth century. The Palace is one of startling immensity and beauty. In it are preserved the ancient royal crown of St. Stephen, the coronation robes, the scepter, and other royal regalia. In the chapel is kept one of the most gruesome yet interesting relics in Europe, the mummified hand of Stephen, the sainted king.

Black Star photo. By K. Mair

BUDAPEST: VIEW OF THE DANUBE AND PARLIAMENT BUILDINGS

PART OF FISH-
ERS' BASTION,
BUDAPEST

Black Star photo. By Il-
lustrated Press, Budapest

Away from the palace, at the other end of the plateau, is the
powerfully built, Romanesque Fishermen's Bastion. This is the
fortress entrusted to the Fishermen's Guild in a much earlier day.
Not far from it stands that exquisite example of Gothic-Roman-
esque architecture, the Coronation Church. Its soft but clear lines
carry the onlooker back many centuries, for this is an ancient
building. There is a legend that parts of the structure date back
as far as St. Stephen's day. In it Hungary's kings were crowned,
and about it cluster the traditions of a proud people. The hill itself is pervaded with the mystery and romance of bygone centuries. Nearly every house upon it bears a memorial tablet set up
by the Academy of Sciences; for these ancient structures are alive
with worthy stories of the past.

In the old city, too, is one of the most vivid reminders of Turkish rule. It is a Moslem shrine; for when the Turks were expelled
from Hungary at the close of the seventeenth century, the Mag-

Black Star photo. By Illustrated Press, Budapest

PARLIAMENT BUILDINGS, BUDAPEST, HUNGARY

yars agreed by treaty to keep inviolate the sacred shrine and grave
of Gul Baba, Moslem saint of the roses. Turkish pilgrims still
come to worship here.

On the Pest side, outstanding sights are the huge Gothic
Parliament Building and the vast grain elevators, which are a reminder that in past years Budapest ranked second to only Min-
neapolis, Minnesota, as the most important milling center in the
world. The mighty St. Stephen's Cathedral, with its large cupolas
flanked by two high steeples, is another famous landmark. The
Parliament Building covers over four acres of ground and has
nearly a hundred statues of Hungarian kings, warriors, and statesmen in it.

A MONUMENTAL CITY

Monuments are not confined to this building alone. They are
to be found everywhere throughout the city. The most famous
one is a statue of St. Stephen, done in Byzantine style, near the
Fishermen's Bastion. Another is of Kossuth and his cabinet. On the
square are four statues, the "four lost Alsace-Lorraines," one at

Black Star photo. By Illustrated Press, Budapest.

THE BEAUTIFUL CASTLE OF VAJDAHUNYAD
Modeled after the original in Transylvania, this structure occupies an important
position on the shore of the artificial lake in the City Park, Budapest.

each corner of the square, representing the provinces which the
Treaty of Trianon gave to Czechoslovakia, Austria, Yugoslavia,
and Rumania.

Budapest prides itself on its immaculate appearance. Its broad,
tree-lined boulevards are so well kept that it is understandable
why the Hungarian believes his capital to be the cleanest city in
Europe. It is said to be the only great city in the world that has
no slums. All the wealth of the nation is concentrated here, and
every important Hungarian has a home in this city, where he feels
he must keep up appearances. So, although the rest of Hungary
may suffer, the capital retains its air of prosperity. The most con-
spicuous objects in the streets of Budapest are the waste receptacles. It is an offense punishable by fine to throw anything on
the sidewalk or street. Next to these ubiquitous receptacles the
glass telephone booths catch the eye of the stroller. These public
pay-stations are placed at convenient spots and are completely
enclosed with spotless and crystal-clear glass.

At night Budapest is at its loveliest. The spacious boulevards
are brilliantly lighted. The hundreds of restaurants and cafés are

filled with talkative people. Strains of joyous gypsy music are heard everywhere. The very Parliament Building becomes a lively, outdoor café. Here, sitting in the great portico under the starlit Hungarian sky, hundreds of the wealthy dine or sip the wine and beer brought from the vast cellars under the building. In such luxurious surroundings one finds the Hungarian dandy at his best. Slim, elegant, usually an officer in a tight-fitting uniform, powdered and even rouged, he is an intriguing figure.

The theater and opera are much frequented. The musical life of the nation centers in the Academy of Music and the Royal Opera House. Numerous philharmonic and chamber-music concerts by world-famous musicians, and splendid choral concerts maintain the high musical standard of the city. Budapest, too, has several fine museums. That of the Fine Arts houses many masterpieces from all countries. The Museum of Applied Arts displays the products of Hungarian national art. The Agricultural Museum is devoted to exhibits of interest to all.

TRUE HUNGARY

Those parts of Hungary described above are the modernized and wealthiest sections. But within half an hour's ride of the sophisticated city of Budapest, one enters the most typical part of this ancient nation—the great *Alföld* (lowland plain). It is a flat, empty, and nearly treeless landscape, given over almost entirely to agriculture. On its fertile expanses, through which sluggishly flow the Danube and her tributaries, are to be found a people who still live in the manner of past centuries. For these farmers are peasants who own a minute portion of the land they till. Little more than serfs, they are governed by feudal Magyar lords who have almost complete power over them. Time stands still in the *Alföld;* for while all the rest of Europe sloughed off its old medieval customs long ago, feudalism held on here.

Between the *Alföld* and the vine-clad foothills lie the steppes of Hungary, called the *puszta*. Almost treeless and not very fertile, they are devoted to the grazing of thousands of sheep and cattle tended by solitary herdsmen. Here, too, are the camps of the gypsies of *Tziganes*. This strange and carefree people has wandered for countless centuries on the steppes, unmolested by the Magyars. From the tents and wagons of the *puszta* have come the magical, wild, and eerie gypsy violinists, whose strange power to enchant their listeners is known the world over. Speaking his own

Black Star photo   By Illustrated Press. Budapest

LONGHORNS OF THE HUNGARIAN PRAIRIE
The poodle dog in right foreground is an expert herder and very useful to his master.

tongue and maintaining his own culture, the Romany still is an integral part of Hungary; for much of the romance of this country lies in its multifarious racial streams, all of which are peculiarly Hungarian. But the nomadic life of the gipsy is passing. In 1918 the government ordered the *Tziganes* to settle in fixed abodes.

A typical city of the *Alföld* is Kalocsa, market center for the surrounding agricultural region. The country in which Kalocsa is located is called rather a strange name: Pest-Pilis-Solt-Kiskun. Standing a few miles back from the Danube, the town rises from the monotonous plain. The markets are carried on here in the most primitive fashion. Tents are set up in the public square, and farm wagons drive in, loaded with their produce. Fairs are held every three months, and merchants from all over the nation come to buy. The town is one of the oldest in Hungary, but it has lost most of the greatness it once enjoyed.

The houses, mainly of a single story, are spacious and comfortable. They are pleasingly colored, usually yellow or gray, and have numerous hand-made ornamentations. The usual color-scheme on the outside includes two bands of blue along the wall, one just above the ground and the other just below the roof. The women of the houses have added painted-flower decorations of red, white, and green. Few cities can boast of such picturesque

HUNGARIAN
SHEPHERD WITH
HIS HERD

Black Star photo
By von Kummer

homes. The most important civic life centers about the church buildings, for Kalocsa is the seat of a Roman Catholic archbishop, who lives in a beautiful and costly palace.

The tourist who comes to this charming town receives a rare greeting, unlike that in most other places. Kalocsa is far off the beaten track, and here the tourist is greeted as a friend; instead of being expected to pay for everything, he is actually an honored guest. Banquets are prepared in his honor, songs are sung, and much wine is drunk.

The gayest social life is enjoyed only by the men, because the woman in the *Alföld* is still held in medieval respect. As in Budapest, there is much hand-kissing and bowing; but the western visitor cannot help but feel that the ladies would prefer less gallantry and more gaiety. However, they express their personalities in their clothes, which are riotous with color. A woman's favorite way of showing off is by the number of petticoats worn. These are piled, one on top of the other, until the women look more like enormous bundles than human figures. A regular occasion for this display is on Sunday, when the Kalocsan damsels wear their best to church. There they can only stand or kneel, for sitting down in all those petticoats is impossible. It is reported that the record number of petticoats worn by any one lady was twenty-three!

From Kalocsa to Szeged is not a long journey but it is an arduous one. The railroads in this region do not provide direct connections, and the overland routes are not exactly all that could be desired. Szeged is the last town of southern Hungary before one crosses the border into Yugoslavia. It is situated on the Danube's chief tributary, the Tisza, and is the second largest city in the country, having a population of 135,000. A well-built modern town, it is a miniature Budapest and a far cry from the medievalism of Kalocsa. Its modern appearance is due to the rebuilding of the city after a disastrous flood in 1879. The restorers laid out the new city in a handsome pattern. There are wide avenues, grand public squares, and stately buildings. Szeged is an important manufacturing center, but it is most noted for its paprika. And what is Hungarian goulash without the right kind of paprika?

THE PROTESTANT ROME

Largest and best known of the typical Magyar cities of today is Debrecen (population 117,000). It is in northern Hungary, about 200 miles by rail from Budapest. In many ways it reminds the visitor of Kalocsa, except that it is much larger and wealthier. Its houses are of one story, and in wet weather many of the unpaved streets are well-nigh impassable. But the thing that makes

Homer Smith photo, Chicago

BUSINESS DISTRICT OF DEBRECEN, HUNGARY

X—21

it different from all other Hungarian cities is its religion. For
Debrecen is the headquarters of Hungarian Protestantism. Because of the pre-eminence of the Reformed Church there, it is
sometimes called the "Protestant Rome." The chief buildings are
the main Protestant church and the great Protestant college. The
church is a shrine for all Hungarians, regardless of creed, because
from its pulpit the national hero, Louis Kossuth, read the resolu-
tion declaring Magyar independence. The college was founded in
1531 and is considered one of the best institutions of higher learning in the country. It has over 2,000 students and a library of
nearly 200,000 volumes.

Outside of Debrecen is the most famous of all the Hungarian
pusztas, that of Hortobagy. Here, it is said, things are the most
typically Magyar. The centuries have changed matters but little
in this lonely wilderness. The great plain extends over thousands of
acres, and immense herds of horses and cattle roam over it. Here,
too, is a famous mirage, called the Fata Morgana, like the one at
the Strait of Messina, because it was once believed to be the work
of Morgan, fairy sister of Arthur and pupil of Merlin the
Magician.

HORSEMEN OF THE STEPPES

Hortobagy is best known for the horses that are bred here and
the men that ride them. The famed steeds of Hungary have been
produced by generations of careful breeding of Arab and other
noble strains. The horses of the Hortobagy are always in great
demand, for the Magyar gallant is immensely proud of his stables.
The vast herds are tended by the Magyar equivalent of our American cowboys, the *csikos*. These men, powerfully built and wearing picturesque costumes, live under the open sky from early
spring till late in the autumn. Most of that period is spent astride
a horse. Seldom has the world seen better riding than by these
csikos. Man and horse seem one as they sweep across the great
steppe.

The Hortobagy offers some of the best hunting in the country.
Wild geese abound and are especially sought. But the hunter is
not limited either to that region or to that game. Because Hungary is still so largely rural and has numerous state and private
reserves and feeding grounds, it offers some of the best hunting in
Europe. Quail, partridge, pheasant, hare, woodcock, roebuck,
stag, fallow deer, and wild boar, all are plentiful.

Homer Smith photo, Chicago

CITY HALL, PECS, HUNGARY

Although by far the majority of her people are tillers of the soil, Hungary is an important producer of minerals, among them coal. Pecs is the chief city of Hungary's "West Virginia," being in the heart of the coal-mining region. Pecs today is a busy industrial city of 62,000 people, located near Hungary's southern border. It is many centuries old. For a century and a half it was held by the Turks, who transformed its churches into mosques. When the Christians returned, the mosques again became churches. The cathedral at Pecs is one of the oldest in Hungary, having been built in the eleventh century.

One of the attractions for travelers in Hungary is seen on the northern border of the kingdom. It is the Baradla Grotto at Aggtelek, the largest stalactite cave in Europe. The grotto is more than twelve miles long, and its greatest hall is over 450 feet high, while the largest stalactite is seventy-eight feet high. There are five underground streams crossed by 104 concrete bridges. More unusual, however, even than these wonders of nature is the fact that the Baradla extends north into Czechoslovakia, Hungary's northern neighbor, and this underground frontier is guarded by an iron grille.

Black Star photo. By Werner Zeymer

SCENE AT A RUMANIAN CATTLE MARKET

RUMANIA is a small and beautiful country in southeastern Europe, a land of towering mountains, winding rivers, fertile valleys, and broad plains of waving grain. On its eastern shore pound the waters of the Black Sea; on the north are the Russian Ukraine and Poland; on the northwest lie Czechoslovakia and Hungary; and on the southwest and south the border stretches to Yugoslavia and Bulgaria.

Within Rumania live people of many nationalities, whose simple lives are enriched by a wealth of folklore and customs. Frequently drenched in blood, Rumania was long the gateway of Asiatic invasions, and her resistance was often valuable in saving Europe from Ottoman encroachments; during the World War her land was devastated. Yet, anyone sitting within the circle of a gypsy campfire, and watching the gay dancing, feels far from all warfare; and listening to the piping of a shepherd boy on some Carpathian mountain slope, one senses the spirit of peace itself.

Rumania's situation has greatly influenced her history. Located as she is, between countries of occidental culture and of eastern tradition, she has acquired a civilization which is an interesting blend of the Byzantine and the Western. The earliest inhabitants of Rumania, the Dacians, believed in the actual geographical migration of souls; and they were called the "Immortals," for they never referred to "dying." They were mentioned by the Greek historian Herodotus as "the bravest and most honorable of all the Thracian tribes." They migrated beyond the Danube River and after centuries of occupation came into conflict with the Roman legions. In 106 A.D., Dacia became a province of Rome, and the country quickly assumed the externals of Roman culture. Schools were built, and cities and aqueducts came into existence. Rumania still shows the Roman heritage in its speech, customs, and dress.

The Roman rule was withdrawn in 271 A.D., and the next thousand years saw wave after wave of barbaric invaders overrun the land. Occasionally there were traces of an emerging Rumanian state, but presently the country fell under Turkish control. There were momentary flares of national consciousness, but during most of the following two centuries the land was ruled by the despotic *Hospodars,* as the appointive Turkish governors were called.

The extravagance of the *Hospodar* style of living is almost unbelievable; it is said that a single costume sometimes represented an outlay of some $12,000. There were occasional attempts at reform. Eventually the country won the right to be governed by Rumanian appointees, and anon the nation of Rumania was officially born: in 1866 Charles of Hohenzollern, a relative of the Prussian King, became prince of Rumania as Carol I. His son Carol II, is the present ruler. The World War resulted in the addition of Bessarabia and other territories to Rumania.

BY THE BEAUTIFUL BLUE DANUBE

Most of Rumania is a level extension of the Black Earth Zone of Russia. The Carpathian Mountains stretch from the north through the central part of the country, then sweep westward in a great curve. Beyond the western limit of the Carpathian Mountains is the Hungarian plain. Bessarabia, in northeastern Rumania, is hilly in the north and mostly level in the southern half. Between the Danube and the Black Sea is the Province of Dobruja, predominantly a spreading steppe land.

Homer Smith photo, Chicago

ROSETTI SQUARE AND PART OF DOWNTOWN BUCHAREST

The great southern plain of Rumania is a gentle slope from the Danube to the Carpathian Mountains, intersected by many beautiful rivers which wind through the highlands to mingle their waters with the Danube. In many respects the Danube itself is to Rumania what the Nile is to Egypt.

"THE CITY OF PLEASURE"

Bucharest, the capital city is light-hearted and sparkling; and its theaters, night clubs, and restaurants have earned for *Bucuresti*, its title, "the city of pleasure." Walking along its boulevards one might think himself at the crossroads of many nations. During a casual stroll one may hear a dozen dialects spoken by natives from the Rumanian countryside, many of them dressed in the colorful costumes of their villages and districts. Shepherds, miners, peasants, fishermen, boatmen, all give the city the air of a great cosmopolitan fair. There is much less of variety and romantic color in the appearance of the upper classes. Most of them speak French; and the styles affected by them, their attitude, and their subjects of conversation show a strong Gallic influence.

Bucharest is laid out with broad and well-paved streets, which extend the entire length of the city. In the central part are ornate and lavishly furnished villas and palaces, belonging to the aristocratic and mercantile families. English and modern architectural styles are widely used in these buildings.

The public buildings are imposing; even the post office possesses a stately entrance, and wide marble halls. The Royal Palace is a long, low building, consisting of three wings facing a narrow courtyard. The interior is carefully decorated with beautiful carvings and rare *objets d'art*. To the west in Bucharest is the Palace of Cotroceni, one of the favorite residences of the royal family. Another building with which every visitor becomes quickly familiar is the shabbily elegant National Theater, where the works of Rumanian and foreign playwrights are presented. The parliament buildings are impressive. One of the great events of the year is the opening of parliament by the king; the entire ceremony is a dazzling display of pomp. The procession arrives in its splendor: the diplomatic corps, with its glittering show of authority; the army officers bearing their weighty medals and gold braid; and the various members of parliament. All these announce the arrival of the king himself, who rides in an open carriage drawn by six matched horses, replete with postillions in red costumes and a dignified coachman.

Bucharest was a city of pleasure as early as the seventeenth century, when it was already widely recognized for its luxury and gaiety, although the settlement was small and in some respects primitive. Today there is much entertaining in private homes, and even more in the public places of amusement. The city's restaurants and coffeehouses are famous. Amusement is one of the most engaging pursuits of the upper class. One pleasure is to drive about the long city streets in an elegant coach; or in winter, in a sleigh. Another pleasure may be found in the cafés on the outskirts of the city, where the music, alternately melancholy and exuberant, played by a gypsy orchestra, stimulates the senses. During the winter Bucharest enjoys a highly regarded symphony orchestra and an excellent national opera company.

The more serious side of Bucharest is shown in the University and the churches. There is great variety of churches: large and small, ornate and simple, Protestant and Catholic, Orthodox, Jewish, Armenian, and Lipovan. The national religion of Rumania is Greek Orthodox, and the Rumanian Orthodox Church dominates the city from its only hill.

Homer Smith photo, Chicago

HARBOR OF CONSTANTSA, RUMANIA
Situated on the Black Sea, Constantsa is Rumania's greatest seaport, from which
are shipped large quantities of oil and grain.

AN HONEST THIEF AND A REED

Travelers in Rumania often go southward to the river from Bucharest, and down that famed river past the cities of Galatz and Braila to the Danube delta.

Beyond Galatz, for long distances on each side of the river, is a wild marshland, an intricate blend of land and water pleasing to the eye. Here are wild birds of great beauty and variety: egrets, flamingos, wild geese, pelicans, herons, cormorants, and cranes. In the swamps and "lost" channels of this wild waste lived the most famous outlaw in Rumanian history, Terente, the Robin Hood of the country. He stole from the rich and gave to the poor; but, being a man of honor and business sense, he never took anything without giving a receipt for it. For years the gendarmes sought to capture this "honest thief." Once they surrounded him in the swamps, but he escaped by remaining under water and breathing through a hollow reed until the search was given up. He was finally shot down, however, when the police lay in wait one night outside his sweetheart's home.

In the delta country are also found many gypsy encampments. Picturesque, itinerant, and crafty, the gypsies are famous for their beautiful music, played on the violin, the flute, and the *cobza* (a lute of outlandish shape); for their beautiful hand-wrought metal-work and their expert carving of wooden trays and baskets. The training of bears has long been a favorite occupation of the gypsies, and they travel from city to city with their ragged animals, which perform crude dance steps to the music of castanets. The gypsy *mira*, or soothsayer, wearing as a girdle the cord and shell, symbolic of necromancy, is sought out by the Rumanian peasant woman with a sick child or by the farmer whose crops are not thriving.

POETRY WITH NEEDLE AND THREAD

From Bucharest one may go north across the mountains to the great province of Transylvania, where the Rumanian peasants spend their lives in simplicity and toil. Everywhere one is charmed by the color of their costumes and delighted with tales drawn from their rich tradition and ancient folklore. The native costumes are worn everywhere in Rumania except in the larger cities; and, while they differ even among localities, all are characterized by bright hues and fine needlework. They are all made by hand,

Homer Smith photo, Chicago

A SCENE ON THE DELTA OF THE DANUBE RIVER

during the long and rigorous winters, by housewives who sew patiently before their firesides and seek to express, with needle and thread, the beauty and gaiety lacking in their lives. Often these ornate costumes become heirlooms and are handed down from parent to child.

The Rumanian peasant expresses his artistic impulses also in the making of brightly colored pottery, lustrous rugs, and skilfully carved objects of wood.

Rumanian folklore shows itself in the fairy tales, legends, magic charms, songs, dances, games, and morality plays of the people. Typical ballads, called *doine*, are sung everywhere in the country and express the soul of the Rumanian peasant. Born in the stress of deep emotion, the *doine* tell of the simple joys and sorrows of life close to the soil.

Important occasions are weddings, baptisms, elections, the visit of the *prefet*, and Sundays and feastdays, when the villagers and peasants put on their festal clothing, and join in a great circle on the village square to dance to gypsy music the graceful *hora*. Easter is an opportunity to celebrate the arrival of spring; and on this day green branches as a sign of welcome decorate every door-

Black Star photo. By M. Vesa

CHARACTERISTIC FOLKDANCE IN A RUMANIAN VILLAGE

Homer Smith photo. Chicago

A LUMBER YARD IN BUCOVINA, RUMANIA

way. At this time the young men often choose their brides; when the unmarried girls, dressed in their best, come to the village, the young men circulate among them, joking and laughing shyly. An invitation to one of the girls to dance is considered a proposal; and, if the chosen one dances twice with the young swain, he is accepted.

FORTIFIED MONASTERIES

All through Moldavia and Transylvania are to be seen the medieval, fortified monasteries, the artistic treasures of Rumania. Because of their isolation these charming buildings are little known to the outside world. Most of them were built by local princes either as a refuge, or to celebrate a victory over some invader; and nearly all of them have high walls, moats, and bastions. In the northern part of Moldavia, called the *Bucovina* because of its great forests of beech trees, there are many monasteries, most of which were built during the late fifteenth century in the brilliant reign of Stephen the Great of Moldavia. On some there can still be seen brightly colored frescoes and terra-cotta plaques, which have weathered the extremes of heat and cold to which all of Rumania is exposed.

THE BEAUTIFUL CITY OF DUBROVNIK (FORMERLY RAGUSA)

YUGOSLAVIA is a name for the group of states molded into one nation by the peace-makers at Versailles in 1919. The intention was honorable. Serbia would form the core of a new Balkan nation to solve the knotty Balkan problem that had acted as the powder keg for the World War. Pieces were whittled out of Austria and Hungary, and the result was a new nation larger than any of the crippled states. Dalmatia on the Adriatic contributed to this new state not only an extensive sea-coast, but also a group of statues carved by Ivan Mestrovic, since then world-famous, presenting in dramatic fashion the Slav fight for freedom.

At the head of the Adriatic is a town called Fiume by the Italians. Before the powers at Versailles could decide where it belonged, D'Annunzio, an Italian poet, had seized the city and later gave it to Italy. Thus a poet had a hand in empire-building. The town of Fiume, as part of Italy, was cut off from its supporting countryside which was made part of Yugoslavia.

Older than the nation of Yugoslavia—in fact, older than some of the nations that were in the conference at Versailles—are the several provinces that were linked together to form Yugoslavia. To tourists perhaps the best-known of these is Dalmatia. In days of ancient Greece this region was known as Illyria, and Shakespeare refers to it by that name.

THE PEASANT'S RIVIERA

Fortunately, however, despite the fact that it has been well known for these many centuries, the native beauty of Dalmatia has not been ruined by attempts to attract tourists as has a similar coast on the Mediterranean, the Riviera of Southern France. Some writers refer to Dalmatia as the "Peasant's Riviera." And so it is. While it was under Austria's grasp, slight efforts were made to attract tourists. Beyond a narrow-gauge railway, constructed to connect the coast with the land beyond the mountains, the efforts brought little change to this beautiful region.

It is estimated that, if the bays and inlets that cut into the Dalmatian coast could be stretched out fully, the coastline would be increased three times its present length; but that would spoil the beauty for which the region is famed. Of all the bays, the most famous is that which was once known as Ragusa. Centuries ago this port was noted for its ships and shipbuilders, and so contributed to the English language one of its most beautiful words—argosy. Ships from Ragusa came to be known as ragusies, and in the careless way people have of pronouncing words it emerged as "argosies," meaning well-built ships bearing treasures from the Orient. Under the new Yugoslavic rule, the name of the bay has been changed to Dubrovnik. The town has an unusual history in a country where even the peasants' homes attain the ripe old age of 600 years and still see use. In 1667 an earthquake destroyed nearly every building in Ragusa. Wealthy Ragusans rebuilt the churches, the Rector's Palace, and other public buildings.

Today the town escapes the busy swing of the economic bustle, of which it was once one of the leading centers. Now much of the trade in the town is carried on by peasant girls bringing in fresh fruit and vegetables from farms surrounding the city.

Everyone who ever ate an ice cream sundae with whipped cream knows that the cherry on top is called a maraschino, but few know that this product makes the town of Zara in the

Courtesy J. Bradford Pengelly

RECONSTRUCTION OF THE MAGNIFICENT PALACE OF DIOCLETIAN
Nearly 4000 people now live within the walls of the palace.

province of Dalmatia world-famous. Zara grows the cherries, and also makes the liqueur maraschino; the citizens of Split and Sebenico trade in these products. These two last towns are, with Zara and Dubrovnik, ports on the Adriatic; but Zara was assigned, not to Yugoslavia, but to Italy, after the World War.

THE TOWN WITHIN A CASTLE

Time must be allowed in Split for a trip through the Roman emperor's palace. Here is where four thousand peasants cram themselves and call it a city. This mammoth of a palace was built by Diocletian about 297 A.D. "Modern" houses, meaning those that have been built within the last six hundred years, surround the town-within-a-castle. Yet, progress is made toward creating a livable city of Split. Electricity, unknown a few years ago, is widely used.

In ships much like those of the Venetians, to whom this area once belonged, thousands of Dalmatians net the Adriatic for fish. About three-quarters of the catch are sardines. By carrying brilliantly-colored sails the ships add beauty to the blue of the Adriatic and to the green backdrop of the harbor towns. Nor is this industry without its hazards as well as beauty. Every Dalmatian sailor speaks in tones of respect of the "bora," the biting cold wind that sweeps from the north and takes a heavy toll of fishermen. These sailors deny that they alone are hurt by the wind, and some tell of the "bora" sweeping through a mountain gorge and lifting a train completely off the track.

PRIMITIVE VILLAGES

Short trips back from the coast reveal extremely primitive villages in the Dalmatian highlands. The gray, arid barren land, fiercely hot in summer and bitter-cold in winter, yields little upon which the hardy natives can exist. The villages are merely stone huts with dirt floors, bunched in hit-or-miss fashion on a level stretch of ground. The inhabitants raise sheep and goats, and from a scanty herd of twenty or thirty a family obtains food and clothing.

Of unusual interest is the little village of Trogir, or Trau, which was founded by Rome and is now noted for its exports

Courtesy J. Bradford Pengelly

THE GREAT PLAIN TREE AT TRES-
TENO, NEAR DUBROVNIK

This tree is more than 30 feet in circumference, and is said to be about 800 years old.

Courtesy J. Bradford Pengelly

FAMOUS CLOCK TOWER AT TRAU
(TROGIR), JUGOSLAVIA

of insecticide. Several shrubs are ground up to provide this product, and, strangest of all, daisies are dried and ground up. Necessity will drive men to extraordinary extremes of using what little is provided by nature.

Travel from the Dalmatian coast to the mountainous wilds of Hercegovina is exciting. Whether the tourist goes by train or car he is in for some roller-coaster thrills and a sense of loneliness and desolation. From the semi-tropical climate of the Illyrian coast the traveler plunges into twisted gorges and under the very edge of out-thrust cliffs, then into the lonely wastes of the Hercegovinan Alps and finally is reassured by the green mountains of Bosnia that there is beauty outside of Dalmatia. The train from Dubrovnik is a small, narrow-gauge affair that pants its weary way over the western mountains, but not without reinforcements. It starts the journey with one engine, but in the mountains in Hercegovina another one helps to pull the train up the steep slopes. Then, before the final destination, Sarajevo, a veritable island in the sky, is reached, two more puffers join the procession, and the number of engines may even match the number of passenger cars.

BLOODY SARAJEVO!

Sarajevo should have a familiar ring even to the ears of a person who claims to know nothing of Yugoslavia. In this little sky-village the shot was fired that started the four bloody years of the World War. Archduke Ferdinand was killed by Gavrilo Princip, whose memory is honored by the Yugoslavians with a simple memorial at the site of the assassination.

On This Historic Spot
Gavrilo Princip
on
St. Vitus' Day, June 28, 1914
Heralded the Advent of Liberty
Narodna Obrana

Narodna Obrana was a Serb nationalist movement of which Princip was a member. But more striking things than the plain marker of a world-wide historical event catch the eye of the newcomer at Sarajevo. The ninety-nine minarets startlingly recall the fact that Bosnia, the province in which Sarajevo is located, is the

Homer Smith photo. Chicago

INTERIOR OF MOSQUE AT SARAJEVO, YUGOSLAVIA

most northern thrust of Islam. Mohammedans have predominated in this city of Serbs for four hundred years. There are no great industries; no rapid means of transportation; in fact, this village perched on the top of the mountains is economically as well as geographically isolated.

Mohammedan customs blend queerly with western innovations. Women wear an outlandish combination of short skirts, and hoods over their faces. The custom of women doing the hardest work prevails. They have the family wash to do at the river bank, the meals to prepare, the babies to tend, and in spare moments spin and weave and embroider new clothes for the family. Here, very young children learn to knit.

In some sections of Yugoslavia great pride is taken in dress, but in others the garments are built to last ten to fifteen years and then patched onto others to strengthen worn places. The men wear baggy trousers, usually of a bright color; in Montenegro, blue is popular. Gay sashes top the pantaloons; over a white shirt, embroidered with fine threads, a red jacket with identifying trim

is worn. In Montenegro, black or gold trim denotes social position; and further signs of a man's place in the world are indicated
by the color of his redingote of dark green or delicate blue, de-
pending on birth and worldly possessions. Women's costumes are
rather dull—often black or dark blue, although holiday outfits
are more colorful.

To return to Sarajevo, however, the next point of interest is
the bazaar, which reflects influence of the Near East. The manu-
facturers are the sellers and make their wares as they wait for
buyers. Beautiful products are turned out by coppersmiths, sil-
versmiths, blacksmiths, cobblers, and rug-makers. This commerce
supports a large part of the population; but another popular enterprise is the ownership of a coffee-shop. An entire section of the
town has been given over to coffee-shops. Again the oriental
influence is apparent in the syrupy drink that is served in these
places: true Turkish coffee.

BOSNIAN TIMBER

Further explorations in Bosnia, leaving Sarajevo behind, reveal
the most valuable economic asset of the region. The stands of
timber are rated with the best in Europe. This comparison means
much when it is recalled that European countries have been prac-
ticing forestry for centuries. In addition to having the timber,
Bosnia is fortunate in having strong streams to bear the logs out
of the forests to the broad Save River, where they can be floated
to the mills. The trees found in these Bosnian forests are the
conifers, or evergreens, and the hardwoods such as beech, oak,
and chestnut. With such excellent timber available it makes it
fairly easy for Bosnians to establish a reputation as the best furni-
ture-makers in Yugoslavia.

In the journey from Sarajevo two more interesting points must
be noted. The first of these is the Karst region. Geologists have
given an excellent description of the type of country found in
the Karst region. "Petrified sponge" they call it, and if you can
imagine a full-sized river plunging into a hole in the heart of
town and then reappearing a few miles farther on, you will have
some idea of the mysteries found in the petrified-sponge kind of
country. Almost as strange as the jack-in-the-box rivers are the
hole-in-the-ground farms. At the bottom of the openings in the

Homer Smith photo, Chicago

SERBIAN PEASANTS ENJOYING THEIR NATIONAL DANCE

VIEW OF THE
DALMATIAN
COAST, KOTOR
YUGOSLAVIA

Courtesy J. Bradford
Pengelly

petrified sponge very fertile plots are to be found. The peasants cultivate these tiny plots with great care, and often these supply all the agricultural wants of a village.

The second interesting place between the interior of Yugoslavia and the Dalmatian coast is the tiny village of Galichnik. This settlement was founded centuries ago by Serbs fleeing the onslaught of the Turkish invader. The men took their families into the mountain stronghold, but found there nothing by which to earn a living. So they left their families secure in the mountain fastness and went into the world in search of work. This custom became more widespread as Europe colonized the New World. Now men from this village travel as far as the west coast of the United States, seeking work to support their families in Galichnik. Each year these long-absent men return to their families for a short stay and then go back to the business world, leaving their wives, the elders and the children in the village.

Just as Yugoslavia takes on more meaning when it is translated as "the home of the South Slavs," so Montenegro means more when the English version "Black Mountain" is given. The ride into Montenegro is a difficult one by automobile, but a most thrilling one. A none-too-wide gravel road races up and down the slopes of the black mountains; bare rocky crags of a uniform gray color swell row upon row, like waves on an angry sea.

TURKISH FEROCITY

Montenegrins are the hardy race that inhabits this desolate area. They have fought for centuries to repel invaders, and they claim they love the land so dearly because so much of their blood has been spilt on its rocks in defense of their homes. Now they

Courtesy J. Bradford Pengelly

ISLAND CHURCHES NEAR RAGUSA
Each of these two little islands on the Dalmatian coast is practically covered by its church edifice.

resent the high-and-mighty methods of Belgrade, Yugoslavia's capital. This tribe of fighters, alone of the Serb forces that sought to block the Turkish invasion, managed to escape the oriental bondage that the rest of Yugoslavia suffered. These men, to whom a pistol in the sash is a necessary part of street clothes, wear a black edge of mourning around the edge of their red hats, in memory of the loss of Serb greatness at the world-famous battle of Kossovo of 1389, when the Turk showed no mercy to the 100,-000 Serb warriors. Here memories are as long as the mountains are high. Women in the town of Crkvenica still wear black clothes of mourning for a family that has been destroyed five centuries ago.

Ruins of Frankopan fortresses are points of interest on the Dalmatian coast on which Crkvenica is a city. Wine and tobacco are the chief articles produced for export in Montenegro. Livestock is raised, but no more than for immediate needs.

Motor travel is again the best way to push into the interior of Yugoslavia. The Occident is left behind as the car travels east. An agricultural mode of living replaces the tough, hardy existence of the mountaineer. The homes are brightly white, with red-tiled roofs that glisten in the sunshine. The interiors of the homes are well kept and spotlessly white.

Obviously a favorite color, white is the predominating tone of the native garb. The men wear a white tunic; white trousers, like pyjamas; *opankas*, a soft sort of mocassin footwear, tied by thongs to the legs. This is the region of the Serbian farmers.

A MINIATURE AMERICAN MIDWEST

Farming in this region, it is true, is not as progressive as that found in the fertile plains in the northern part of Yugoslavia, but it is a vast improvement over the hole-in-the-ground methods of the Karst region. Cereals form a large part of the year's crop and a surplus is left for export purposes. The chief cereal is maize, with wheat, barley, and oats following in about that order. The land is rolling and prairie-like, and has sometimes been called a miniature of midwest American farmlands, but such a comparison is more truthful when drawn between the northern part of Yugoslavia and the prairie states of the United States.

In addition to the waving fields of grain, green orchards dot the landscape, and indicate that fruit crops are not missing. Vegetable-raising is pursued by most of the farmers in the region,

Homer Smith photo, Chicago

GRAPE HARVESTING NEAR SMEDEREVO, YUGOSLAVIA

with the sugar beet as an unusual addition. Mulberry trees are cultivated for their silkworm value.

OLD-FASHIONED WOODEN PLOWS

With better pasturage available than to their mountain neighbors, the Serbian farmers can fully develop livestock breeding. Hogs form the greatest part of the stock population, followed by cattle, horses, and sheep, the latter really an upland animal. The part of Bosnia that comprises this same general type of land and climate is a backward imitator of Serbia. Steel plows are gradually replacing wooden plows, but it is a slow and bitterly fought step toward modernization of agriculture. The reaping is still done by men with scythes.

This region is a part of the fertile valley known to geologists as the Pannonian Basin. It runs northward as far as the Danube River, but, before wandering up that way, we should first observe the southern influence on life. As the southern edge of Yugoslavia is approached, it becomes more and more apparent that sunny-south products are replacing the produce of the temperate-climate farms. Rice fields appear in this area called the Morava-Vardar Depression. Poppies are grown for opium, although it is claimed that the country has no opium addicts. Cotton, that staple of the southern states of the United States, makes its appearance as does tobacco.

In addition to fairly good agricultural possibilities this area is fortunate in having considerable mineral resources including coal, copper, silver-lead, chrome ore, iron, and antimony. These have by no means been developed to the fullest extent, but they are there to be utilized some day. Livestock flourishes in the hillier sections of this region. The principal animal kept is the sheep, largely for the wool that is spun and then woven into beautiful rugs, of which those at Pirot are renowned for their color and design.

A CROWDED POPULATION

Chief city of this southern Serbia region is the antique town of Skoplie. History dates its beginning at something like two thousand B.C. But today the scene is undergoing drastic changes. Half of the town is new since the World War and the other half contains the Mohammedan section. This factor and the large population (70,000) prepares the traveler for the sight of Belgrade. Speaking of populations, we may note that the census puts the population of the country at about fourteen million persons. This is not very many when the country has several large towns, but when they are as small as those in Yugoslavia it means that the farmers are crowded on the land. The average population per square mile is 125 persons, almost the same as in the state of Illinois. It must be remembered, however, that Illinois contains a mammoth city and very fertile farm lands, and so the comparison fails to give an adequate idea of the crowding found in a nation like Yugoslavia where large towns are few and much of the land is unfit for use because of rocks or mountains.

Cities often show a remarkable ability to stage a recovery in the face of the greatest difficulties. Ragusa recovered, stronger than ever, from an earthquake. San Francisco accomplished the same thing. Chicago was rebuilt even better after a great fire. In Yugoslavia of today, Belgrade is in the midst of a recovery. It has been nearly twenty years since the war, but with the added worry of being the capital of a new nation, Belgrade's slowness in becoming a "city beautiful" is rather pardonable.

Homer Smith photo, Chicago

BUSINESS SECTION OF BELGRADE

THE TOLL OF WAR

With the possible exception of some Belgian towns, no other European city suffered so greatly from the World War as did Belgrade, the capital of Serbia. The Austro-German artillery opened fire on this city in the early months of the war. The Serbs made a valiant defense until attacked from a new direction by their old foe, Bulgaria. The Serbs had to yield in the face of such odds and the city passed into the possession of the Central Powers. War, disease in the form of two typhus epidemics, and starvation, took a heavy toll of the population.

Following the creation of the Yugoslav nation in 1918, Belgrade began its meteoric rise to the present population of 350,000 from the 25,000 at the close of the war. Some of the suburbs of Belgrade are larger than the central community was twenty-five years ago. Belgrade is distinctly a boom town—a boom town like the western mining towns of the United States in gold-rush days. But Belgrade promises to be more permanent. That does not mean that the town will not change. The very construction of the buildings indicates that they will soon have to be replaced,

Paul's Photos, Chicago

VIEW OF DIBRA (DEBAR), YUGOSLAVIA
Dibra is the center of an important agricultural district.

for they are of cheap construction, made of concrete because Germany sent great amounts of concrete as partial reparation for damages in the World War. Since Belgrade took the place of Vienna as the economic center for millions of buyers and sellers of Yugoslavia after the war, there has been this over-rapid development, with too great a rise in prices, and a serious housing shortage.

Belgrade is ideally located at the confluence of two great rivers, the Danube and the Save, the latter of which, throughout its entire length, flows through Yugoslav territory exclusively— from the Alps to Belgrade. The two rivers are navigable for hundreds of miles. The Danube flows through Europe for about 1800 miles, and its shores owe allegiance to nine different countries, of which Yugoslavia is one.

Not only is the river a very important artery for freight-transportation, but it is an ever popular tourist route. Canoe trips are a preferred method of sight-seeing, especially among the younger people, and large steamers are likewise used for gay pleasure-jaunts.

THE GREAT GORGE OF KAZAN

Down the river, to the east of Belgrade, may be seen signs of the early occupation of this valley by the Roman legions. Through the great gorge of Kazan, where the Danube, closed in between two massive walls, flows swiftly, the Emperor Tiberius led his legions in 33 A.D., after building a military road with tremendous difficulty. Still farther down the river is another gap, where the river seems to have cut through the mountains, the famous "Iron Gate." Beyond lies Bulgaria.

In the other direction from Belgrade, to north and west, lies the wonderful farm country of Voivodina, a region offering great economical advantages. In this land farmers employ distinctly more modern implements and methods than elsewhere in the country. Also in industry there is to be found excellent advancement. Some of the potential water power has been tapped. Flour mills are operated; sugar is obtained from the sugar beets; brewing and distilling is carried on; rope-makers utilize the home-grown hemp, and linen and silk manufactures flourish.

This does not mean that the region is greatly industrialized. It does mean that the small manufacturer is busy utilizing water power to operate his small plant. In this area is the second largest city of the nation—Zagreb. It is a ten-hour journey by railroad. The country through which the train travels is comparable to the prairies of America.

Catholicism reigns supreme in this section. The land is inhabited by four million Croatians who represent a strong minority party in opposition to the Serbian rule. In fact, Zagreb, with its 185,000 inhabitants, forms a strong core around which an anti-Belgrade feeling is built.

If possible, there is one man in Zagreb to be visited. He is Ivan Mestrovic, world-famous sculptor. He gained fame by his mammoth pieces for the Kossovo memorial. Since then he has hewn out more than six hundred and fifty monuments. Two of them are in commanding positions on the most famous boulevard in the city of Chicago: two huge Indians on horseback, Mestrovic's contribution to culture in midwestern America.

Moreover, the Croatian people have established no mean reputation as craftsmen. Their embroidery work for decorating cloth is famous in all parts of Yugoslavia, and they excel in batik work on fabrics. Hard-carved figures decorate in a beautiful fashion the furnishings of the simple and clean homesteads. Even the plows, wagons and other farm tools are beautifully painted.

Zagreb is the home of the oldest printshop and bookshop in the northern Balkans. The town also boasts the best university, the largest library, the foremost art academy, and the best opera performances in that section of Europe.

YUGOSLAVIA—AN UNTOUCHED CIVILIZATION

As a way out of Yugoslavia, the railroad alongside the broad river Save offers one of the most beautiful and swiftest exits. Like a funnel, the river valley narrows and pours the train forth into a three-nation corner at the head of the Adriatic.

As the train carries the thoughtful tourist out of the newly knit union of Slavs his mind will be pondering the possibilities of a permanent nation. He will find no ready answer to that problem. But he will be able to tell questioners at home that Yugoslavia has much to offer the tourist in the form of historical, cultural, and thrill-seeking interests; beautiful scenery, an untouched civilization of bygone days, and any of the many attractions for which people travel afar.

Courtesy J. Bradford Pengelly

ANCIENT AND PICTURESQUE FORTIFIED TOWN OF KRUJA

RARELY ON EUROPEAN HIGHWAYS, but occasionally in the files of the world's diplomatic portfolios may be seen the new official abbreviation "M. S." indicating "Mbretnia Shqiptare" (Kingdom of Albania); for the Albanians do not call their land "Albania." They are Shqipetars, and their country is Shqiperia, which means "people of the rocks." Only a single small district near Kruja, the ancient fortress of their great hero, George Castriota, called Scanderbeg, is known locally as "Arbenia."

Tucked into the western part of the Balkan peninsula, just opposite the heel of Italy, lies Albania. This country stretches along the blue Adriatic Sea, backed by lofty mountains and bordered by Yugoslavia and Greece. Tradition calls the people "sons of the eagle"; and the proud mountaineers, perching in their remote crags, like the eagles in their aeries, live up to the old legend.

But there are productive plains, too, in the valleys of the westward flowing rivers. The interior is still wild and difficult of access, although vigorous attempts at westernization have provided the land with some fifteen hundred miles of fairly good highways.

Within Albania's present boundaries are less than a million inhabitants, which number includes half of the Albanian people. Approximately eighty-seven thousand live in southern Italy and Sicily; and fifty thousand are in the United States.

About twice the size of Massachusetts, Albania is a land where rugged mountains alternate with extensive valleys. The dales are very fertile and produce grains, tobacco, and fruit; but only a small fraction of the earth is under effective cultivation. When in 1923 the Albanian parliament passed a grant of land for an agricultural school and later gave over this project to the Albanian-American Schools of Agriculture, the first step was taken toward developing these resources. Today American apple seedlings and other plants are sent in quantities from the New Jersey Agricultural Experiment station at New Brunswick, to supply the needs of the Near East Foundation in its program of developing Albania.

OLDER THAN ROME

Before 1912, when, following the Balkan War, independent Albania first appeared on the map of Europe, few had known that such a country existed. Yet the Albanians have lived in this area, never completely subdued by any other nation, since many centuries before Roman times. In the Roman period there were many flourishing towns, villas, and seaside resorts in Illyricum, as the land was then called; and the Romans built a military road across the land, leading to Constantinople and Asia Minor, some of whose bridges are still in use.

During the Middle Ages the mountain tribes were largely left to themselves, though Byzantine and Roman warriors repeatedly attacked and occupied part of their territory, and Serbs and Bulgars at various times overran it. In the fifteenth century the Turks gained a degree of control over the country and maintained it until 1912. Lack of harmony and unity among the wild tribes allowed the Turks to gain their foothold; but for more than twenty years all their attacks were repulsed by the efforts of many clans fighting together under the great leader, Scanderbeg, the national hero of Albania. Between 1444 and his death, in 1468, Scanderbeg kept Albania free. In respect for his dauntlessness, even the Turks used bits of his bones for courage-charms; while in token of reverence for him many Albanians of today wear a

HARBOR AT DURAZZO, ALBANIA
Large sums of money, loaned by Italy, were spent by the Albanian people on this
harbor from 1930 to 1937.

cloak modeled after his, the "Scanderbeg jacket"; and his colors, black and red, are the national colors of Albania.

While Albania was a Turkish province, many of her sons served in the Turkish government as able officials and administrators. But after Albanian independence had been recognized in 1912 and the confusion and disruption of the World War followed, the country had difficulty in establishing a firm central government. Not until Ahmed Zogu became president of the

Courtesy J. Bradford Pengelly

BISHOP'S VILLA, ALTA ANTIVARI, ALBANIA

Albanian republic, later to be proclaimed king in 1928, was Albania, the foundling state of Europe, really instituted.

Albania may be classed as a Mohammedan state, the only one in Europe. In a population of about nine hundred thousand there are about six hundred thousand Mohammedans. King Zog is of this faith. The Mohammedans live chiefly in the south and are generally called the "Tosks." The "Ghegs," who are generally Christians, live in the north. Towns are few and contain small populations.

VENDETTA!

It has been said that in Albania a man never goes without a gun or knife. The general aspect of lawlessness and the habit of the men, especially in the mountains, of bearing arms openly is due to the existing blood feud, a vendetta or *gjak,* which keeps the participants on the alert but seldom causes inconvenience to visitors.

Many of these feuds are continued on the grounds of some remote, past offense, such as the failure of a suitor to marry his betrothed, or an accidental homicide whereby the tribe became involved in feud and pledged vengeance. Yet no Albanian would think of discharging the blood obligation if his prospective victim were accompanied by a woman or a child; for women, although without legal rights, are held in high esteem, and children are carefully protected.

Albania is a land of craggy mountains, swift-flowing rivers, and singular customs. The native garb varies widely in the different sections. Some of the costumes have been copied by other lands, as has the *fustanella*, or short, pleated skirt, which for male attire was worn in the south of Albania and has been borrowed by the Greeks.

TOWNS OF INTEREST

Albanian towns do not thrill the traveler with grand and stately buildings; but each town has some peculiar interest. The southern towns have far-famed horse-markets. At Argyrocastron are great Cyclopean ruins from ancient times; at Valona is a good harbor; and at Korcha, in its mountain bowl, is Lake Malik. To the north is Berat, with its mountain stronghold perched high above the River Semeni, and at Tirana is the relatively new capital. In Durazzo are found even yet the relics of Roman builders and reminders of the medieval splendor that prevailed when the Counts of Durazzo played their part in Italian politics. And at Kruja the crumbling fortress of Scanderbeg may be seen.

The traveler, to secure safe passage, must gain not only the hearty hospitality of the people but also a *bessa*, which means a truce in the blood feud. To the extreme north, on its ancient lake, lies Scutari, a market town with a strong fortress.

Homer Smith photo, Chicago

SOFIA, CAPITAL OF BULGARIA

BETWEEN the Danube River and the Macedonian Mountains lies little Bulgaria, a state about the size of Indiana. The Bulgarian people form a branch of the Slavic race, although, because of past conquests, a small admixture of Mongol blood flows through their veins. Once a great empire during the Middle Ages, the country was overrun by the Turks; and not till 1878 did Bulgaria gain its independence.

Bulgaria is a land of farming villages, picturesque peasant women in native garb, and native dances.

A Bulgarian proverb says: "If you visit the village, you must join the dance." And so it is. The people love their dances. The men and women in their unique costumes dancing in either a row or a circle, are led in the singing, clapping of hands, and dancing, by a leader, who in peculiar fashion twirls and rushes around and through the group, waving a colored handkerchief on the beat of the music.

Unlike their sisters in some of the surrounding countries, the Bulgarian girls have a good deal of social freedom. The great social gathering place is the village well, where the peasant youths and maidens obtain the daily water supply. Here they meet, and tarry much longer than it takes to fill the pails of water, which are carried on yokes on the shoulders. They may arrange to

meet at the "Sedanka," where the young people sit around a large
fire, sing their melodious Bulgarian songs, and eat boiled corn.
The feast may end with the "Horo." Before dispersing, at times
a dramatic event takes place. Some strong peasant may capture
the girl of his choice, carry her off to his home, and the next day
marry her.

The capital of Bulgaria is Sophia, up to seventy years ago a
mere village; hence the city bears a modern aspect because
it is entirely new. At present it has a population of a quarter-
million inhabitants. Yet the city has an air of peasant conserv-
atism, so characteristic of the entire Bulgarian people. The center
of life and parades is the great square.

TIRNOVO—MONASTERIES

The tourist will find Tirnovo, ancient capital of Bulgaria, of
greater interest. The city is situated on the Mount of Eagles, and
overlooks the winding Yantra river. By a narrow isthmus it is
connected with the Hill of the Tsars, where a wall formerly
hemmed in the Tsarist palace. Nearby is the Preobrajenski Monas-

Homer Smith photo, Chicago

THE CITY OF LOM, BULGARIA, AND THE DANUBE RIVER

tery, which is famous for the exquisite murals which adorn it both inside and outside. The same is true of Batchkovo Monastery, which has seen within its walls during succeeding centuries the Byzantines, Crusaders, Turks, and Bulgarians. Rilo Monastery in the past was fortified like a fortress, and has been a focal point of Bulgarian culture.

When in Bulgaria, the visitor should not neglect to visit the famous "Rose Valley," where the peasants of two hundred villages cultivate and harvest more than twenty thousand acres of roses. During the flowering season a sweet fragrance hangs over the entire valley. The roses are raised for their product, attar of roses, a sort of rose oil, used as a base for various perfumes. The rose petals are harvested by the peasants and brought to the factory in wagon loads, where by means of an elaborate process the oil is removed. The visitor obtains a most picturesque view of peasants and their women sitting in the midst of a load of dark red rose petals on their way to market.

Homer Smith photo, Chicago

TYPICAL BULGARIAN COSTUMES

Paul's Photos, Chicago

THE HARBOR OF PIRAEUS, FAMED PORT OF ATHENS

ON THE WAY TO ATHENS

ONE should approach Greece by water, for the sea has been so intimately linked with the story of this glorious country. When the ancient Greeks set out to conquer Troy, to seek the Golden Fleece, or to defeat the horde of Persian barbarians, the sea was always their highway. When the rest of the inhabitants of Europe were still in a primitive state, the Greeks had sailed far abroad to establish colonies along the distant shores of the Mediterranean Sea.

Even as the ancient Greek galleys sailed past Cape Sunium, capped by its graceful and milky-white temple to Poseidon, god of the sea, and into the Bay of Phaleron, so may the traveler follow their route, to round a point of land and come upon a familiar scene—the Acropolis with Athens nestling at its base.

There it is, that monument which has represented beauty and wisdom to the millions of inhabitants of the civilized world for ages past. There stands the Acropolis like a mound of brown marble topped by a glistening pile of opals, shimmering under a brilliant sun shining from a sky of an unfamiliar blue. We dock at Piraeus, the ancient port of Athens, and anxiously clamor for a

Black Star photo   By Fritz Henle

THE ACROPOLIS, ATHENS, SHOWING FRONT OF THE TEMPLE OF NIKE

closer view of the most glorious city in the ancient world. But what a shock awaits us. Before we see "the glory that was Greece," that is, ancient Greece, we must pass through some of the squalor that is modern Greece. The harbor is jam-packed with all sorts of moving vessels, the shores are lined with people, all engaged in some sort of activity, and behind it all are dirty buildings, dusty streets, ragged men, and all the other accompanying features of an industrial and commercial community.

MODERN SONS OF SOCRATES

Passing through Piraeus, on the way to Athens, disappointment begins to recede when one realizes that there is something rather attractive about these surroundings and the people—especially the latter. They are a pleasant, smiling, handsome, quick-moving lot with mischief sparkling in their brown eyes. The cab driver, who deposits his passengers in Athens after a hectic ride through the crowded streets, provides our first experience with one of the people. He tries to charge three times too much, but when we hold out for the proper price, he gives in with a smile and wishes us a pleasant stay in his city. That is easy for him to say, for any stay in Athens is bound to be a pleasant one.

The Athens just outside our hotel door seems to be a modern replica of the ancient city. All around the Syntagma, or Place of the Constitution, a pretty little park, are men standing, walking, or sitting together and no matter whether they are moving or standing still, the lips of all are in motion. Just as Socrates and his pupils discussed the highest of philosophies, so are their modern sons discussing, not philosophy especially, but politics and business, national and international.

HISTORY IN STONES

On one side of the Place of the Constitution is an impressive building which, like many of the other structures in Athens, has been used for many things, but is now being put to its intended use—as the Royal Palace. In a historical sense it was yesterday the parliament of the Republic, the day before a hospital and a museum, and before that the residence of the kings. Other structures throughout the city give a clue to the historical episodes which have taken place in this city of Athena, goddess of wisdom. For instance, Hadrian's arch tells a story of the Roman conquest; the monastery on the top of Lycabettus Hill, the summit which dominates the city, is a Byzantine relic; many ruined and abandoned mosques recall the terrible days of the Turkish domination and oppression; the broken pillars of the most glorious ruin, the Parthenon, remind us that a Venetian shell struck a Turkish powder-house that was hidden there in the sixteenth century; and the Pnyx, the small hill at the side of the Acropolis, is a rocky monument to St. Paul, who addressed the Athenian crowds from its summit in the first days of the Christian Era.

In walking about this enchanting city, one cannot go ten minutes without coming to a spot where Plato instructed his pupils, or where Socrates was imprisoned and drank the hemlock, or where Pericles sat when he watched the production of the ancient Greek tragedies and comedies in the theater of Dionysus.

"THE GLORY THAT WAS GREECE . . ."

Although not the highest point in the city, the Acropolis, by its beauty and its weight of historical associations, is the center of attraction for everyone's eyes. In order to enjoy the full beauty of the scene, wait until sunset and then start to mount the long line of white marble steps that lead to the top. Before passing through the Propylaea—the rather massive, yet exquisitely lovely, marble gate that leads to the inner grounds—turn to the west to drink in the golden and violet glory of a Grecian sunset. The sun seems to be sinking into a huge bowl of fire and flames in front of which are the purplish and hazy outlines of the mountains of the Peloponnesus. Between them and the observer lie the now shimmering-golden, now deep-blue waters of the Gulf of Aegina, while on our side of the Gulf the tiny yellow lights of the Athens street lamps are feebly puncturing the evening's mists with their flickering flames.

Just below and to the right, the last rays of the sun are turning the Theseum, the best-preserved temple of ancient times, into a tawny diamond, so lovely that Athena and Hephaestos, the goddess and god to whom it was dedicated, must still feel that they are appreciated even in this commercial twentieth century. Close by, the gate to the Roman market place can be seen, while inside the market is the Tower of the Winds. The Tower is a small, octagonal building, each of four of its sides facing toward a point of the compass, which originally housed a water clock, a weather vane, and a sundial. Each wall is decorated with

THEATER AT THE FOOT OF THE ACROPOLIS, ATHENS

a statue of a figure which represents the wind coming from
that direction. Thus, Boreas, the north wind, is an angry-looking
old man who is dressed in a heavy cloak, while the west wind,
Zephyr, is a handsome young man scattering flowers. All around
the market place are remnants of walls, towers and gates left by
the ancients and which are now being partially used by the very
poor moderns as their dwellings. Along the walls of the building
that the Roman Emperor Hadrian built as a famous library are
poorly constructed hovels made of gasoline cans and rags in which
these unfortunate descendants of Socrates and Pericles still read
the classics.

To the west the mountains and the Gulf are now lost in dark-
ness, but behind us the moon has made a silver garden of the
marble columns of the Acropolis. To one side is the seemingly
square and angular Parthenon, but actually there is not a straight
line in that architectural gem. Although the structure is quite
large, the ancient Greeks, who did not like large and ungainly
things, curved all of the lines slightly to make this temple to
Athena appear small and graceful. In the moonlight the soaring
columns topped by the fine capitals, both made of creamy
Pentelic marble, throb and glow and seem to give off a light of
their own.

TREASURES OF THE ACROPOLIS

To our right is the Erechtheum with its famous portico of the sculptured maidens. The Caryatids are pillars in the form of shapely women supporting the roof on their heads. This is the only instance in architecture where human figures are successfully employed as supports. These maidens not only hold up the roof but are extremely beautiful figures to look upon. All are made of the whitest of marble and are exquisitely carved so that their robes fall in flowing curves around their bodies. No, there is one exception. The third from the left does not belong with her sisters. About a century ago, when Greece was still ruled by the barbarian Turks, an English lord came to Athens and acquired several of the statues and sculptures on the Acropolis and sent them to the British Museum in London. Among other things, he took a Caryatid, and in her place stands one which is supposed to be an exact copy, but being made by modern hands the differences from her foster sisters are immediately recognizable.

A third delightful building on the Acropolis is the diminutive temple of Athena Nike. Nike means victory and the statue was erected by the Athenians after they had defeated some of their enemies. Its delightfulness lies in the fact that it is so small and

Courtesy J. Bradford Pengelly

THE PARTHENON, ATHENS

perfectly constructed. Although it was mostly destroyed by the Turks, archaeologists have reconstructed it so that it gives as much pleasure to the Athenians of today as it did to the citizens of Athens in the days of Praxiteles, the great sculptor.

At the base of the Acropolis, on the south side, lie two theaters; one small, white and graceful, the Grecian; and the second, massive, brown and powerful, the Roman. Both are open-air amphitheaters in which performances of the ancient plays are still given. Farther on stand fifteen enormous columns, remnants of the one hundred and four that supported the huge temple built to the Olympian Zeus by the Romans. Just beyond this temple is the stadium which seats 50,000 people and is built entirely of marble. Ancient Greece was filled with stadiums, but this one is quite modern in that it was reconstructed by a wealthy Greek citizen of the nineteenth century, although he used the site and followed the plans of the ancient stadium exactly. It was here that the Olympic Games of 1906 were held. Nearby, on the eastern side of the Acropolis, is the monument to Lysicrates, who won a prize in games similar to the Olympics, but in the year 334 B.C. It is a handsome little building that resembles a small circular temple surrounded by columns.

Paul's Photos, Chicago

THE FAMOUS CARYATIDS
AT ATHENS
Classic portico of an ancient temple in Athens showing the use of statuary instead of columns as a support for the cornice.

At some distance from the Acropolis is the Ceramicus, or cemetery, dating from the days of the Golden Age of Greece. It is interesting not only because there are so many famous people buried there, but also because some of the statuary and sculpture representing the deceased is as beautiful as anything to be found in the museums of the whole world.

However, all of Athens is not ruins dating from the Age of Pericles or the Romans. There are many remains of the Middle Ages, especially the Byzantine chapels. For some reason these tiny, distinctive churches with their many domes are like jewels dimmed with age and put in a modern setting of harsh metal.

Many of the churches built by the Byzantines were very large, but, strangely, those that remain in Athens are small and neat. Much like the temple of Nike, on the Acropolis, they are so small as to be perfect. When the modern Greeks built the metropolitan's cathedral, the Mother Church, they set it next to one of these Byzantine jewels. That was unfortunate, for, although the cathedral is very impressive by its size and dwarfs the tiny chapel, it is to the chapel that the lover of beauty first goes.

CLEANLINESS NEXT TO GODLINESS

Other remnants of the Middle Ages are the few Turkish mosques which still stand. At one time there were a great number of them; but when the Turks were driven from Greece, the Greeks immediately demolished many reminders of their recent Moslem rulers. All minarets were pulled down, but a few mosques were spared. These are now used for museums, houses for the poor, or Turkish baths. The Turks managed to leave many mementoes of their stay. The Greek language, food, clothing, music, and customs have all been affected by the Turks. In some parts of Athens you can still find men who smoke hubble-bubbles, or water-pipes, wear baggy trousers and fezzes, and eat Turkish food as they listen to the whining of pipes and the pounding of drums —music typical of the Near East.

On the other hand, it is only a short walk to University or Stadium Street, where people dress in the latest occidental styles, eat food which might have been cooked in Paris, and dance to music which *was* written in New York. Modern Athens is just as modern as any other large European city. Its charm lies in the fact that you can enjoy the glories of the ancient world, the mysteries of the dark ages and the Near East, and the conveniences of the present day by merely walking once around the block.

SIDE SHOWS

Another delightful feature of Athens is that the neighborhood near at hand abounds in interesting spots which are only a short journey from the city. Marathon, the site of one of the most famous battles of the world, is one of these. As Byron says, "The mountains look on Marathon, and Marathon looks on the sea." We have the brown mountains of Attica behind us and the blue waters of the Gulf of Aegina before us. Between these two features lies the coastal plain where, in 490 B.C., 10,000 Athenians under Miltiades preserved Western civilization by defeating an army of Persians which outnumbered that of the Athenians

Paul's Photos. Chicago

IN MODERN ATHENS

FIRST MARATHON WINNER
Loues, winner of the first modern Marathon race in 1896.

many times. All that remains of this heroic event is a mound under which the bodies of 190 of the noble Athenian warriors were buried. Another monument in the vicinity, of less historic value to be sure but of great utility, is the Marathon dam, built by an American engineering firm to assure the modern Athenians a good water supply. Southward from Marathon are the mines of Laurium, where gold was obtained for the Athenian mints, and the temple on Sunium standing on the lofty peninsula. The temple was a welcome landmark for the sailors of the olden days. As soon as they could see its white columns they knew that they were close to home. On one of the columns is cut the name of Lord Byron, the English poet who died fighting for the freedom of Greece.

Stretching westward from Athens is the road to Eleusis. Before we reach Eleusis we pass the Byzantine monastery of Daphne. The monastery is not only a perfect example of early Byzantine architecture, but it contains some of the best mosaics in existence. One shows a very lifelike representation of Christ, while another depicts the sea so realistically that you can almost hear the roar of the waves. Eleusis itself is a great aggregation of temples, walls, towers, shrines, and palaces, all devoted to the ancient mysteries. People came here from afar to take part in religious ceremonies and initiation into the mysteries, which, by report of the ancient historians, were very impressive and had much to do with dancing girls. However, the initiates never told all, because the mysteries are as much a mystery now as they were then.

THE PELOPONNESUS

Peloponnesus means the land of Pelops. It was connected by such a narrow isthmus that most people thought it to be an island. As a matter of fact, it is now an island, for in 1893 a canal was finally dug across the isthmus. This is the Corinth Canal which we cross on our way to the south and the lands of the ancient Greeks other than the Athenians.

In the far southern part of the Peloponnesus lies the site of Sparta. Here was a town which was famous for its military strength and leadership. While Athens, the center of knowledge and light in the days before Christ, was producing great architects, sculptors, poets, historians, dramatists, and philosophers, Sparta was rearing famous generals. As fate would have it, Sparta finally conquered Athens, but to no avail, for Athens is now recognized as the seat of highest culture in Greece and is visited for its famous and beautiful buildings, while Sparta is now no more than a meager collection of stucco huts. The most impressive of these is a two-story hotel run by an American-Greek who once lived in Brooklyn.

A short distance south of Sparta the opposite condition remains. Just as Sparta is a living village with no ruins to remind us of its past, so is Mystra a dead town, all in ruins, with neither present nor future. Mystra is the Pompeii of Greece. Here on the mountainside is a complete city containing everything from large cathedrals and palaces to the huts of poor peasants. Everything is intact and in place, just as the Byzantines left it when they

CORINTH
CANAL

were driven out by the Turks. The city was first started by a
crusader in 1250 A.D. The Byzantines soon took it over and
under their control it grew to be a famous and important town.
It was surrounded by thick and high walls and contained numerous large buildings, two cathedrals, many churches of great
beauty, and market places and streets which were thronged with
people at all times. But now the streets have the silence of death;
the market places are overgrown with grass, tall and beautiful
cypress trees grow in the courtyard of the palace, while the
churches are overgrown with ivy. It has come down to us as a
veritable graveyard of late Byzantine art and architecture with
everything as it was when it was first built.

THE FIRST OLYMPIC GAMES

In the northwestern part of the Peloponnesus, a considerable
distance from Sparta, is the site of Olympia. Here is the place
made famous by the innumerable Olympic Games, the gigantic
forty-foot statue of Zeus, carved by Phidias, and one of the most
beautiful statues still in existence, the Hermes of Praxiteles.
In the olden days athletes from all of Greece and the whole
Hellenic world, which included many of the Mediterranean lands,

Courtesy J. Bradford Pengelly

STATELY COLUMNS AT OLYMPIA

came here to compete with one another. These competitions were especially memorable because all wars had to cease in order that the games might proceed. Now, the games are postponed on account of wars. Olympia was important also because it contained the most holy temple in the whole land of Hellas. In it was the enormous statue of Zeus to which the athletes and spectators made offerings.

When the games originated in the ninth century B.C., they consisted of little more than foot races. As the centuries passed, other events, such as boxing, wrestling, discus throwing, and horse racing were added until the exhibition assumed the proportions of a large circus. For a while even debates and oratory by the famous philosophers were added; but after the Roman conquest degeneration set in with the coming of professional athletes, and the games were finally suppressed in 394 A.D.

After being discontinued for many centuries, the games were resumed in 1896 and were held in the land in which they originated. Thus, the Olympic Games constitute another feature which ancient Greece has given to our civilization. In these new games it was fortunate that a Greek won the marathon race, for that was the last time that a Greek athlete has won that event in the games originated in the land of his fathers.

MUSIC FROM THE HILLS

As we gaze upon the foundations of the temple and the still distinct oval, which was once the stadium, the slanting rays of the late afternoon sun cast long shadows and help us to build in our minds the wonderful collection of marble edifices which once stood on this spot and were called Olympia. As the scene grows in the imagination, another element is added which makes the picture all the more realistic. From the sere, brown hills behind us there comes a sound which in days of mythology must have made the nymphs and naiads want to dance and gambol like young lambs on the greensward. The sound comes from shepherd pipes which are of the same kind as were played by the god Pan as he wandered over hill and dale coaxing the fairies of the forest to dance for him while he played his enchanting pipes. This time it is a small shepherd boy who is playing the eerie notes and it is we who are enchanted.

As the afternoon draws to its close the shepherds are wont to herd their sheep for the night and then express their melancholy

Above: ENTRANCE TO WORLD-RE-
NOWNED ANCIENT STADIUM AT
OLYMPIA

Right: PEASANT WOMAN OF KOS-
TRAKI, NEAR METEORA MONASTERY,
BALABAKA

by blowing these weird and mournful tunes on their pipes. The
silvery notes, sliding up and down the scale, are coming closer
and presently we see the shepherd boy with his flock placidly following him. He seems to have them charmed by his piping, for
he easily leads them to a corner of one of the ruins and there shuts
them up for the night. Then he walks, a lonely figure dressed in a
brown, hairy robe, tight and fuzzy woolen pants, and up-turned
shoes, to a gnarled olive tree and leans against it, still playing.
He drops the pipes and picks up the tune with his voice and with
a perfect imitation of the fluid pipe notes, pours out, in a now
wavering, now smoothly flowing, liquid rhythm, the pathetic
story of a disappointed love.

THE LAND OF CURRANTS

The sinking sun reminds us that it is time to leave Olympia
and the sad shepherd boy to their pasts, for we must either catch
the last train for Patras or sleep in the fields with a marble pillar

for a pillow. So we pile onto the tiny puffing train with its shrill whistle that makes it sound more like a peanut stand than a dignified means of locomotion, and proceed to Patras in the center of the currant country.

Patras, the fourth city of Greece, lies near the western end of the Gulf of Corinth in the section of the country which is famous for its currant crops. Incidentally, the name "currant" is a corruption of the name "Corinth." Patras, because of its exposed position on the sea coast, has seen more than its share of the warfare of the world. Since very ancient times it has passed from the hands of one nation to another but always after a stiff resistance. Finally, in 1821, the first Greek flag was raised as the sign of the beginning of the war of liberation with the Turks. Since then, with the exception of a few minor revolutions, Patras has enjoyed an undisturbed century of peace. In the past the town was destroyed so many times that nothing remains to remind us of its history except part of a Roman aqueduct and the Venetian fort, which is now used as a prison.

WHERE MOUNTAINS MEET THE SEA

From Patras we journey eastward along the southern shore of that beautiful arm of the sea, the Gulf of Corinth. Our carrier is the narrow-gauge railroad which seems to be about half the width of an American track. It couldn't be any wider because some of the places through which it passes seem so narrow that it appears as though we might put one hand out the window and touch the sea while the other could pick flowers off the side of the mountain. At one spot the mountain recedes a few feet so that it is possible to climb off and set foot on a small patch of level ground. It is here that we change trains for Megaspelaeon and Kalavryta.

Perhaps we were wrong in thinking that the train was small, for before us rest a locomotive and three cars that would delight the heart of any child. It is so little that it would seem to fit in your front parlor and at the same time so powerful that it is able to carry us up the sides of some of the steepest mountains in this part of the world. The tiny cars hold only six people each, so a nineteenth person would have his choice of riding in the cab with the engineer or waiting until the next trip, which occurs on the next day. The natives, well aware of this limitation, advance on the toy train in a great rush; but there are only a few of them, so we are able to tuck ourselves into one of the midget compartments and away we go at the breakneck speed of three miles an hour up the side of a deep gorge.

A GREEK ROLLER COASTER

Although the train is advancing at only a snail's pace, it surpasses any roller coaster in Coney Island for thrills. Even though there is nothing to be seen to the right or to the left except the rocky walls of the steep gorge, the view up and down is breathtaking. Above, seemingly many thousand feet, are the snowy crags of the very mountains up whose sides we are traveling. Below there is a sheer drop of several hundred feet to the bottom of the gorge where a turbulent mountain stream is churning itself into a white froth as it flows over its rough and rocky course. After some twenty minutes of terrific struggle, the little engine finally arrives at some land which is comparatively flat. Then the thrills really start. The train starts to pick up speed so that we are thrown from one side of the compartment to the other as we round the sharp corners, roar through tunnels (fourteen of them in eight miles), shoot through the air over narrow trestles with nothing under them but space and lots of it, until our toy train snorts and rattles to a stop. Our sigh of relief comes at the same time that the shrill whistle of the engine announces to the villagers the completion of another difficult but successful trip.

THE GREAT CAVERN

This is the stop from which we start our trip to Megaspelaeon, the Great Cavern, the most important single monastery in Greece. As we uncurl ourselves from our compartment a crowd of villagers, farmers and shepherds gathers to watch the foreigners who have come from far-away America to see the Great Cavern. The watchers with their beards, baggy knee pants, white stockings, short cloaks, and tiny caps, form a very interesting group. A few are dressed in the fustanella, the national costume of Greece, which consists of a crushed fez, a short, gaily-embroidered jacket, ruffled blouse, fluffy ballet skirt with innumerable pleats, long, white, woolen skin-tight trousers, and shoes with up-turned toes and pom-poms. All are straight, stalwart and dignified and yet all of them have twinkling, jolly eyes. At the first opportunity they ask from what part of the "States" we come. They probably

have very hazy ideas about the geographical location of Tokyo,
Calcutta, Moscow, or Berlin, but they very definitely know all
about such towns as Brooklyn, Buffalo, Birmingham, or Berkeley,
California, for those are the towns where their sons, grandsons,
or nephews are running restaurants and fruit stores. If we hap-
pen to come from towns where relatives of theirs work, we become their close friends and must visit at their homes and partake
of their hospitality.

Instead we must refuse their kind invitations for lack of time
and content ourselves with the food served in the "restaurant"
which this town of one hundred souls boasts. There is very black
bread, white and strong goat-milk cheese, Turkish coffee, and a
glass of oozo. The last mentioned is a colorless, innocent-looking
fluid made from grape skins and is the Greek equivalent of whiskey. We drain our glasses in a second and then wait a full ten
minutes in order to recover our voices and balance. After our
heads have returned to their normal size, we feel very much prepared to scale the side of the mountain to see the Great Cavern.

That, however, is not to be considered, for all foreigners ride
up the mountainside astride the flanks of a skinny donkey, and
who are we to go against the tradition of ages? So, resigned
to fate, we climb on to the wooden racks which go for saddles
while the guide, the woman who runs the "restaurant," literally
stones our mounts up the path. She first beats them with a thick
stick and then when they go no faster, hurls boulders and curses
at them. Even then the poor beasts go no more rapidly but, at
least, she is doing her work. On reaching a high point in the
path, the guide points with pride to the Great Cavern. Search
as hard as we may we can see no cave or cavern but only a very
unusual structure which looks like a five-story tenement house
built flush into the perpendicular face of a wall of rock. One
learns, however, that the unusual building is the monastery which
has been built across the front of what was once a huge, gaping
hole in the mountainside.

It seems that in the fourth century a group of monks were
seeking seclusion and security in order to contemplate the beauty
and mystery of the Greek Orthodox faith, and they chose this
great hole because of its inaccessibility. They built up the front
with apartments and still had room behind for a large church, re-
fectory, library, arsenal, and a barrack room so large that it could
easily accommodate a regiment of soldiers. Instead it houses wine
casks apparently about the size of the boats in which Columbus

THE LITTLE TOWN OF BATHY, ISLAND OF ITHACA, LEGENDARY
HOME OF ULYSSES

first sailed the Atlantic. In these the monks store their liquid treasure, the proceeds from the sale of which help to keep the monastery running.

"FREEDOM OR DEATH"

Farther up the valley, near the town of Kalavryta, lies another monastery, much smaller than Megaspelaeon, but of great historical interest, nevertheless. If we are in a hurry and have the courage to avoid both donkeys and train, we can make very good time on foot. We are admitted to the monastery, called Agia Lavra, by a very earnest monk who proceeds to demonstrate how the first call for Greek freedom was sounded. Standing in the same spot where his patriotic predecessor stood a century ago, he seizes the same flag and sword, waves them above his head in a dramatic manner and cries, *"Eleutheria e Thanatos!"* that is, "Liberty or Death!" After this stirring demonstration by the robed and bearded friar, we return to the sea on the toy train, an even more thrilling trip going down, catch the boat, and steam across the silvery waters of the moonlit Gulf of Corinth to Itea, the port of Delphi.

DELPHI AND ITEA

Delphi, one of the most important places in ancient Greece, lies in one of the most beautiful spots in the whole country. Its importance was due to two distinct facts. The first was that here was a hole in the ground through which noises came. The noises were said to be the voice of the Sibyl who foretold the fortunes of men and kingdoms. There were also cold springs and many draughts of mountain air in the neighborhood; so the ancients came to think of the region as mysterious and sacred. Its importance was further heightened when the Greek cities and states established the headquarters of a "league of nations" there. If an argument arose between any of them, representatives would come here and settle it peacefully—sometimes. These features, and the superb grandeur of the surrounding scenery, made it a place where all sorts of temples were built. So famous and important did Delphi become that it was famous not only in Greece but along all the shores of the Mediterranean.

Itea, the port, is little more than a small country town, but the road that leads outwards and upwards from it is one that takes us through scenes of ever increasing charm. The whole picture is that of a harmonious blending of plains, mountains, and sea so that the colors of all form a landscape that no artist could reproduce. The mountains, first a dry brown, change to a brilliant green and then become a dark blue until they fade, range upon range, into the hazy distance. The plains are a patchwork of tawny plowed fields, stands of amber grain, and great sweeps of green produced by the orchards of olives which thrive here. The Gulf of Corinth, looking more like a river than an arm of the sea, is of the blue that is found in the waters and skies of Greece alone.

As if inspired by this scene, there arose here one of the greatest collections of temple buildings in Greece. It was second only to the Acropolis, but such conquering armies as those of Alexander the Great, Sulla, and Nero, not to mention some of the later ones, passed by and took whatever they could and destroyed the rest. Now Delphi lies as a flat ruin of marble blocks and columns. But the barbarian conquerors could not mar the natural grandeur of the spot, and so it still remains an exceptionally beautiful place in a beautiful country.

CORINTH

Across the bay from Delphi lies Corinth, the city which had the reputation of being one of the most wicked in Roman days. The story is told that because of its sin it was destroyed. Destruc-

ACRO-CORINTH
The mighty mound
behind the city of
old Corinth.

Courtesy J. Bradford
Pengelly

tion certainly came, because today there is not much more of it than there is of Delphi, a holy city. Of the many acres of its widespread buildings, only seven small columns remain standing in the places where they were originally erected.

Old Corinth enjoyed a very profitable location. It was placed so that it controlled all trade that passed into the Peloponnesus over the Isthmus of Corinth, and at the same time could utilize the water route that existed on either side. As might be expected, Corinth grew to a position of great commercial importance. Just as Athens was known for her high intellectual level, and Sparta for her military greatness, so was Corinth famous all over the ancient world for her affairs of business.

One of the most imposing sights in the neighborhood of Corinth is the massive mountain of stone that arises abruptly from the level plain all around it. As the walls of this block of stone rise straight into the air, the ascent is very difficult, but the view from the top is worth twice the effort. Below may be seen, through the gaps in the ruined medieval fortifications that ring the top of the mountain, the pattern of streets and buildings of Old Corinth. Beyond the old city, lying right on the water's edge, is the modern town of new Corinth. There is nothing really wicked about the new town, but nevertheless it has been twice destroyed in recent years by earthquakes. Immediately behind us, covering the mountain top upon which we stand, are the ruins of Acro-Corinth, or High Corinth. This was the citadel that guarded Corinth and many furious battles took place here when the invading armies sought to dislodge the defenders.

To the south lie the brown and blue mountains of the Peloponnesus and to the east gleam the waters of the Gulf of Aegina and beyond them the blue Aegean. In this same direction lie the ruins of Mycenae and Tiryns, two towns that were old when the ancient Greeks, who were at the time barbarians, came down from the north. A very remarkable reminder of the inhabitants of Mycenae and Tiryns is their architecture. The city walls and many of the buildings were built of blocks of stone so large that they weighed from four to five tons apiece.

SOUND EFFECTS

Still farther to the east, almost on the shores of the Gulf, is the most beautiful and best preserved Greek theater in existence. This is the theater at Epidaurus which rises tier upon tier so high that a person standing in the center at the bottom feels like the smallest of midgets. It is built entirely of pure white marble and set, in open semicircular fashion, into the side of a

Courtesy J. Bradford Pengelly

ANCIENT BOURDZI CASTLE IN BAY OF NAUPLIA

FAMOUS CLIFFS NEAR BALABAKA, GREECE
Centuries ago hermits lived in the caves of these cliffs.

hill which is covered with a dense growth of dark green pine trees. Credit must be given to the ancient Greeks, not only for selecting a wonderful site and building an architectural masterpiece, but also for a knowledge of acoustics. It is possible to stand on the topmost row and hear a pin dropped on the stage scores of feet below.

MONASTERY IN THE CLOUDS

Thus far, the Greece which we have been enjoying was mostly connected with the glories of the ancient Greek city-states. Now, as we move northward to the mainland again, past noble Mount Parnassus, over the plain on which Thebes rose to power and then fell, and through the pass at Thermopylae, where the three hundred Spartans held off the Persian hordes, there are fewer and fewer reminders of ancient times and more and more of the Middle Ages. This is still Greece and the inhabitants are still Greeks, but the charm is of another kind.

In the central part of the country there is a valley walled on one side by the Pindus mountains, whose slopes seem to rise vertically from the valley floor, and on the other side, the eastern, by gentler but higher mountains of which the mighty Olympus is the highest. At the northern end of the valley are some rock formations of a very peculiar sort. They are solid masses of rock, something like thimbles with straight sides, which rise three to four hundred feet straight into the air. The natives call them Meteora because they seem to have fallen from heaven. Although the sides of some of these tremendous rocks are so steep and smooth that it is impossible to climb them, on the tops of the highest and steepest are monasteries—the Hanging Monasteries of Meteora.

As we move between these massive columns made by nature, we come to one that has a rope hanging down the side. A pull at the rope is followed by the tiny tinkle of a bell, which seems to come from the clouds. Then a creaking and groaning of ropes and pulleys, and in a surprisingly short time a basket, large enough to hold several people, rests on the ground. The passengers climb in, the creaking recommences, and the basket slowly starts skyward. Surely this is an easy and comfortable way to attain heaven! At the top one finds that the crude elevator was pulled up by six perspiring monks in much the same manner as water is raised by a crank from wells. Despite their exertions they are glad to have visitors and immediately invite inspection of their heavenly home. What is most surprising is to find many gardens and even a pasture on which sheep are grazing, all atop this rocky plateau. The view is magnificent from this exciting perch where one may sit on the edge of a cliff and contemplate the sheer drop of four hundred feet. This is really sitting on top of the world.

The cordial hospitality of the cheerful monks is not matched by the quality of their food. The fare consists of a fiery drink called chiporu, cold macaroni, fried octopus, and very sour wine. The hungry guest might well eat sparingly of this rather queer food, at least if he wants to enjoy the beauties of the delightfully constructed monastery and chapel, both built in the finest style of the early Byzantine Empire. But in spite of the beauty, the odd mixture of liquor, wine, and octopus is likely to make a nap seem especially alluring.

No one can look upon the gentle foothills and then the steeply rising slopes of Olympus, which come to a climax in the three magnificent, cloud-wreathed peaks, without forgetting oneself entirely. It is no wonder that the gods chose Olympus for their home. The genial, black-robed hosts bid farewell to their guests with a gracious blessing. After another drink of the liquid fire and a pinch of homemade snuff, an offering of pennies is dropped into the collection box, and the visitors are gently lowered down to earth once again.

THE COVETED CITY

Lying to the north, at the mouth of the Vardar River, is Saloniki, the second city of Greece and from time immemorial a town which was coveted by all nearby nations. The approach to Saloniki from the sea brings to mind pictures of the Middle Ages. Rising up a steep hill, surrounded on three sides by thick walls and guarded by an ominous fortress at the water's edge and another on top of the hill, the city is a reminder of the days when attacks by barbarians and sieges by enemies occurred frequently.

The old city is a galaxy of white walls, red-tiled roofs, and green and graceful cypress trees. The many domes of Byzantine churches, the solitary spire of a minaret, and the incongruous steeple of a New England church are all framed by the crumbling battlements of the formidable fortifications and dominated by the sinister citadel, the present-day prison.

Outside the walls the new city has avoided the hillsides and has spread in a crescent shape around the shores of the bay. This newer part is a mad mixture of gas tanks, fine villas, refugee shacks of wood and tin, new buildings after the latest styles of Paris and Berlin, which may be seen through the forest of masts and funnels of the shipping which makes Saloniki a great port and important city.

In the city itself are to be found the church of St. Sophia, an exact duplicate of the mother church of Eastern Christianity in Constantinople; and the cathedral of St. Demetrius, now gutted by fire but still containing a fine collection of mosaics and architectural evidences of the glories of the once great Byzantine Empire. There are also the White Tower, a fortress built by the Venetians, converted into a torture chamber by the Turks, and now used as headquarters by the Boy Scouts of Macedonia; and the Temple of St. George, first a Macedonian shrine, then a Roman temple, a Christian church, a Turkish mosque and finally a museum of antiquities. Another interesting feature is the arch which Galerius, a Roman emperor, built over the ancient Roman road, the Via Egnatia, to commemorate his victory over the Persians. The Via Egnatia was an important artery which connected Rome and Constantinople via Saloniki. Over it marched the Roman legions on their way to the east to subdue the rebellious tribes

HARBOR OF SALONIKI, ON THE AEGEAN SEA

of the Near East. Now street cars run its length and its sides are lined with shops selling radios and Bibles, but its name is still the same.

Saloniki, the old Thessalonica of the Bible, contains thousands of Armenians, Jews whose ancestors were driven from Spain in the fifteenth century, white Russians who escaped the revolution that shook their country, Albanians, Macedonians, and even Americans who operate an American school. The school, Anatolia College by name, occupies a position on the hills just outside the city so that the students can look up from their English lessons to see Mt. Olympus across the bay, the amazing city at their feet, or cloud-covered Mt. Hortiati behind them.

THE HOLY MOUNTAIN

Eastward from Saloniki, on the mountain that tips the third finger of Chalcidice peninsula, we find a spot that has been preserved as a perfect example of medieval times. This is Mount Athos, the holy mountain, covered from one end to the other with monasteries built a thousand or more years ago and which still maintain the traditions of the days in which they were erected.

The monasteries occupy high crags, lofty summits and other

Courtesy J. Bradford Pengelly

COURT IN THE MONASTERY OF SAN STEPHANOS AT METEORA

inaccessible spots. They are built like fortresses, the better to guard the wealth and treasures which lie inside. For centuries the nations of the orthodox faith have poured in gold, silver, and precious stones as a means of showing their devotion and appreciation of this holy mountain—holy because the Virgin Mary is said to have appeared here in the fourth century A.D., to locate the site of the first monastery. So the monasteries, mostly Greek, but also Russian, Bulgarian, and Serbian, display their wealth on certain occasions in a fantastic array of glittering splendor that amazes the modern onlooker as much as it did the people of the tenth century.

In order to maintain the purity of the holy precincts, and incidentally remove all temptation from the monks, no women are allowed to set foot here. In fact, it wasn't until a few years ago that cows or chickens were allowed to exist there in any form other than on a platter, well cooked.

"WHERE BURNING SAPPHO LOVED AND SUNG"

Some people have maintained that while the mainland of Greece is one of the most interesting and inspiring regions on this globe, it is the Isles of Greece that constitute the real charm and beauty of the country. Be that as it may, such names as Lesbos, Chios, Rhodes, and Corfu conjure pictures of real beauty and charm. While Athens was achieving heights in intellectual greatness, the islands of the Aegean were following her by producing great men and buildings. Some of the temples built on the promontories of the islands, graceful pictures with blue sky for a background and bluer sea for a foreground, have inspired poets throughout the ages.

Some of the isles are so tiny, only a few square miles in area, and so remote from the shipping lanes of the Aegean, that they have had little contact with the outside world and have preserved their ancient ways. In fact, it is in some of these spots that a language very little different from classic Greek is spoken. Nevertheless, as we tramp the cobblestone streets of some of these fairyland towns with their tiny but sparkling houses and churches built up the steep side of a hill, we can at any minute expect someone to greet us with, "Hello Mister. How do you like it here? O. K.?" Just another Greek who has been to America, made a small bit of money, and returned to his native land for a little luxury and rest before he dies.

"THE GREAT GREEK ISLAND"

Crete, known as the Great Greek Island, has had a history different from that of her smaller sister isles of the Aegean. Crete

Courtesy J. Bradford Pengelly

ST. PANTELEIMON OR RUSICON MONASTERY, MT. ATHOS
Before the World War this old Russian monastery was reported to be the richest and most aristocratic in the world.

Courtesy J. Bradford Pengelly

THE FAMOUS ISLE OF THE DEAD WITH A PICTURESQUE CHURCH,
ON THE DALMATIAN COAST

was large enough to support a sizable population so that when
Egypt was in her glory, Crete had a civilization which was as
great as that of the country on the Nile.

At Knossus, capital of the ancient realm, the massive palace,
much of which stands today, contained bathrooms with running
water for the comfort of the kings. On the walls are murals
which still retain the grace of line and beauty of color in which
they were originally painted.

Corfu, which lies on the western side of the country, has a
charm of its own and is an exact replica of the scenery which
the ancient poets described. To walk down the road from the city
of Corfu to the one-time palace of the Austrian emperors, is to
find oneself in a place where meeting a nymph, a centaur, or even
one of the gods would not occasion too much surprise. In the
city the mixture of Greek and Italian architecture is especially
interesting. But there is no question as to its being a part of
Greece, for over one of the doors of a shop is a word announc-
ing that the doctor specializes in eyes, ears, noses, and throats. The
name is "ophthoötorhinolaryngologos." The Greeks had something there.